MATCHLOCKS TO FLINTLOCKS

Matchlocks to Flintlocks

WARFARE IN EUROPE AND BEYOND
1500–1700

William Urban

Foreword by Dennis Showalter

Frontline Books, London

FRONTLINE BOOKS, LONDON

Matchlocks to Flintlocks: Warfare in Europe and Beyond, 1500–1700

This edition published in 2011 by Frontline Books, an imprint of
Pen & Sword Books Limited, 47 Church Street, Barnsley, S. Yorkshire, S70 2AS
www.frontline-books.com

ISBN: 978-1-84832-628-6

For more information on our books, please visit
www.frontline-books.com,
email info@frontline-books.com
or write to us at the above address.

Typeset by JCS Publishing Services Ltd, www.jcs-publishing.co.uk
Printed in Great Britain by CPI Antony Rowe

Contents

Illustrations

Photo Credits

1, 6 & 8: Reubens, Peter Paul. *P. P. Rubens; des Meisters Gemälde, in 538 Abbildungen*, edited by Rudolf Oldenbourg, Stuttgart: Deutsche Verlag-Anstalt, n.d.

2 & 3: Spofford, Ainsworth Rand, Frank Weitenkampf and John Porter Lamberton. *The Library of Historical Characters and Famous Events*, Boston: J. B. Millet, 1902.

4: Hackett, Francis. *Francis the First*, New York: Literary Guild, 1935.

5: Van Marle, Raymond and Charlotte van Marle. *The Development of the Italian Schools of Painting*, The Hague: M. Nijhoff, 1923–38.

7: Glück, Heinrich and Ernst Diez. *Die Kunst des Islam*, Berlin: Propyläen-Verlag, 1925.

9 & 13: Rembrandt Harmenszoon van Rijn. *Rembrandt; des Meisters Gemälde, in 643 Abbildungen, mit einer biographische Einleitung*, edited by Adolf Rosenberg and Wilhelm Reinhold Valentiner, Stuttgart: Deutsche Verlag-Anstalt 1909.

10, 11, 12, 15 & 16: Weisbach, Werner. *Die Kunst des Barock in Italien, Frankreich, Deutschland und Spanien*, Berlin: Propyläen-Verlag, 1924.

14: Horne, Charles Francis. *Great Men and Famous Women: A Series of Pen and Pencil Sketches of the Lives of More than 200 of the Most Prominent Personages in History*, New York: S. Hess, c.1894.

Foreword

In his preface William Urban remarks that 'readers who prefer narrative accounts to academic studies will be more likely to send me appreciative notes.' Like many authors, he misunderstands the book he has written. *Matchlocks to Flintlocks* is indeed narrative in format. One might even call it story-driven. And in that the book fills a significant gap in the military history of the early modern world. For over fifty years the subject has been idea-driven: the nature, scope and existence of military revolution; a Eurocentric perspective versus a global one; war in the context of the rise of the fiscal-military state – these macro-issues structure scholarship and presentation. They have been unusually successful integrating military themes into the big pictures discussed in general histories. In that process, however, the specific subject of early modern warfare has been fragmented at best, at worst mined for data supporting broader constructions. Urban has returned to the roots of his subject. The result is a story of war, and the persons and institutions that waged it, during the two key centuries when warriors became soldiers and soldiers became servants of the state.

In *Matchlocks to Flintlocks* events shape paradigms. And those events are discussed and analysed in a uniquely balanced comparative framework. In the early modern world three dominant cultures of war were shaped by a synergy of their internal and external interactions. One was Latin Christian western Europe. Another was Ottoman Islam. The third, no less vital for so often being overlooked, was east-central Europe: Poland/Lithuania, Livonia, Russia, the freebooting Cossacks, a volatile mixture of variations on a general Christian theme.

Mughal India, Ming/Manchu China and Tokugawa Japan were formidable enough on their own terms, but also marginalised, essentially outside the cross-fertilising loops that shaped and defined military effectiveness in the early modern world. Their presence in this work is correspondingly and appropriately limited. The same is true for Urban's treatment of European global reach, which in this period was primarily commercial, with armed force a secondary instrument of power projection.

The result is a book that gets to the heart of its subject – not least, in passing, because of a perspective that marginalises the familiar Anglophone viewpoints. Urban convincingly eschews another familiar approach: ranking the participants. His large body of earlier work on the Baltic Crusades stands him here in good stead. Years spent in close study of small-scale combats has led him to the conclusion that Bellona is no one's trull – that victory on any given day is less likely to be the triumph of a system than the result of a spectrum of particular events, predictable or otherwise. Latin, east European, Muslim: each system had its own qualities; each adapted to and borrowed from its opponents.

Urban understands as well that nobody shows up to lose. The result is an integrated account of early modern war at the sharp end: of campaigns and battles, soldiers and generals. Temporally it extends from the French invasion of Italy in 1494 to Austria's Balkan victories culminating in the 1718 Treaty of Peterwardein. Geographically it covers ground from the Low Countries to the depths of the Ukraine.

That narrative in turn focuses Urban's major analytical points: the replacement of 'crowd armies' by professionals, and the professionals' integration into crown armies: government-supervised, bureaucratised institutions that structured dress, maintenance, training and above all pay – regular pay generated by systematic taxation and distributed by reasonably honest administrators. The key to this process was the mercenary. Originally recruited because the obligations of feudal levies were too limited, mercenary forces evolved operationally into skilled users of an increasingly complex gunpowder technology in ever more complex tactical situations. Institutionally they developed into contract armies, linked across specific obligations by a guild identity as masters of war. By the end of the seventeenth century, soldiers were identifying with the states and the rulers they served.

The process was not complete. It was, however, a crucial step in a modernisation that was not entirely built on economic liberty and personal freedom. Urban makes the telling point that modernisation also was a product of passions: religious, ethnic and political. During the two centuries covered in this book, not liberty and freedom but civil strife and intrastate warfare were the dominant forces. The eventual development of professional armies firmly in the hands of the rulers did not usher in an age of amity and concord. Nonetheless, a monopoly of effective public violence did keep the era's long-running, mutually exhausting conflicts from becoming the first step to entropy.

Perhaps that manifested Hegel's 'cunning of reason'. Or perhaps it reflects Bellona's fine-tuned sense of irony. Urban's demonstration of both possibilities merits wide attention and general recognition.

Dennis Showalter

Preface

To the Readers

This volume enlarges on themes set out in *Bayonets for Hire* (Greenhill, 2007), illustrating how war affected economics, intellectual life and society between 1500 and 1700, but is less focused on mercenaries than on the evolution of the military arts that slowly transformed soldiers of fortune (as mercenaries were once, rather inaccurately, called) into servants of the state.

As armies became less ad hoc collections of bodies of horsemen and infantry, it became more important for rulers and the commanders of their armies to make long-term provision for feeding, housing, clothing and training professional military personnel. This is a complex subject. While everyone today understands that armies travel on their stomach, we have largely forgotten what went into stomachs during those centuries. The rather bland medieval diet of commoners was becoming richer, or at least more varied; and military fare mirrored – because soldiers or their camp followers cooked for themselves – what civilians consumed. But even here there are surprises.

As meat became more available, consumption actually declined; spices made good cooking possible, but they were used less after they became cheap. When distilling technology produced brandy, widespread drunkenness increased, but beer production countered its harmful effects, giving way to wine whenever the economy improved. The desire for sugar led to the African slave trade and naval wars for control of Caribbean islands; tobacco, tea, coffee and chocolate were newly popular among people with money, but cereal crops became more expensive, so that the poor could often afford only gruel, or, when times were truly dire, only meat. Everyone had to have salt and it was usually imported – two characteristics that made it the perfect commodity for newly powerful rulers to tax.[1]

Technological advances were uneven. The development of the spring – the result of much-improved metallurgy – made possible the matchlock musket, and improvements in clockwork led to the wheel-lock mechanism that made a cavalry pistol practical. Eventually the flintlock musket proved so much more convenient than the matchlock that everyone adopted it. Warfare was more than technology, of course – in the right circumstances old fashioned weapons were superior. And there was little change in dynastic intrigue, personal ambition, religious rivalry and ancient hatreds – subjects less exciting than the clash of armies, but more likely to change the way we see the past.

The readers most likely to enjoy this book will be those who are eager to learn more about a somewhat familiar subject, warfare, but to see it in unfamiliar places and perhaps from a different point of view. Readers who prefer narrative accounts to academic studies will be more likely to send me appreciative notes.

To the Subject

This is a book about warfare, a subject that seems easy to define until one tries to do it. As Bert Hall says in *Weapons and Warfare in Renaissance Europe*, warfare is the most confusing enterprise pursued by humans. Moreover, to call war an armed conflict between states is more appropriate after the Peace of Westphalia in 1648 than a century and a half earlier, when dynasties claimed the allegiance of nobles and clerics and the financial contributions and services of commoners. In 1500 there were kingdoms and one emperor in Latin Christendom, but the numerous smaller political units – towns, abbeys, confederations, free knights – had not yet been completely brought into the larger framework that we usually envision. The right of private individuals to make war had been circumscribed, but not eliminated. Even the most powerful rulers were not yet firmly in control of their own lands, and diplomatic representation was rudimentary. Only the pope had a Europe-wide network of informants, and only the Venetians had a good spy system.

The Islamic states were somewhat better off, though the Ottomans, Persians, Mamluks and Tatars seemed to be mired in a state of continual warfare. Perhaps this reflects our tendency to note the rise and fall of dynasties rather than the continuity of states; our Western view might simply see the dynamics of non-European politics incorrectly. Central

Asia was important, too. The fierce nomadic warriors of that vast region often fell on Persia, India, Russia and Poland. Other nomadic warriors dominated the military history of North Africa.

In short, this was a period of continual conflict, not only between dynasties, but between rulers and their most important subjects, against bandits and pirates. If we are confused about the differences between warfare, the suppression of lawlessness and insurrection, and random violence, we can excuse it because people living between 1500 and 1700 were sometimes confused too. They responded to foreign invasions and domestic crimes with demands for protection and for law and order, demands of such intensity that territorial rulers who were able to provide stability and security made themselves powerful. Sometimes these rulers – eventually called, with some exaggeration, 'absolute monarchs' – prevailed by appeals to reason, bribery, mutual concessions, threats and force.

It was not possible for European rulers to achieve this by reliance on traditional methods – neither feudal taxes nor feudal armies were up to the task, and local warriors were likely to resist efforts to create a proper army and the bureaucracy necessary to pay for it. Rulers who proved successful usually turned to mercenaries whose principal allegiance was to their paymaster.

Many mercenaries were less skilled in the use of cutting weapons or archery than nobles and even commoners who had trained with those weapons from childhood, but they could learn to use firearms and cannon relatively quickly. By 1500 advances in technology had recently improved these weapons, not just in making them somewhat lighter and more dependable, but in providing more effective and more stable gunpowder. Still, not everyone was persuaded that firearms could be depended upon in pitched battles – matchlocks were unwieldy and slow under the best of circumstances, and the fuses were liable to blow out in wind or get damp in rain. While cannon were effective in sieges, they were difficult to transport to battlefields and to protect from infantry and cavalry long enough to blow holes in opposing formations.

A combination of arms became important – employing cavalry, infantry and artillery together was not new, but now it was becoming more complicated. Through the first half of the sixteenth century, commanders were still trying to figure out how to combine horsemen, cannon, pikemen and musketeers most effectively; and how to feed and house the men and animals until the day of battle. Mercenary officers who understood the new system found employment easily.

At this same time rulers needed soldiers willing to fight farther from home than a feudal array of knights and militia would. Accompanied by a veritable army of camp followers, a mercenary army was like a moving city – with many of the amenities of a large town. Women and boys (the derided camp followers) were essential to the army's effectiveness, gathering supplies and watching the tents while the soldiers were on duty.

Mercenaries

This book is not primarily about mercenaries, but since European armies of this era included many of them, they cannot be ignored. Many think that a mercenary is someone who fights for money, for any employer willing to hire him. That definition works for Hollywood, which portrays the mercenary alternately as a hero and as evil incarnate, but – as this book indicates – reality is more complex. Morally, we still see the mercenary as one who sells his soul for lucre, the servant of violence and often a supporter of tyranny. Such is the viewpoint of the Geneva Convention (as amended in 1949 and 1977) and the United Nations' Mercenary Convention of 2001. This definition does not fit the practices of Europe, Africa and Asia between 1500 and 1700.

A stimulating effort to define these practices in the period before 1500 can be found in John France's *Mercenaries and Paid Men*, the very title of which suggests that defining the roles of military employees is no easy matter.[2] Does accepting money make one a mercenary? Certainly the old definition that combined 'fighting for pay' and 'being a foreigner' is less cut and dried than before.

In *Bayonets for Hire* I wrote about mercenaries in Europe from the Wars of Religion to the eighteenth century. The present volume looks at new regions, not only to southern and eastern Europe, but also Africa and the Indian Ocean. European rulers found it more practical to send mercenaries on these ventures rather than to risk valuable subjects; some of these mercenaries went into the service of non-Christian rulers or became pirates.

Then there is the question of employers. Kings and prelates often led armies in battle, but they were not, by education or preference, interested in the raising or training of such forces. For that they relied on people who specialised in the business of war. So, when was the making of war taken from private entrepreneurs by royal bureaucrats?

National Armies

Because it has been argued that mercenaries were a part of the process of modernisation in early modern Europe, I wanted to test the notion that the military profession assisted in the creation of the national state.[3] I think it did. However, I also conclude that this process of slow change cannot be equated to the situation today, where many new nations are dominated by military elites that have become frustrated by the corruption and inefficiency of civilian institutions. Today's emerging nations seem to have more in common with the declining Roman Empire than with the Holy Roman Empire or France during the period 1500 to 1700. Mercenaries did not attempt to overthrow the government, or at least, when they participated in a coup, they handed it over to someone with a dynastic claim to the throne.

For much of this period mercenaries looked upon themselves as somewhat disinterested professionals. That is, they fought hard for their employers, but they were not enthusiastic about dying for them.[4] When Germans attempted to surrender, they cried out 'Kamerad!' (comrade), implying that all soldiers were fighting for employers whose cause was less important than professional solidarity and the shared desire to survive the trials of battle. It was not unusual for prisoners (or even entire units) to enrol in the victorious army.

When soldiers began to identify with their nation-state, warfare changed significantly. This did not immediately end the employment of mercenaries, but from that time on mercenaries could not change paymasters easily. Kings may have sensed that the nation-state would eventually turn them into figureheads, then into headless figures, but the cheering of crowds made them ignore such worries.

Changes in European warfare, but especially those leading to the creation of national armies, track the development of the modern state well. New weapons and new tactics required more supplies than had been necessary before. After 1650 procuring supplies from the homeland became more important than taking them from those unfortunates who lived near the battlefields, and transporting and storing these supplies became more business-like and efficient. In short, the military bureaucracy became more than a simple means of guaranteeing that officers obtained their subsidies and their share of the loot. This was an aspect of modernisation in the sense that armies came to be more like those of today.

To Modernisation

The way modernisation is defined has implications for today's world. The long-respected ideas of Talcott Parsons (1902–79), emphasising the central role of economic liberty and personal freedom, are being challenged by advocates of despotic rule and anarchism. This affects our understanding of the European world of 1500–1700 that was marked by somewhat similar contests over authority. As great states coalesced, peoples unwillingly annexed to them sought independence, and nobles and burghers demanded some role in government. The push towards parliamentary systems had the immediate result of encouraging class warfare and religious strife.

Holding traditional institutions together proved as difficult as stabilising new ones. The universal church of 1500, as the popes saw their flock, was shattered by that culmination of long-developing demands for reform that we call the Reformation. Reuniting the Church by persuasion or force was the ambition of Paul III (1468–1549), a pontiff more at home in the fifteenth century than in that of his papacy, but still a man of great knowledge and competence. By 1536, his second year as pope, he was torn between a wish to call a council to reform the Church, anger that Emperor Charles V was tolerating Protestants in Germany and his interrupting the war against the Turks to deal with French aggression, and fear that King Francis I would be so angry at the papal alliance with the emperor that he would become a Protestant.

Just when suspicious Lutherans and Evangelicals in Germany were feeling secure enough to resist binding negotiations with Catholic church-men, Charles understood that he could not fight wars without Protestant help. The result was that both sides accepted the religious status quo as a temporary measure. Then, with the pope as intermediary, the emperor and French king became bosom friends. Within two years, however, the constellation of problems evolved into new and unrecognisable configurations, and five years after that Copernicus proposed a new vision of the heavens that outraged Catholic and Protestant theologians alike. The best that Paul III could do was to appoint new cardinals, hoping that in time they could move the Church in a new direction.

Unable to refrain from the traditional practice of enhancing his own family, Paul III wed his grandson to one of the emperor's illegitimate daughters. Personal talks with Charles and Francis bore little fruit, and the passing of time diminished the reputation of both the pope and the French king (Francis's open co-operation with Ottoman naval forces in raids on Italy and Spain was obvious treason to the concept of Christendom, but no pope dared condemn him too loudly). It is easy for us, with hindsight to guide us, to criticise the pope in general terms, but what policies would we have recommended? Paul III had to deal with the day-to-day issues as much as the long-term strategy.

Meanwhile, eyes were drawn to the Mediterranean, where Muslim corsairs were falling on coastal villages and towns, surrounding them before daylight, then subjecting them to robbery, murder and rape before carrying the survivors off – often employing them immediately as galley slaves. Stories of such atrocities did not lend themselves to arguments that the Church should give more emphasis to pacifism, but they do explain why Charles V spent so much time and treasure, and even risked his own life repeatedly, in attempting to occupy the North African coastline, and why Suleiman the Magnificent (1494–1566) wanted to retake it. Christian pirates were active, too, some of them members of military orders operating from strongly fortified island bases, their every atrocity praised by popes and even distant Protestants. Modern readers may think religion irrelevant, but no one in the sixteenth century made that mistake.

There are good reasons for our not confusing this era of religious wars and absolutism with its successor, the Enlightenment. The generations of 1500–1700 possessed religious convictions more violent than would be known again until our own times. Reformation passion was matched by Counter-Reformation zeal, and contending parties shouted 'anti-Christ' and 'heretic' at each other. Majorities became intolerant, minorities revolutionaries. Visions of heaven justified mortal sins and venal ambitions.

The desperate struggle with Ottoman navies and armies made it easy for Catholics to perceive Protestant rebellions as an effort to undermine Christian unity – what difference was there between a Turkish sapper and a Lutheran minister? Or a French engineer in the sultan's service?

While the Inquisition in Madrid was burning heretics, Muslim equivalents were perishing in Istanbul. Individuals who saved themselves by conversion faced horrible deaths if captured by their original countrymen; those who refused to abandon their faith faced slavery, exile or heavy taxes. Yet, awkwardly for such generalisations, there were examples which proved the opposite – Greeks and Jews often preferred Muslim rule to Catholic, trade could trump religious ideology, ransom could be more attractive than revenge, and political realities led to interfaith alliances.

The most passionate feelings about religion and nationality were shared just as strongly by mercenaries. Money was important, but it was not everything. Most mercenaries considered ethnic and religious interests as important as the quality of the coins they were offered. Protestant Germans could fight the Turk, then turn quickly against their Austrian Catholic ally, accepting pay from Catholic kings of France who held such great love for German lands that they wanted more of them. National interests would then draw them back to the service of the Habsburg emperors, until they remembered that their real allegiance was to whichever corner of the Holy Roman Empire they called home. This pattern was repeated across Europe, from Britain, to Poland, to Italy. The names and circumstances changed, but the principles remained the same.

Most of these emotions burned out in wars that exhausted everyone, and eventually many agreed that only an iron hand could bring the last fanatics under control. Afterwards logical argument and ridicule persuaded those whose opinions counted that strong beliefs were no justification for killing anybody.

To Today

What has this book to tell us about our world today? What can we learn from a story of Christian Europe – Orthodox and Roman Catholic – fighting against the Islamic empire of the Ottoman Turks. We should take care to avoid thinking that it is a story of good Christians and bad Muslims (or the other way around), for it is not a story of heroes fighting villains, but rather human beings struggling in webs of their own making, or caught in those woven by previous generations.

The European world around 1500 managed to produce in one nation both Ignatius Loyola and Cervantes, each with very different ideas about their times – it was a world that after 1700 produced in one nation Voltaire and Rousseau, and, to their east and to their west, Leibnitz and Newton. Between those two eras were sweeping changes in society, technology and thought. In 1500 the Christian world was inferior to the Islamic world in many respects; by 1700 it was not.

The Islamic world encompassed great cultures and magnificent traditions, but its interactions with the West were such that it was perceived as both exotic and dangerous.[5] We, living in a far better-informed era, can surely have a more nuanced understanding of the goals and potential of various conflicting states – without succumbing to the tempting belief that everyone and everything is equal, and equally good, at every time and every place.[6]

All scholars agree that the Ottoman Empire was entering a long and ultimately fatal decline. Why this happened is not clear. Was it a parasite state, able to exist only on the taxes and services of unwilling subjects? Were internal conflicts among the ruling elite to blame? Was it class conflict? Was there something in Islam, something that discouraged innovation and capital accumulation, which caused economic decline? Or was economic failure a part of the sultan's state organisation that had nothing to do with religion? Was it perhaps a preference for rural life that disparaged industrial production? Without question, government policies limited the entrepreneurship needed to produce military wares or taxes. What was not sponsored by the state simply did not happen.

Certainly, there was no universal sense of being Ottoman, much less Turkish. The *millet* system, which gave local authority to minority religious leaders, was popular, but it was less attractive to minorities than having an independent state of their own. Nationalism, though still in its earliest stages, worked against the Ottoman Empire. There was no unity in Islam, even though from 1517 onwards the sultan was also caliph – Shiites resisted Sunni domination, there were sects and cults, and the army had to be ready for war at any place, on land or sea, at any time. It was a classic example of 'imperial overstretch', a phrase popularised by Paul Kennedy in *The Rise and Fall of the Great Powers*.

The Habsburgs had the same problem. From the Balkans to the Low Countries, to Italy and Spain, the emperors had to contend with problems that combined religious and regional feelings; they had to be ready for war at any time, even in the New World and Asia. Geography made the shipment of goods expensive, which limited commerce, and, in turn, kept government revenues from taxes and tariffs low. The existence of two superpowers required each to strain every resource to keep up with the other, leading eventually to mutual bankruptcy.

The shift in relative strength initially favoured the Habsburgs, then later the kings of France. As Christian infantry formations evolved from the Swiss phalanxes to the Spanish *tercios*, and eventually improved on the Swedish linear formations, new forms of army organisation appeared. By the end of the period under study generals were arranging infantry in long lines only a few men deep. This permitted more mobility, easier employment of artillery and more effective use of combined arms to weaken and then rout a foe.

The debate on this is far from over. Max Boot, in *War Made New*, suggested that Western arms did not become decisively better than those of competing cultures until the early nineteenth century; William McNeill, in the *New York Review of Books* (January 2007), placed that moment earlier. Or was this issue even important? Charles Tilly, in *Coercion, Capital, and European States*, says that war-making led to state formation – a more important development than improvements in the technology of slaughter.

In contrast, Steven Gunn and David Parrott in *European Warfare, 1350–1750*, emphasize negotiated relationships between the ruler and his nobles, each gaining advantages from creating a more permanent military establishment and raising new taxes. No one purchased a commission or a regiment without an expectation of profit. We might call that corruption, but it saved the crown a great deal of money. In theory, the king controlled the bureaucrats, the bureaucrats the officers, the officers the army; in practice, the system ran pretty much on its own, and changing it was difficult.

Nowhere does the rapid evolution of the military arts appear faster than the states fighting over the Low Countries. This densely populated and productive region belonged to the Habsburgs – first to the Holy Roman emperor, then the king of Spain, then again to the emperor. Each had to defend that land against the king of France, while fighting Protestants in Holland as well.

Bringing troops to the Low Countries was not easy. Spain found the sea lanes too dangerous in wartime – there were English, French and Dutch navies and privateers to cope with – and the 'Spanish Road' from Italy over Switzerland, Alsace and Lorraine was in danger of being cut off by French advances to the Rhine. This supply line could be best protected by hiring local soldiers and local princes. It was best attacked by the same means. For mercenaries, business was good.

William Urban
Lee L. Morgan Professor of History
and International Studies
Monmouth College

'I tell you, captain, if you look in the maps of the 'orld, I warrant you shall find, in the comparisons between Macedon and Monmouth, that the situations, look you, is both alike. There is a river in Macedon, and there is also moreover a river at Monmouth: it is called Wye at Monmouth; but it is out of my prains what is the name of the other river; but 'tis all one, 'tis alike as my fingers is to my fingers, and there is salmons in both. If you mark Alexander's life well, Harry of Monmouth's life is come after it indifferent well; for there is figures in all things.'

Captain Fluellen to Captain Gower,
King Henry V, Act IV Scene VII

This book was written at another Monmouth, the one in Illinois with a college that is sometimes confused with a newer one in New Jersey. It does not have a river, though the Mississippi is not far distant.

Acknowledgements

Few people write a book by themselves, and usually I have so many to thank that I hesitate to name anyone lest I overlook someone. This time, however, I need to recognise the assistance of my college roommate, Marshall Morris – retired director of the Honors program and the Translation program of the University of Puerto Rico at Piedras Negras – and my daughter's father-in-law, Richard Spencer, a retired lieutenant colonel in the United States Air Force, college professor and essayist. I also wish to thank the anonymous readers and editors who smoothed the rough edges off the manuscript, then helped to polish it.

CHAPTER ONE

Warfare in Europe and the Mediterranean in 1500

The general outline of future national, dynastic and religious conflicts became apparent in the first decades of the sixteenth century. What would change most over the course of time was that contests once centred on Italy would spread to new theatres of conflict – to the seas, the Balkans, to the steppe bordering Russia and Poland, and to the very heart of Europe. But at its onset the great game of imperial and dynastic politics was played south of the Alps, with French, German and Spanish rulers understanding that Italy was the great prize, with Italian inventiveness prominent in every aspect of culture and commerce. Even the Turkish sultan, who was too distracted by Persian and Egyptian competitors to do more than encourage pirate raids on the coasts and to seize Italian island colonies, was eager to hire Italian artists and architects, and to take the profits of Venetian, Genoese and Florentine merchants, or at least to tax them.

This was an ambition that Bajazet II (1447–1512) shared with the Valois dynasty of France, the Habsburg dynasty of Austria, and the king and queen of newly united Spain, only he could do little about it at the moment – his attention being focused on his rebellious brother, Cem.[1] The first to intervene in a decisive manner was Charles VIII (1470–98) of France, in 1494.[2] During the long wars with Burgundy Charles's predecessors had seen the advantages of a combination of feudal cavalry and mercenaries, but the time had not yet come that they could rely on patriotic sentiment and sufficient revenues to create a true national army, which was essential for overcoming regional claims to autonomy and curbing powerful nobles. The cost obliged them to use their armies sparingly, but when they did, as in the Italian campaigns after 1494, the results were impressive.

Ferdinand and Isabella of Spain were doing the same in the Americas, sending ambitious young men there who saw no future at home. Among these men was a class of unruly *hidalgos* – young nobles – who had been largely unemployed since the victorious end of the *Reconquista* in 1492 with the capture of Granada, the last Muslim state in Spain. This had set entire populations in motion: large numbers of Moors and Jews emigrated to Africa and the Ottoman Empire, poor knights looked for honourable work in Europe and the New World, and Castilian peasants sought alternatives to hard labour and heavy taxes. Queen Isabella employed mostly Castilians in her overseas empire, while her husband used Catalans (from Aragon) to hold the kingdom of Naples against French claims.

Nobles, who understood that their status rested on their near-monopoly as a ready-to-go armed force, resented mercenaries, and were not useful for much apart from fighting.[3] Feudal cavalry could be deadly on the battlefield, but it took strong personalities to keep their attention focused on victory rather than going after loot and prisoners or undertaking some foolhardy venture in search of honour and glory. Italians could have provided lessons in command and control – and caution – but national military traditions and pride stood in the way.

Condottieri – as the commanders of Italian mercenaries were called – lost favour with city-states and powerful lords in these years, not because of any failure to adapt to new technologies but over demands for higher pay. As private entrepreneurs, they had pressed their employers for ever more money, and often they failed to live up to the terms of their contracts.[4] However, it would be wrong to blame them alone. Military units had organised along the lines of modern labour unions to protect their rights, especially their expectation of receiving regular pay, and had then chosen leaders who could drive hard bargains; they always overreached, causing employers to seek other ways to raise armies. The solution – a long time coming to fruition, partly out of institutional inertia, partly because the rulers could not extort sufficient money or obedience from their subjects – was the state-commissioned army.

It is hard to fix a date for the beginning of this change, since dissatisfaction with the contract warrior had long existed, but 1494 is a good date to use, as that was when Charles VIII of France crossed the Alps with his siege guns; afterwards the days of the armoured knight, the high-walled castle and independently owned armies were numbered. Draught horses for pulling cannon and supplies were suddenly in more demand than war horses.

Local knights and militias, even when led by *condottieri* with good hired troops, were unable to slow the French king's advance down the Italian boot. The rulers of Spain and Austria, dismayed by Charles's swift occupation of Milan, Florence and Naples, had to intervene – they understood that otherwise the balance of power would be permanently upset. The hurried alliance between Spain and Austria ultimately resulted in a worldwide Habsburg empire with the resources to support magnificent armies, although this was not the case when the Valois–Habsburg conflict over the possession of Italy, the Rhineland and the Low Countries began.

Charles VIII's successors, believing that France was essentially surrounded by a ring of Habsburg possessions, sought to break the encirclement by striking initially into Italy, then into the Low Countries (the commercial heart of Europe and a major source of Habsburg income), and again into Aragon and Navarre. However, Louis XII (1462–1515) lacked the vitality to be successful at such an ambitious project; he clung to life, but not to his Italian lands.[5] The search for allies against the Habsburgs would lead Francis I (1494–1547) to support Protestant princes in Germany and Scandinavia, and to enter into an unofficial alliance with the Ottoman sultan. Francis offered subsidies to German and Italian princes, making the nobles almost mercenaries. Though everyone explained that the connection was common political interests, not money, it was still a precedent that would increase in importance. While French kings would have preferred to support allies only in time of war, to guarantee that princes would be available then, they had to pay them in times of peace.

Francis was a spectacular ruler – a brilliant combination of everything that Anglo-Saxons find irritating in the French. He was handsome, vain, witty, frivolous, attractive to women and courageous. He wanted to rule Italy because he was honour-bound to continue the policies of his predecessors and because he thought it was his right. It would also confirm the high opinion that he had of himself – that he was an extraordinary man, from whom extraordinary feats were expected.

His chief opponent was Charles V (1500–58), the ruler of Spain, Germany and the Low Countries. Despite Charles's efforts to be a chivalrous crusading prince, he was comparatively dull and plodding; happily for him, those characteristics eventually worked in his favour.[6]

Other princes were nuisances, but not particularly dangerous. Henry VIII of England (1491–1547) was flashy, but unsuccessful in his continental wars. Italian princelings and cities cancelled out one another's efforts, as did German princes and prelates. Although the outcome of the struggle between the Habsburg and Valois dynasties was long in doubt, even when the wars ended in 1559 with a Habsburg advantage, France was clearly destined to be the political and social leader of Europe.

The Islamic World in Turmoil

Beyond the European horizon, though not forgotten, were powerful Muslim states. Turks were excellent cavalrymen, as were some of their subject peoples, and they could always call on Tatar horsemen or even more distant Arabs. Infantry was the problem because Turks were free men who considered fighting on foot tiresome, dirty and dangerous – in short, dishonourable. The sultans resolved that problem by imposing a tax on Christian subjects in the Balkans – a tax payable every four years in the form of young boys.

The Ottoman sultans employed captive Christians because they could be removed if they performed poorly, while Muslims often had friends and relatives to speak on their behalf; Christian slaves could even be executed, but Islam went so far as to forbid enslaving a fellow believer. Lastly, there were few Turks who could be called middle class – the group that filled minor governmental posts in Europe – and while no Ottoman wanted to trust a non-Turk, a child slave trained to become a Turk was acceptable. Lastly, cultural traits of the Turkish military class made them unsuitable for methodical and dull administrative tasks.[7]

Ottoman tax collectors selected boys from Christian subject peoples in Bosnia, Serbia and Croatia, converted them to Islam and taught them Turkish. Unlike ordinary Christian males taken prisoner, who were often just castrated and employed in households or used for heavy labour or as galley slaves, these boys were trained to serve in responsible positions, even within the imperial administration; those possessing exceptional strength became janissaries, the best infantrymen of the era.

The Arabs, who were the first to employ slave soldiers, lost control of their army and became servants to their slaves. These Mamluk (Mameluke) warriors, magnificent cavalrymen, made Egypt a powerful rival of the Persian and Turkish empires; their example made Ottoman sultans worry about how to limit the influence and importance of their own slaves.

The Turks also hired an occasional European military expert, especially for dirty work such as artillery; some Frenchmen went east as a combination of mercenary-adventurer and representative of the king; others, mainly Italians, served in the sultan's navy. Bajazet II, seeing the Christian advantage on the seas as his greatest military challenge, scaled back operations in the Balkans in order to hire Christian pirates. His military policies were so unpopular at home that the army ultimately rebelled and put his son Selim I (Selim the Grim, 1467–1520) in command. However, at that time, 1512, given that the greatest challenge was from Persia and Egypt, it was impractical for Selim to advance into Europe.

The most important suggestion that French military experts had to offer the sultan and grand vizier at this time and later – that a *national* army be created, or at least an army of mercenaries – was not something that any sultan was willing to hear. The Ottoman state was a multinational empire, and since a national army would have to have Turkish as the language of command and Islam as the religious 'cement', the minorities would object; in turn, Turks were not willing to allow minorities to hold positions of command. The janissaries were an exception – they spoke Turkish, were Sunni Muslims, and were loyal to the sultan. On the whole, traditional arms supplemented by the janissaries seemed to be a force well able to deal with all traditional challengers – and by 1520, when Selim died, he had defeated both Persia and Egypt.

Until this time, Europeans – Venice excepted – could ignore the Ottoman presence.[8] This changed after the army of Suleiman I captured Belgrade in 1521 and Rhodes a year later; henceforth, the ambitions of the sultan would complicate every political and military consideration in western and central Europe. Suleiman's successors – and, more importantly, their grand viziers – learned that janissaries, combined with Turkish horsemen and the forces of local subjects, Christian and Muslim alike, could deal effectively with enemies at all points of the compass.[9]

The Persians were not equal to the Turks in numbers; moreover, their principal concern was with Turcoman and Uzbek nomads in Inner Asia. Consequently, they traditionally recruited units of light horsemen, which were at a disadvantage against properly led Ottoman infantry and siege guns. Thus, the Persians' frequent military defeats probably had little to do with their well-deserved reputation for being lovers of art and comfort. What saved them was their willingness to burn the food and fodder across what is today Iraq and Azerbaijan, then employ light cavalry to harass Ottoman units on the march. Baghdad would remain in Turkish hands, because supplies could be brought to the garrison by boats and because the great city lay in the midst of a rich agricultural area that allowed the governors to keep the granaries filled. But elsewhere the Turks had to expect desert heat, arid marches, ambush and harassment.

Only in the 1600s did the Safavid dynasty of Persia find it desirable to employ many firearms, but when the shahs copied the practice of training foreign slaves as musketeers, they used some as dragoons, who rode horses and camels into battle, then dismounted to fire deadly oversized muskets.

The rulers of the three powers fighting for control of Italy in the early 1500s – France, Spain and Austria – had each promised that once they were victorious, they would lead a crusade against the enemies of Christendom, meaning the Ottoman Turks. However, before any of them could employ land and naval forces in the Balkans and the eastern Mediterranean, they had to win the struggle for hegemony. To do this, first they needed mercenaries, and second they had to deal with the leader of western Christendom – the pope.

The Struggle for Control of Italy

Julius II (Giuliano della Rovere, 1443–1513) used a shifting combination of private armies and regional allies in his efforts to recover papal territories: first the Holy League of 1508 (League of Cambrai, with France and Austria against Venice – an expanding land power at that time), then the Holy League of 1511 (Spain and Venice, and later Austria, against France – which had controlled Milan from 1500 to 1513). Complicating his policies were ambitions to win fame as a warrior and builder and to enrich his family. His reign contributed much to the demands for reform associated with the early Reformation.[10]

Julius did not command troops personally, but he drove his generals hard. Since he was temperamentally incapable of remaining safely in Rome and awaiting news, he journeyed into the field to share the sufferings of his soldiers, as well as their risks. He expanded the existing practice of making churchmen with military talents into cardinal-deacons (i.e., cardinals who were not priests, but were used primarily as legates, generals and administrators). He assigned Christopher Bainbridge, the archbishop of York, command of the papal army; he used the talents of Frederico Sanseverino, the son of a *condottiere*, until he went over to the French. Worried that cardinals representing the leading families of Italy, though often competent, tended to be more interested in advancing their own families rather than expanding papal authority, he rewarded Matthäus Schiner (c.1465–1522), a German-speaking professional soldier from the Swiss Confederation who intensely disliked his French-speaking countrymen, with a cardinal's hat, then gave him command of the papal-Venetian mercenary army. Almost immediately Schiner had the challenge of a lifetime – a French invasion aimed at recapturing Milan and the rich lands of Lombardy. The pope urged him to prevent this, and, at a distance, Maximilian I (1459–1519), the ruler of Austria and Holy Roman emperor, promised support.

Habsburg–Valois Rivalry

Maximilian can be understood by his motto, AEIOU, which meant in both Latin and German that Austria would rule the world.[11] While he preferred to work towards that goal by marriage alliances rather than military conquests, there was still Italy to consider. His grandson and heir, the future Charles V, was being reared in Burgundy, with Maximilian overseeing his German lands and Ferdinand of Aragon (1452–1512) acting as regent of his Iberian inheritance. Maximilian planned to defend imperial claims to oversee Italian politics using German landsknechts (pikemen) and feudal and hired cavalry, allied with the pope, along with Spanish troops provided by Ferdinand. Money was short, of course, since the gold and silver of the New World were still a vague hope rather than a reality – and what there was of that would go to Spain, anyway – and the princes of the Holy Roman Empire were reluctant to authorise taxes.

Maximilian's role in the Italian wars was indirect – his claim on Milan had not been forgotten, but the Sforza dynasty had gained a new lease of life in 1513 when Maximiliano Sforza (1493–1530) was brought home by Swiss mercenaries. Since twenty-year-old Maximiliano was an inept politician, no general at all, and had no children, the future was unclear. Milan was impoverished by war, the French were clearly coming back, and past marriage alliances had given almost everyone a claim on any inheritance should Maximiliano die, as was expected; the emperor had Maximiliano's cleric brother in waiting, should he need a figurehead to hold Milan for him. The emperor, however, was not well himself, either physically or psychologically – he carried a coffin with him everywhere – and he was fully employed arranging a double marriage with the Jagiellonian dynasty in Hungary that would eventually expand the Habsburg holdings across central Europe. While he could not ignore the Italian wars, he could leave the fighting to his generals and to Ferdinand of Aragon, who not only had a long-standing alliance with Genoa, but realised that to hold Naples he would have to expand his authority to the north – a preventive war, since the French were certain to make another effort to reclaim his southern Italian kingdom.

Everybody was hiring mercenaries at this moment and no one was more effective than Francis I, whose boyhood dreams of battlefield valour and chivalry were encouraged by his ambitious mother, Louise of Savoy (1476–1531). In reviving the dreams of his predecessors, Francis hoped to weaken his Habsburg rival; by occupying Italy, he would divide his enemies geographically and deprive them of that region's rich human resources; perhaps he could even make the pope subservient again, as his fourteenth-century ancestors had done during the popes' long exile in Avignon. Pope Leo X (Giovanni de'Medici, 1475–1521), however, had plans of his own – he would use the Holy League to recover territories from Venice, then turn on the French while using the potential of a French alliance to keep Spain and Austria in check. If lucky, the de'Medici pope could acquire territories for his nephews. It was an artful game, but too clever – it would succeed only against stupid opponents.

Few can follow the twists and turns of policy in the Holy League. The silk thread of continuity was Leo X's effort to protect the Papal States, using private armies supervised by cardinals acting as papal legates. Some observers, appalled by the papacy's cynicism and worldliness, began to cry out for a reformation of the Church. Germans, who were asked to pay tithes and taxes for Italian politics and palaces in Rome, began to pay attention to an obscure monk in Saxony, Martin Luther, who argued that if papal authority justified such behaviour, then Christians should rethink the doctrines underlying it.

Leo X counted on being able to manipulate the rulers of small Italian states and the leading *condottieri*, and to play the various kings against each other. Maximiliano Sforza was a pawn of his Swiss troops, who treated him as the mere figurehead he was. The duke of Savoy, Charles III (1486–1553), hoped that his control of the Alpine passes between France and Italy could restore his family's ancient prestige; however, in choosing to join the imperial alliance, he risked French anger. Venice was creating a land empire as insurance against the loss of its commercial empire to the Ottomans, an effort that brought them into conflict with the emperor and the pope. Minor despots profited from choosing the right side at the proper moment.

Francis of Valois cared little about such scheming. He owed his crown to an ancient rule, Salic Law, that limited the royal succession to male heirs; it passed to him as head of the Orleans branch of the dynasty and as the husband of Louis XII's daughter. He might have been happy with a life of selfish pleasures, like his male ancestors, but his mother possessed the determination and political skills that he lacked. Francis was handsome, athletic, a lover of art and poetry, an easy conversationalist and a connoisseur of music, wine and women. He was also incredibly rich. In short, he felt himself to be the perfect Renaissance man. Being conversant with every art and science, he imagined himself a master of the military arts as well. There was nothing he would not do if it furthered his ambition to be the master of Italy, or at least of Milan and Naples. In the spring of 1515 he left France with an army that contemporaries estimated at more than twenty thousand landsknechts, mostly drawn from the northeast provinces of France, carrying eighteen-foot pikes, with ten thousand Basques and Gascons, mostly armed with crossbows, and an equal number of Bretons and elite royal soldiers. Trailing along were feudal knights, a vast number of servants and camp followers, several dozen huge bronze cannon and some hundreds of men bearing firearms. His opponents – the pope's general, Schiner, Roman strongman Prospero Colonna (1452–1523), and the dukes of Milan and Savoy – had forty thousand Swiss pikemen and Italian mercenaries, and they controlled the Alpine passes.

Estimates of the numbers of troops varied widely, larger numbers being given by contemporaries, smaller ones by modern authors. This may be explained by the propaganda value of large numbers, as well as mercenary commanders having no incentive to understate the number of men being paid. Given losses to disease, desertion and preliminary skirmishes that every military unit experienced, a huge army at the beginning of a campaign could dwindle to a handful by the time it went into battle. Thus, both estimates might be close to the truth.

The crossing of the Alps was considered one of the great French military achievements of the era. Much credit for this went to Gian Giacomo Trivulzio (c.1440–1518), a Milanese noble in Francis's pay. It helped that the snows had largely melted by August, so much so that mountain torrents were now mere streams. Much like Hannibal centuries earlier, Trivulzio found an obscure pass, the Col de Larche, built a road of sorts and led the army over it.[12] This movement was not detected by the defenders, who were concentrating on the forces of Charles of Bourbon (1490–1527), Francis's cousin and a highly competent soldier, who was moving along the coastline. Duke of Burgundy and constable of France, Charles of Bourbon was high up the line of succession, behind only the king's young sons. Juvenile mortality being high, Charles of Bourbon could easily imagine himself wearing the crown – though that would require Francis also meeting an early death.[13]

The first French soldiers into Italy captured Prospero Colonna, who could not conceive of their crossing the mountains without being detected. Trivulzio said, 'My Lord Prosper, the fortune of war! Lose one time, win another.' The Roman nobleman replied that he had always wanted to visit France. Colonna was one of the foremost *condottieri* of his time, and, thanks to his family connections and to his ability to change sides abruptly, he had been able to acquire lands for himself in Naples. Francis later allowed Trivulzio, who had fought in nineteen battles for him, to die alone and out of favour. The fortune of war!

Schiner's Swiss were caught between two French armies – the one commanded by Charles of Bourbon, which they had been facing, and now Trivulzio's, threatening their rear. Escaping the trap by falling back to Milan, the Swiss then explored the potential for changing sides. In this, the mercenaries seemed rather more dependable than their employers, who were also reconsidering their options. The problem was that soldiers facing defeat were less likely to accept promises in lieu of payment than those who saw victory and booty ahead.

Bourbon, sensing that his opponent's troops were ready to mutiny, tried for weeks to persuade them to take his bribes and go home. However, the Swiss – though badly divided between the mountain cantons wanting war and urban cantons wanting peace – voted to accept Maximiliano Sforza's promise of future payment. This army, less a few units that returned home, marched immediately on the French king. Francis, suddenly facing an advancing army, ordered his own mercenaries to form ranks, only to be informed that they would do so only if allowed to plunder Milan and keep a third of the booty. Francis, unhappy to see that the principle of threatening a strike while negotiating wages had been grasped so quickly by his own men, said no, that he wanted Milan intact, but he would give them a month's additional pay.

The battle at Marignano, in early September of 1515, was a desperate encounter. After Francis's artillery and Bourbon's timely cavalry charge blunted the Swiss advance, neither side was willing to give ground; the conflict continued through the hours of darkness, though at a less intense pace, then resumed at dawn. At mid-morning word arrived that a hastily raised mercenary army was approaching from Venice to join the French king. This came as a surprise, since it was well known that the Serene Republic had run out of money; however, the councilmen had hurriedly raised the funds for twelve thousand troops by auctioning off positions in the government. That was a desperate measure, but if the army of Italian and Swiss mercenaries were to be victorious, Venice might lose its independence. The battle was now even more hard fought than before. At nightfall the exhausted victors fell asleep on the field, surrounded by sixteen thousand or more corpses and countless wounded men from both armies. In the morning the *condottieri* retreated, allowing Francis to occupy Milan. Maximiliano Sforza held out in his family's citadel for a month before surrendering, then went into exile in France – enjoying a generous pension from the king for the rest of his life.

Marignano was, according to some military historians, the first modern battle – the first in which firepower overcame traditional weapons. It also suggested that France, with a population equal to Spain and the Holy Roman Empire together, was now the leading power in Europe. Not surprisingly, when the emperor, Maximilian, died in 1519, Francis presented himself as a candidate for the imperial crown. He had good prospects – Maximilian's grandson, Charles, was fully occupied with secessionist movements in Spain, there were rebellions of knightly corporations in Swabia and reports of religious dissent in north Germany; most importantly, several electors had promised Francis their votes.

The setback caused Leo X to make a hurried tactical, temporary alliance with the French. This was opposed by Francesco Maria della Rovere (1490–1538), the hot-tempered duke of Urbino who now commanded the papal army. As a nephew of Julius II, della Rovere had not taken well to Church leadership coming into the hands of the de'Medici family. When della Rovere argued for continuing the imperial alliance, Leo X transferred the army to a pair of newly minted cardinals – Giulio de'Medici (1478–1534), the pope's nephew and a skilled diplomat (though no general), and Bernardo Dovizi, who knew almost nothing of war.

Although Leo X thought that it would be an easy task to replace della Rovere in Urbino in a similar fashion, with his own nephew Lorenzo, that proved to be an expensive and, in the end, impossible project. Della Rovere obtained Spanish aid and that was that. Dovizi's plan to talk della Rovere into abandoning his ancestral lands ended when della Rovere warned him that priests kill with cups of wine, soldiers with a sword. Since Dovizi knew that della Rovere had murdered a cardinal four years earlier,[14] he did not offer him anything to drink. Della Rovere received his lands back and was paid for all his expenses.

After Leo's two nephews died (memorable only for the fact that Michelangelo designed and decorated their tombs), he reverted to traditional papal policy – protecting the Church's lands by expelling or assassinating the minor lords who had made cities their own. Among his victims – according to the chatty and inventive Sienese chronicler Sigismondo Ticci – was Cardinal Alfonso Petrucci (1491–1517), whose sins were as minor and distasteful as his political contributions. When Leo X replaced the cardinal's thuggish brother in Siena, on the grounds that he was unpopular at home and refused to follow the papal lead in foreign affairs, Petrucci plotted to poison the pope. Leo is said to have used a safe-conduct to lure Petrucci out of his refuge with the Colonna family to discuss restoring the family properties, then imprisoned him in Castel Sant'Angelo in Rome while he tortured information out of his agents; after obtaining confessions, the pope turned Petrucci over to a giant Moor wielding a scarlet cord. Leo, like Petrucci, not wanting blood on his own hands, had a Muslim perform the strangulation. The two cardinals who had conspired with Petrucci were fined heavily – Leo X wanted to placate other, obviously nervous churchmen who were willing to trade cash for their lives – and thus escaped execution. This unsavoury scandal distracted the pope from dealing with the rise of Luther in Germany at the same time that it encouraged Protestants to believe that the papacy was totally depraved.

German Problems

Francis easily persuaded Leo X to lift the long ban on church services in France, and even to grant him the tithes of the French Church for three years (for a new crusade, both parties said); he was also allowed to continue the Pragmatic Sanction that gave him primary control of the French church and made the pope a secondary authority. However, no sooner had the king returned home in 1516 (with Leonardo da Vinci in tow) than struggles began, which soon became familiar. First, there was the French *parlement*, a judicial body whose consent was necessary to ratify the agreements with the pope; the lawyers, many of whom were clerics fearful of royal tyranny, resisted royal blandishments, threats and shouts for months. Second, Francis was spending too much money on friends, palaces, mistresses and luxuries. Third, the contest for Milan resumed – Maximilian had sent troops to take the city, but the combination of Bourbon's skill and Austrian poverty caused the siege to fail. Then, in 1519, the emperor died. The ensuing election paralysed German politics, for nothing could be done until a successor was elected – the favourite was Maximilian's grandson, Charles, just nineteen, but whose upbringing in Brussels gave him a good understanding of German politics.

The first step in selecting an emperor was for the electors to choose a German king (emperor-elect, or king of the Romans) from among the candidates. Most candidates could claim at least one emperor among their ancestors, but the Habsburgs had a considerable advantage in having several. Moreover, although Austria did not have a vote, the archduke – Maximilian's second grandson, Ferdinand (1503–64), named for his Spanish grandsire – had also become the king of Bohemia, the most prominent of the four secular electors (the others being Brandenburg, Saxony and the Palatinate). The three archbishops were never seriously considered.[15]

The second step was to be crowned by the pope. Historically, this was the most difficult step, since the popes resisted performing the ceremony until they could extort concessions and promises. After 1530, and the coronation of Charles V, this was less a problem – the Habsburgs simply dispensed with the practice. Technically, each emperor was only emperor-elect, but nobody would dare call them that to their face.[16]

Each election occasioned a political crisis, sometimes a serious one, and at times even a war. This was certainly true in 1519. However, after Charles's Flemish mercenaries put down resistance in Spain, highlighting that Charles would be a powerful figure, the electors welcomed him as a German-born candidate whose ancestors had long held the office – someone, moreover, who was willing to give larger bribes than his French competitor.[17] Moreover, German Protestants objected to Pope Leo X backing Francis and to royal efforts to repress demands for religious reform in France. They did not believe Francis's explanations that his persecution of Protestants was only a political matter and did not really concern theology, though there was much truth to that.

The new emperor was young, inexperienced, bug-eyed and slack-jawed, but he possessed in abundance a determination to defeat his dynasty's ancient enemies (France, Turkey and various Italian princes) and, later, to bring new ones (the pope and Protestant Germans) to heel.[18] While plans to achieve this were at first surely more rhetorical than practical, he was more intelligent than people believed and he was deeply committed to performing his duties. There seemed to be no limit to his prospects – he could surely even defend Belgrade and Rhodes from the Turks – but more immediate events required him to give his attention to Muslim pirates who were carrying away people from every coastline in his Mediterranean lands.

The Church, meanwhile, temporarily ceased to cause him problems. Leo X's premature death in 1521 was followed by the reform party's triumph. A dour Dutch churchman became Adrian VI (1459–1523). A close adviser of the emperor, Adrian abhorred ostentation, corruption and war. Holy war was a different matter – he was ready to mount an expedition to break the Turkish siege of Rhodes and to protect Belgrade, but he had no money to hire troops and sailors, nor could he persuade Charles V and Francis I to put their war aside to lead a joint crusade. Consequently, both Rhodes and Belgrade fell. In short order the cardinals, the bureaucracy and the nobles came to hate Adrian; and the common people despised him – two defects that Machiavelli (1469–1527) had warned princes to avoid. Being neither loved nor feared, when Adrian died, he was not missed. His successor was Leo X's nephew, Giulio de'Medici, who took the name Clement VII. His principal goal was to guarantee his family's possession of Florence through the troubled years ahead. A bit of corruption helped raise the funds he needed.

Valois versus Habsburg – Again

Francis meanwhile had overplayed his hand on the French frontiers, suffering two setbacks. That had persuaded Leo X, in one of his last political gambles, to join with Charles V to recover Milan. Fittingly, the army was led by Prospero Colonna. Foolishly, the king chose this moment to alienate his best general, the recently widowed Charles of Bourbon; desperate for money and worried about Bourbon's growing importance, Francis confiscated the rich properties of Bourbon's late wife and suggested that, rather than Bourbon marrying a woman of his choice, he could have the queen mother, who was obviously past the age of childbearing but infatuated with the heroic warrior. This was the culmination of years of growing estrangement. The king's need for money (and Louise of Savoy's jealous anger at Bourbon's rejection of the proposal) drove the proud constable to conspire with Charles V, then flee into Habsburg service.[19] In 1524, while Francis was struggling desperately with bankruptcy, Charles of Bourbon, after recognising Henry VIII of England as king of France, led the imperial army west along the coast as far as Marseilles, while the English king was to advance on Paris. The widespread conspiracy failed – it was easier to find men ready to talk treason than to commit it. Bourbon's plans fell apart. Even his invasion failed. It was not the last time that imperial armies would press into Provence, only to be forced back by famine, disease and a revival of French patriotism. Francis pursued the Habsburg army back into Italy.

Francis now had many Swiss in his service, facing Germans, Spaniards and Italians – it was a more natural arrangement for the Swiss in any case, since the Habsburg dynasty had long been the principal threat to their independence – but there were difficulties. When Francis ordered money to be sent to his troops, he discovered too late that his mother had taken it as repayment for her Neapolitan inheritance that had been squandered.

Charles V, meanwhile, had been in Spain, trying to learn the language, customs and personalities of his divided kingdom (Catalonia was not happy to be, as Catalans believed they were, subordinate to Castile). The most important of his generals in Italy was Fernando d'Avalos (1489–1525), the marquis of Pescara, whose connections with prominent *condottieri* went back to his Spanish ancestors in Naples and his marriage to Vittoria Colonna (1490–1547). Vittoria was one of the most prominent women of the era, important in art and culture as well as in politics; her father was a prominent mercenary, as was his cousin, Prospero Colonna, and her grandparents were the rulers of Urbino, Federico da Montefeltro and Battista Sforza. Pescara was, in short, a king-maker.

By now Francis had recognised his personal limitations as a general, but the close friends he entrusted with command were no better; what was worse, the king failed to supply his army properly. An epidemic of syphilis – deadly in its early form – had felled countless warriors and may have incapacitated Francis for a while. The contest would turn on the ability of his Swiss pikemen to prevail over German landsknechts, Spanish infantry, the best Italian mercenaries and more artillery than anyone had ever seen. There was supposed to be a secondary front in the north, with Henry VIII of England (who was married to Charles's aunt) once again pressing towards Paris, but the English king was soon halted by mutinies among his unpaid troops. In this contest of exhausted treasuries, Pescara and Bourbon had the initial advantage, but Francis was able to restore the balance, largely due to fear of Habsburg power that had made an ally of the new pope, Clement VII. Francis easily occupied plague-ravaged Milan (forty thousand citizens had died – as many people as were in his army) because the imperial army had wisely declined to take refuge there. With one imperial army at Lodi to the east, Francis chose to besiege the second, at Pavia. He then made an amateur's mistake – thinking that Italy was his for the taking, he sent part of his army to occupy the kingdom of Naples.

The commander of this army was John Stuart, duke of Albany (1481–1536), regent of Scotland until 1524. The king was generous in granting him exile in France later, because the expedition to Naples failed ignominiously. Francis had not only weakened his own army, but he had entrusted command of the detached army to a nincompoop.

Charles V, meanwhile, had authorised Georg von Frundsberg (1473–1528) to recruit an additional twelve thousand German landsknechts – many of them Protestants – to break the circle of forts around Pavia. Frundsberg was one of those famous Swabian knights who had rebelled in 1519, largely because they had been treated as irrelevant by Charles V. Like many others, Frundsberg had been a mercenary soldier with a distinguished record; he was also an enthusiastic follower of Martin Luther. Perhaps partly because the pope was a French ally and Frundsberg was a German patriot, he accepted employment in the Habsburg army – in any case, Charles V and his brother Ferdinand were the only employers in sight (though Spain was far over the horizon, and every proposed action had to be approved in Madrid before it was backed by money).

An even more important mercenary captain, Franz von Sickingen (1481–1523), was no longer available.[20] When unemployed at the end of the 1519–21 war, Sickingen and other Protestant Swabian knights had attempted to seize Church properties and make themselves territorial lords. When their effort failed, a whole generation, a whole class, went to its doom.

Entering papal service now was Giovanni de'Medici (1498–1526), the commander of the famous 'Black Bands' (which his men wore on their arms to mourn the death of Leo X). Unhappily for him, while visiting Pavia to offer advice to Francis, Giovanni was shot in the heel, requiring him to return to Rome for medical treatment. Before he left, taking his men with him, Giovanni told the king that he needed deeds more than advice. Francis, however, dithered, his army becoming weaker by the day.

In February of 1525, as the imperial army reached Pavia, the stage was set for the greatest battle of the era. The king's generals wanted to wait behind their fortifications, but Francis insisted on moving to a walled park outside the city, with the intention of attacking the imperial camp. He was also motivated by a chivalric desire for battle, and perhaps by a fear that he lacked the money and supplies to stay in place; also important may have been a misunderstanding of Giovanni's counsel, or perhaps mere impatience.

Moving the army out of its trenches was a mistake. However difficult Francis's situation had seemed, the imperial army had been worse off – Pescara and Bourbon could not retreat without angering their soldiers, they lacked the money for a siege and they dared not attack the French trenches and forts. However, once Francis came out to meet them, the customary struggle for positions, slowly wearing the opponent down, was unnecessary. Pescara saw the opportunity – he suggested that they break through the park wall and force a fair fight between the two armies.

This battle was very confused: partly because it was fought without much order, the Germans having advanced in the dark; partly because of the thick fog that Francis attempted to exploit in his dawn counterattack; partly because personal accounts reflected the experiences of very different parts of the battlefield and the human tendency to enhance one's own deeds; and lastly the desire of later generations to see here a decisive moment when foot soldiers and firearms triumphed over cavalry – a conclusion that may not be warranted.[21]

The imperial army was breaking into the French camp when Francis formed his infantry into ranks – six thousand Germans, eight thousand Swiss, seven thousand French and six thousand Italians – and took personal command of the cavalry. When his artillery caused the imperial van to recoil, the king led his heavy cavalry forward, hoping to turn the retreat into a rout. He captured the Spanish cannon, but his advance masked his artillery, making it useless; encountering rough terrain, his horsemen then came to a halt, allowing the imperial infantry to realign its ranks. When Francis's cavalry flinched from the gunfire on its flanks, the Spaniards went on the attack, breaking his Swiss pikemen, who were reluctant to press on to certain death. The king led repeated unco-ordinated cavalry charges on the centre, but was unable to make an impact on the serried ranks of the advancing German pikemen. To the king's credit, he fought valiantly, even after his magnificent warhorse was shot from under him, then he was surrounded and wounded. While the Germans and Spaniards cheered, the French army collapsed – and most of their commanders died. The French losses could only be approximated – seven to ten thousand, maybe even thirteen thousand; it was the greatest French military disaster since Agincourt, and Francis was taken prisoner.

The Sack of Rome

Although Clement VII was an experienced diplomat, his military experience was hardly deeper than having become a member of the Knights of Malta: he had been in nominal command of several armies, but being a papal legate hardly prepared him for command. He ended his initial alliance with France after the battle of Pavia, then changed sides again in 1526 in the hope of keeping Charles V from dominating Italy. That was a gamble, but he had two armies that he thought he could rely on. The first was commanded by Francesco della Rovere, the experienced campaigner with fine troops. His duchy at Urbino had little to offer except beautiful scenery – it was difficult to attack though it was easy to sally out from. However, della Rovere had lost Urbino briefly to the previous de'Medici pope and was unwilling to risk his life for this one. Between his dislike of the pope, his normal slothfulness and his Venetian employers' caution, he had reasons to avoid exerting himself.

The second army belonged to the pope's kinsman, Giovanni de'Medici, who had recovered from his wound sufficiently to walk. The only general willing to serve the pope unreservedly, Giovanni was sent to keep the German armies from breaking into central Italy. However, while leading an attack on disorganised imperial troops trying to cross the Po River, he was struck by a cannonball and mortally wounded. His men halted their attack, then fell back to Rome.

The Habsburg army had not been taken seriously until this moment. Georg von Frundsberg had been given only three weeks to recruit his landsknechts, and, having received insufficient funds from Charles V's administrators to pay each soldier an enlistment bonus, he had borrowed money in his own name and even sold the family silver and jewellery. When he crossed the Alps with twelve thousand Germans and Lowland Swiss on schedule to join Charles of Bourbon, he found that the emperor had provided him with no pay and few supplies, and that the Spanish troops – largely arch-Catholics – were unwilling to trust his Protestant mercenaries. Surely, Pope Clement must have thought, such an improvised and impoverished imperial army would dissolve.

When Bourbon and Frundsberg ordered their unhappily united armies to march towards Rome, Francesco della Rovere trailed after them without enthusiasm or hope of slowing their march.[22] Indeed, his Italian mercenaries were behaving every bit as badly as Machiavelli had predicted. No one was willing to die for the pope – at least not this pope – except the Swiss guards, and even they could do no more than retreat inside the fortifications of Rome and await the arrival of the imperial forces.

When the campaign began, Bourbon and Frundsberg had reason to believe that they could join with the forces of Cardinal Colonna, a supporter of Charles V who had turned his supporters loose to create chaos in Rome. Clement, however, had struck back quickly, routing the cardinal's mobs and destroying many of the Colonna palaces and estates. Contemporaries thought this was only just – that ancient family had always acted as though Rome belonged as much to them as to the papacy, and they had controlled the papacy as recently as 1431. Clearly, Cardinal Colonna was not the equal of his late cousin Prospero as a military commander or a political analyst.[23]

Bourbon and Frundsberg, in contrast, were brilliant generals. All they lacked was money, a problem they resolved by allowing their Spanish and German mercenaries to sack almost every place they captured, even at the cost of slowing their advance southwards. When this endangered the whole campaign, they stood up to their own rebellious men; during one protest for back pay, Frundsberg suffered a stroke. While Charles of Bourbon was able to persuade Frundsberg's men not to sack Florence, but to take money instead, he could not save Rome in the same way – Florence was a city with a trained militia ready to fight in its narrow, twisting streets, whereas Rome was divided by ancient family rivalries and lacked Florence's commercial resources and banks. Moreover, the mercenaries already saw Rome's legendary wealth as theirs. When the pope offered 150,000 ducats to spare the city, the mercenaries promptly demanded twice as much. Desperate, the pope began to name rich churchmen cardinals, hoping that the fees he would charge them would allow him to meet the soldiers' demands. The ploy would have worked had the pope had more time, but the mercenaries were howling to be let into the city immediately.

Though resistance in Rome was poorly organised, it should not have been hopeless. The pope had his Swiss guards, the now disorganised Black Bands, and the thuggish mercenaries of his cardinals and those Roman families that had a long-standing feud with the Colonnas. He hoped to negotiate with Charles of Bourbon, with Cardinal Colonna as mediator, but that prospect vanished in the dark and fog of 6 May 1527, when Bourbon was shot while leading his men in an assault on the walls. After that there was no way to protect the city.

The most exciting account of Bourbon's death was written by Benvenuto Cellini (1500–71), who at that time was still a lowly musician in the papal household. According to his autobiography, Cellini persuaded a friend to join him in taking a look at the fighting; like every sensible person of the day, they each brought an arquebus. His friend gave the tumultuous scene one glance and wanted to leave, but Cellini, who was by nature as much an adventurer as an artist, persuaded him and another friend to join him in firing a volley at the leader of the storming party. Though they could barely see through the fog and smoke, they fired two shots each, took one more cautious look over the parapet at the confusion in the imperial ranks, then retired. He learned the next day that some anonymous shooter had slain Charles of Bourbon.

When the imperial mercenaries broke into the city, the Colonna mobs emerged from hiding and ran amok. The Swiss guards took a stand near the Vatican, fighting desperately against Spanish swordsmen who ducked under their pikes and cut them down. The guards managed to get the pope through the elevated covered passage to Castel Sant'Angelo, the solid circular fortress on the Tiber River, but of those who made a stand at the foot of the high altar in St Peter's, only forty-two survived.

After that the mercenaries became distracted, none wanting to miss out on the looting. Why risk being killed when there were opportunities to break into cardinals' houses and search for money, to torture wealthy men and women, to taunt priests, to rape nuns and worse? Most of all, perhaps, after days of hunger, they could get something to eat and drink. The mercenaries were lucky that none of the pope's commanders was willing to strike while they were dispersed throughout the city, intoxicated and disorderly, or desecrating the bodies of the late popes. But all the papal officers did was helplessly witness outrages on their wives and children, and the destruction of their homes.

In any case, Castel Sant'Angelo could not be easily taken, and the surviving imperial commanders understood that Charles V would not want the pope slain – as some of the Protestant troops yearned to do. Cellini claimed to have taken command of the papal artillery, using it effectively against the besiegers until the pope could arrange the surrender of the fortress – a process that was hastened by knowledge that Spanish engineers were digging a mine shaft under him that they would fill with powder; the Germans gleefully taunted the defenders that the pope and his cardinals would soon be blown to hell (the directions of heaven and the underworld having become somehow reversed). Cellini boasted of incredible feats of marksmanship during the siege and reported that the pope had been so overjoyed at witnessing his exploits that he raised his hand in blessing and pardoned every act of homicide that he had committed.

Such marksmanship was impossible with a typical smoothbore.[24] However, three years earlier Cellini had made a fowling piece for himself that he boasted was extremely accurate, with careful loading enhancing its performance. In defending Castel Sant'Angelo he used the demiculverins on hand, taking great care to load the eight-pound shot in his own artistic manner. After peace was concluded, Cellini boasted that he marched away with three hundred men, but turned down the offer to become their commander. He had greater ambitions – to be a famous artist. (No one ever successfully accused Cellini of modesty, and anyone who doubted his feat would probably have been stabbed to death immediately – Cellini's temper had a hair-trigger, as his arquebus probably did, too.) He went to Florence, which rebelled against de'Medici rule two years later, then he returned to papal service as an artist, sexual adventurer and troublemaker; he ended up at the French court, alternating art with abuse, and defending the honour of his native land by insulting his hosts.

Pope Clement – who, like his predecessors, had been clean shaven – now grew a beard as a sign of mourning for the people who died in the sacking, imitating Julius II's example after the loss of Bologna in 1511. Henceforth, for almost two centuries, all popes wore a beard.

While partisan historians have long made Charles's Protestant troops the villains of the sacking of Rome, contemporary records suggest that the Spaniards were no better. Up to twelve thousand Romans died, countless churches and abbeys were looted, and ordinary citizens were robbed, raped and murdered. Afterwards, the mercenaries could not stay in Rome, stinking as it was from the piles of bodies, as well as being the scene of plague. Their march south to Naples was marked by burning villages, by the corpses of their own men who had perished from disease and heat, and by deserters looking for employers with money.

They were followed by a French army led by Odet de Foix, vicomte de Lautrec (1485–1528), an experienced campaigner who had moved into the vacuum in Lombardy, captured Milan and Pavia, then pressed south towards Naples. He needed naval support, but the Genoese admiral, Andrea Doria, was so angry over not being paid that when his contract expired he went over to Charles V. Lautrec's men died by the thousands in the siege of Naples, almost all of them from disease. When Lautrec himself perished, order in the French army collapsed. Those who had survived so far fled wildly for home – few made it.

It had not been a good summer for these mercenaries, although, in fact, these were poor years for mercenaries everywhere.[25] The profits were good at times, but the money went out even faster than it had come in; and while private contractors had few sources of income other than pay and plunder, kings had taxes and popes had tithes – that is, rulers had greater expectations of future income than any private entrepreneur could have. Bankers appreciated that, and only bankers were able to make the immense loans needed to raise and pay armies.

Once imperial authority was established in Rome, Clement VII quickly agreed to crown Charles as Holy Roman emperor. Pope and emperor-elect each had common enemies now – Frenchmen, Protestants and Florentine republicans – and both agreed that it was necessary to bring peace to Italy and to the Church. Afterwards Charles insisted that the pope replace his bodyguard with Catholic German landsknechts. Pope Clement agreed, on the condition that he be allowed to retain at least a few of his experienced Swiss guards – after all, they knew Rome and the dangers that awaited popes who were not cautious. The emperor agreed to this request, though at first the pope could only find twelve who were willing to serve along-side Germans. His successors quietly ignored the emperor's wishes, slowly increasing the numbers of Swiss. Later popes encouraged Spanish, Austrian and French military actions against Protestants and Muslims, but they never possessed a significant military force themselves. They might fume at the insolence and disobedience of their royal subjects, but they were utterly incapable of stopping wars between Catholic Frenchmen and Catholic Spaniards and Austrians. The most they could do was to cajole, to plot and to denounce. As Stalin would famously ask, how many divisions did the pope have?

As far as soldiers went, no pope had more than a handful of gaily dressed guards. The uniforms were probably not designed by Michelangelo, but they date from 1548, with significant simplifications made in 1914. Swiss mercenaries did not lack for employment, however – they were in high demand as bodyguards and for ceremonial occasions, even among Protestant rulers; the Bourbon kings valued French-speaking Swiss mercenaries very highly.

A New Master in Italy, Pro Tempore

After the great turn of the wheel of fortune at Pavia few of the expected changes in the political balance happened. In France Louise of Savoy maintained calm and order, much to the dismay of Charles V's advisers, who had been told by Bourbon to expect an uprising.[26] This allowed Francis, then a prisoner in Madrid, to turn his considerable personal charm on Charles V, who was beginning to rely on his own judgement in matters of state rather than on experts. In early 1526 Charles – eager to finish arrangements for his marriage and to take possession of disputed territories along the French borders – accepted Francis's two sons as hostages and released the king. As Charles's advisers had warned, Francis quickly repudiated the peace treaty. The emperor awkwardly insisted on directing his armies from Spain personally, despite the time lag required to send messages back and forth.

As Italians came to realise that the distant Charles V was their new master, many began to call on fellow nationalists to drive the foreigners – Austrians and Spaniards now – out of the country, but it was Machiavelli's appeal to patriots, immortalised in *The Prince*, that became most famous. Pescara, who had been badly wounded at Pavia, was approached as the most likely leader of the new coalition's army, the incentive being that he would become king of Naples. This was not an outrageous suggestion, but, being cautious, he neither agreed nor dismissed the proposal. Instead, he immediately wrote to warn Charles V. Months passed, during which he heard nothing from the emperor, received no reward for his services, and no pay for his troops. When Pescara died from his injuries, his widow received a handwritten letter from the emperor, but no money. That was an additional warning to mercenaries that they were much like tailors – their services were necessary, but not important enough to be paid for in a timely fashion.

The war resumed in late 1526, when disintegration of all the great armies led Clement VII to believe that the emperor's grasp on his conquests was weak. He persuaded himself that it was possible to return to the days when small papal armies could tip the balance of power. However, according to David Chambers, he simply lacked the money to raise any significant force. Parts of the Papal States were held by local tyrants; the men he had made cardinals so that they could supervise the mercenary armies were now dead or were going over to the French; and his alliances had suffered military defeats. As unpaid mercenaries plundered Italy from one end to the other, Clement VII slipped from one failed policy to another. His inability to master the situation or even hold to a decision cost him the confidence of his supporters. This contributed to a general feeling that even his good ideas were doomed to failure. Luck, as Clement could have learned from a closer perusal of Machiavelli's manuscript, *The Prince*, was essential to military and political success. Clement was not a lucky pope.

Because Clement eventually managed to recover Florence for the de'Medici dynasty, he could believe that his papacy was at least as successful as those of his predecessors. However, his plans for a new crusade failed totally. Benedetto Accolti (1497–1549), whom he had appointed cardinal to command Spanish troops at the siege of Florence in 1527, was arrested in 1534 for having stolen the funds raised for the holy war.

Crusading was the cry of the moment, though not such an obsession that it distracted anyone from local or dynastic politics. The advance of Ottoman armies on Serbia and Hungary had consternated even western Europe in the fifteenth century, but the conquest of those regions after the battle of Mohács in 1526 made it clear that the next battleground would be Austria; the fall of Rhodes in 1522 allowed Ottoman navies to threaten Venetian commerce and southern Italian coastlines.

Clement was the last pope who could have made himself the leader of western Christendom; he was also the last who could have made compromises with the Protestants – hard ones, but those made by the Council of Basel in 1436 to bring an end to the Hussite wars in Bohemia were not easy, either. Had the councilmen made similar concessions to the Greek Church, Constantinople might not have been lost to the Ottomans in 1453

– or, at least, there might have been less impotent anger and resentment.
The papacy, however, was itself part of the problem, and Clement refused to
make significant changes in traditional practices. When reform came, at the
Council of Trent, it was too late – the moderates had already lost hope or
been silenced. This schism would divide western Christendom well into the
twentieth century, when the passions associated with the divorce had cooled
sufficiently to allow for an approximation of polite conversation again.

It was not the end of the militant papacy. Though no pope appeared on
the battlefield, all encouraged taking strong action against Protestants and
Turks, and all supplied princes that were willing to fight with copious sums
of money. In the 1600s the popes managed to realise the dreams of Julius
II and Leo X by occupying all the disputed territories of the Papal States;
afterwards, though, the lack of an obvious enemy made the idea of a heavily
armed papacy somewhat ridiculous.

Still, the enormous financial power of the papacy was not to be
discounted, once stability returned sufficiently for tithes and taxes to be
collected. Even the loss of the Protestant states – where economies boomed
– did not seriously limit popes' abilities to funnel money towards friendly
rulers (usually Habsburgs) who could oppose the advances of the Ottoman
Turks. It was not yet clear that Turkish raiders would not overrun Italy
– and Clement had made it clear that he would die in Rome before
abandoning the city.

The popes were not alone in facing financial troubles. Gold and silver
from the New World caused an inflation of prices that eventually drained
precious metals out of the Ottoman world. Chinese and Indian potentates
similarly expected Europeans to pay in silver and gold, but some European
states could earn hard currencies by exploiting new colonies and expanding
trade with Africa and Asia. When the Portuguese came to dominate
the Indian Ocean, the Islamic world lost both access to Asian goods and
the monopoly on spices that allowed them to charge high prices. This left the
sultans with no alternative but to devalue their coins and collect more taxes;
it was a downhill path that no one imagined would last as long as it did.

The future lay with the great states, with dynastic rulers who could assure
a continuity of policy – whereas papal policies were more a reflection of the
personalities of each pope. The great states also had the population and
wealth to raise and support armies, while the popes had to rely on foreign

contributions that dried up in moments of crisis. Lastly, the Church did not understand that the growing gap between rich and poor was essential to maintaining a large army. Prices rose rapidly, wages did not; as food became expensive, consumers went hungry. Though royal revenues doubled or tripled, then doubled again, those sums were insufficient to keep up with inflation and perceived needs. Kings built palaces, roads and bridges, fortresses and churches – partly from pride, partly from perceived necessity, and partly as work projects – then justified taxes as necessary for these projects. While impoverished peasants drifted to urban slums, which had more crime and disease than jobs, turned to vagabondage or enlisted as mercenaries, kings turned to bankers who were flush with money from investors desperate to find some place to employ it before inflation eroded its value.[27]

It was not brute force alone that allowed monarchs to become masters of the situation, but also their manipulation of public opinion. Kings could impress their subjects through elaborate displays, magnificent palaces and military parades. This helped persuade their nobles, clerics and subjects to raise taxes for armies that defended what more and more people saw as the interests of the realm, not just those of the dynasty.

The role of the military contractor changed. From now on they would be selected by the territorial rulers; and if they decided to change employers, they did not take their units with them.[28]

The great struggle between France and Spain did not end with the peace settlement of 1559, but it could no longer be pursued with the frenzy of the earlier decades. France was momentarily exhausted and torn by religious strife, Italy was prostrate and Spain was fighting a naval war against a newly energised Ottoman Empire.

In the end numbers were what mattered. France not only had stability, but also more good land, hence more people, hence more soldiers and taxpayers – more than Spain and Austria combined. However, France was not yet unified – regions, classes, religions and noble families worked to defend themselves and their liberties, ancient and new. This gave the Habsburgs opportunities to continue to strive for European leadership.

The new battlefield was in the Low Countries – modern Belgium and Holland – not Italy. The rich lands south of the Alps remained objects of desire and ambition, but the opportunities for royal acquisitions seemed better to the north, where there were no mountains in the way, only rivers that may have been barriers to marching armies, but were means of transportation for men and supplies. While Italian commercial networks were shrinking before the advance of Ottoman navies and Algerian pirates, the Low Countries were sending ships to the Baltic and the Americas, even to the Indies.

Geography and Destiny

Spain and France were separated by a range of mountains, the Pyrenees, that formed a substantial barrier to armies, except where they approached by sea. At various times small states had straddled the mountains, but by 1500 these had been crushed between the two great powers. Moreover, it was not in Aragon (Catalonia) and Navarre that Spain and France mainly collided, but in the Low Countries. France had long coveted that region, with its rich lands and richer commerce, and Flanders was largely French in language and culture. Marriage contracts had delivered those lands to Austria, then, in the division of Habsburg domains after the death of Charles V, they went to Spain. Geography had invited French aggression for centuries, the only natural barriers being mighty rivers, most importantly the Rhine. What kept the French kings at bay was the determination of the inhabitants to retain their independence in local matters and commerce.

The unity of the region – never very strong – was shattered during the Reformation when a large minority became Calvinist Protestants. Charles V had tried to suppress this movement peacefully, but in 1567 Philip II (1527–98) sent a more forceful governor, the duke of Alba, Fernando Alvarez de Toledo y Pimentel (1507–82), who brought to bear the traditions of a powerful monarchy and a triumphant Church, as well as a powerful mercenary army.

CHAPTER TWO

Armies and Personnel

Mercenaries were common in the early medieval world. They were, in fact, necessary to rulers, taking care of their three most important duties – to protect subjects against foreign enemies, to arrest criminals and to defend the Church. Anything else the government could provide was welcome but not essential: social services could be left to the Church and local authorities. It was not until about AD 1000, when the economy began to rebound from the destruction of barbarian invasions and civil wars, that western kings, petty nobles, prelates and cities had sufficient money to hire soldiers regularly. Afterwards mercenaries were part of almost every army. Although vassals and loyal subjects usually helped enforce the laws and collect taxes without objection, mercenaries were essential for dealing with unco-operative vassals and subjects; mercenaries could even be employed against the Church, because although they saw themselves as devout Catholics, they were realistic about the hypocrisies of churchmen, who were not only individually ambitious, but also often assisted relatives in pursuing dynastic interests. Mercenaries were complex men – one just had to know how to handle them.

Mercenaries became even more important in the fifteenth century, especially in Italy and in the duchy of Burgundy, but also in France and Hungary. Burgundy – which is central to almost every study of warfare in this era – included the rich lands of the Low Countries (literally the Netherlands), the seventeen provinces where most people spoke variations of the Low German language family, most importantly, Dutch and Flemish; a minority living in Liège, Namur and Flanders spoke French. All provided taxes that allowed the dukes to hire professional soldiers who were superior in many ways to traditional forces. The dukes of Burgundy became deadly enemies of the kings of France, allying themselves first with England until the Hundred Years War was lost in 1453. Afterwards Charles the Bold (1433–77) attempted to reconstruct the long-vanished middle kingdom of Lothar – who gave his name to Lorraine – stretching from the Low Countries into Italy.[1] This brought him into conflict with the French king, the Habsburg emperor and the Swiss.

Charles had used his immense financial resources to hire German and French cavalry and English archers. Englishmen in those days were routing every opponent they faced – in France, even in Italy – and Charles had assumed that their firepower would cut all opposing forces to pieces. He especially did not believe that Swiss fighting in a phalanx would be dangerous. His archers would create great holes in their formation that his horsemen could then disperse. What he did not count on was the speed at which the Swiss marched into battle, or the men wielding halberds, a combination of spear and axe, or swinging a two-handed sword. He lost successive battles to the Swiss, eventually being slain in combat himself during a snowstorm.

Victory thus went to the French, though not total victory. Louis XI (the Spider King, 1423–83) had expected that he could force Charles's daughter, Mary, to marry his deformed son, Charles. However, she elected to marry the Habsburg heir, Maximilian, who retained the Low Countries after her death in 1483. This was one of several reasons for the later wars over the Low Countries.

In 1494, when Charles VIII cobbled together an impressive army from royal and feudal resources and equipped it with large artillery pieces, contemporaries recognised that this was different from any previous invasion force. Italy had been invaded many times before – by German emperors, by French supporters of the popes against Germans, and by Hungarians claiming the Neapolitan throne occupied by Frenchmen. But local strong points had held up the invaders until heat and disease struck down their men. Moreover, there was now the special class of mercenary captains, *condottieri*, whose armies were more effective than knights and local militias had ever been. Charles VIII's army was not superior to these forces in every aspect, but clearly only large states had the resources to raise and equip large armies – a point that Machiavelli made repeatedly, calling in vain for Italian unification.

What the *condottieri* contributed to future warfare was the kind of specialisation appearing elsewhere in society. Since the transition from medieval to early modern was occurring fastest in Italy, that land was seen by the newly powerful rulers of Spain, France and Germany as a highly desirable prize, a prize that was not organised to defend itself. Quite the opposite – there were always Italian princes eager to welcome foreign assistance against rivals, even when that involved some risk of the foreigners becoming their masters.

The revival of trade that made Italy wealthy also provided the money necessary for that rebirth of classic attitudes that we call the Renaissance.[2]

Renaissance Mercenaries

Italy had ancient traditions that lent themselves to the rise of mercenary captains. Since every city was divided into factions – most importantly over whether to support the pope or the emperor – city councils avoided complaints of party favouritism by hiring a foreign *podestá* to supervise the judicial system. This magistrate usually hired soldiers as policemen, but was limited in his military duties – there was a justifiable fear that if he had too many soldiers, he would just take over the government. Therefore, in time of crisis, city councils hired some powerful noble for a short period. However, when this, too, appeared too dangerous, they called upon *condottieri* with small private armies. Some *condottieri* were professional soldiers who had risen from the ranks, aided by a smattering of courtly manners and education; others were minor lords who had turned a part-time occupation into a full-time profession. In a very real sense, then, a *condottiere* was a private entrepreneur, an individual less threatening than a hereditary noble or a territorial ruler.[3]

The armies of *condottieri* rarely got out of hand as the 'Great Companies' in France had during the lulls in the Hundred Years War: masses of unemployed warriors terrorising entire regions, defeating every army sent to control them. The Italian mercenary units might have originally arisen spontaneously, but they understood that long-term employment was superior to short-term enrichment. Therefore, they trusted that the magnetic personality and business acumen of their leaders would provide a steady income without risking danger unnecessarily. Professional leadership soon proved its worth to both employers and employees. The Italian model, however, had one weakness: *condottieri* did not, as a rule, rely on large numbers of professional foot soldiers, nor did they have many heavy cannons; hence, after Charles VIII invaded Italy in 1494 with an immense army and an impressive artillery train, they were, in effect, priced out of the market.

Artillery required an investment of capital that no private army – nor even a small state – could afford, much less the cost of building artillery-resistant fortresses. Therefore, the battlefields of the future would be peopled by the armies of the great states. The economy of scale allowed for cheaper weapons – Milan was one important centre for producing armaments – and distributing taxes over a wide area meant that merchants would have been bankrupted if their competitors had not been obliged to pay the taxes as well; they were willing to pass it on to customers as an ordinary cost of doing business.

Although there is a tendency to think of the *condottieri* as having had only a short period of importance, they made substantial contributions to the military arts. First, they were very good at recruiting and training men; secondly, they knew how to avoid the effects of fatigue, dehydration and surprise that could undo all their preparations; lastly, they knew that pitched combat was wasteful – even a victory was purchased at the cost of valuable men and expensive equipment. If the same result could be achieved by manoeuvre and negotiations, why risk battle? *Condottieri* acquired a reputation for not fighting – thereby stretching out their employment contracts – but it would be better to think of them as capable, cautious commanders. Such men knew how to teach recruits to conform to the needs of the unit, to overcome enemies at minimal cost, and, when necessary, to lead their troops into the horrors of battle. They understood that soldiers had a natural reluctance to put their lives at risk, but that they would fight well if reasonable steps had been taken to assure victory.

Armies that expected defeat were much like mobs – or 'crowds'. While cavalrymen who sensed danger could ride away, infantry could escape only by throwing away their weapons and fleeing – once dispersed, they were difficult to rally. This is why armed peasants were so ineffective – they knew that they were not warriors, and when their immobile masses were flanked by knights, they fled in such panic that they were easily slaughtered in great numbers.

The term 'crowd' may be unfamiliar to readers of military texts, but everyone understands that a mob is usually excited and unruly, while a crowd is more passive – more like onlookers. Since only a fraction of any army is directly involved in deadly combat, the units out of the zone of conflict and the support personnel are by definition onlookers. Certainly there was some potential of their becoming involved in the fighting – their commander could order them forward at a critical moment, or the combat units could break and run, leading, as it were, the enemy right to them, but usually they contributed little to the fighting beyond assuring the fighting units that somebody was covering their backs.

In crowd armies the commander – usually a king or prominent noble – had to be at the head; if he fell, the men fled. Any army is prone to panic, but crowd armies are especially so. In a professional army the commander should be *behind* the troops, ready to move units about and to commit the reserve. Crowd armies have no reserve, and usually there is only a pretence at combined arms – a cavalry force may use a mass of foot soldiers as a momentary barrier to rally behind, but when the fight seems to be going badly undisciplined foot soldiers will quickly take to their heels. Thus, the importance of the 'pep-talk' before the fight began, to whip up enthusiasm and confidence – armies of 1500 were still small enough that a commander stood some chance of making himself heard, and of giving the impression that he knew what he was doing.

Trained professionals disdained civic and peasant militias because so many were essentially crowds – barely mobile, fearful and easily driven from the field. They feared them only when assaulting city walls, when their own cohesion necessarily broke down into individual acts of valour or into individual searches for loot. Once over the walls, the professionals knew that their reputation for brutality would terrorise most militiamen into cowering submission; if the resistance was too courageous, they would reinforce the lesson that civilians should stay out of the business of war.

The replacement of crowd armies by professionals was one of the most important developments in European military history. Although Renaissance armies were so small they could have achieved nothing against the well-organised large armies of Asia, small bodies of Spanish professionals overthrew both the Aztec and Inca empires. Firearms and horses were important in those epic adventures, but without enthusiastic native allies and the spread of epidemic diseases, they would have failed. Still, on battlefields filled with crowds of native warriors fighting one another, it was Spanish discipline and generalship that made the difference; and Spanish administrators were ready to take over when native empires collapsed.

The transition to a professional army involved a total restructuring not only of military practices, but of the government, the economy and the education of the public. Most of all it required discipline. Experienced troops understood that their units could not be allowed to dissolve into crowds; and officers needed training and experience. We have long underestimated the skills needed for success on the medieval battlefield, but those skills were not sufficient for the longer and more complicated campaigns of Renaissance armies, much less those of the French, Austrian and Spanish forces that began to fight over Italy in 1494.

Hiring mercenaries was not easy. Convicts and misfits were always available, but an army had to be more than a collection of criminals, drunks and runaways working for irregularly paid wages – certainly more than youths given weapons just before being sent into combat. Scars and missing teeth might be impressive, but what employers wanted were military *units* ready for combat from the moment they arrived, not individual warriors of questionable background and in need of training. The question was: with the *condottieri* unsuitable for raising armies outside Italy, who could do so?

The answer was experienced officers from Swiss cantons and Upper Germany who raised volunteers without formal authorisation, then sought employers. When early units failed to abide by the promises of their officers, employers were disconcerted; what guarantee was there that the troops would not demand increased wages just before joining battle? For a long while rulers had no alternative to hiring whatever forces were at hand – any one unit was much like the others. Moreover, since each contractor trusted only himself to command his units, a representative of a distant monarch could not easily give him orders. In time the rulers took over the business themselves, much as Italian despots had done with the *condottieri*, but that brought new problems. Command and control always sound easy. Many difficult tasks do.[4]

In the past rulers had commanded armies themselves, despite most of them lacking talent for war or experience in leading large bodies of men.[5]

While mercenary generals offered more hope of battlefield success, that hope came at a price – and at a risk. No one could guarantee that a hired general would perform as expected, or even, if he had a claim on the throne almost as good as the ruler's, that he would not use the opportunity to put himself in power – for example, Francis I's fear of Bourbon.

Hiring an expensive mercenary army was occasionally a case where the cure was worse than the disease – if abandoning a disputed point would make peace, that might be the cheaper and wiser course. Since many rulers preferred to use their money on safer projects such as palaces, artists and mistresses, and they were likely to lose the war anyway, this was what they did. Of course, if neighbours concluded that a peaceable lord was an easy mark, they were likely to press him hard. Thus, fighting had the benefit, even if the war was lost, in that those who fought back were likely to be respected.

Choices had to be made on imperfect or even false information, and so important was the role of Fortuna that everyone understood that the final arbiter of success and failure was often pure chance. Here a change in weather, there an apparently random cannonball, and yonder a messenger who lost his way or whose mount foundered. How easy it was to throw up one's hands in despair or to raise them in prayer. Holding up a sword worked better, but many just held hope aloft.

The promise that hope offered over logic was especially influential on individuals who saw themselves as knight-errants, chosen figures that God would protect no matter what the odds. Some, such as Louis II of Hungary, led their nation to disaster. Others, such as Charles V, missed opportunities to prevail. Then, as today, there was no universal rule – the weak made their way as best they could, the strong failed to realise their limits; since circumstances varied greatly, some judged poorly whether they were weak or strong.

A prince who could have been profitably emulated was Ferdinand of Aragon, one of Machiavelli's models for *The Prince*. He was a master of politics and war who had limited goals and therefore was rarely distracted into fanciful ambitions. Although Ferdinand's power came from his ability to employ mercenaries effectively by land and sea, Machiavelli regarded them as almost useless. No wonder that professional soldiers found Machiavelli's views of history interesting, but considered his proposals for military reforms foolish. Historians have found Isabella more interesting than her husband, because Ferdinand was too focused on Italian affairs to think about exploring for a new route to India, while she financed Columbus's expeditions to the New World.

In sum, the Renaissance was a period of significant change not only in art and architecture, but in military practices. These changes took place over so many years that it might pay to remember the phrase 'the moveable Renaissance'. The Renaissance that we are used to thinking of as beginning in 1300 with Dante and Giotto has been shoved by historians into the 1500s, and Jakob Burckhardt, whose concept of the Renaissance was widely accepted by the public as late as a generation ago, is rarely mentioned by scholars today.[6] In short, there is often a wide gap between what the public believes and the changing fashions among scholars. Bert Hall's *Weapons and Warfare in Renaissance Europe* not only eloquently summarises many of the commonly held ideas about the era, but his chronological repositioning of the Renaissance echoes what many medievalists have long argued – that there was no Renaissance; that Europeans just slipped from the Late Middle Ages into the Early Modern era.

Swiss and German Armies

The Swiss, having few natural resources other than scenery, which was of little value in that era, discovered that they could earn good money as mercenaries, and bring home valuable loot as well. They were courageous beyond belief, especially in comparison to the cautious mercenaries of Italy, who were willing to risk their lives when necessary, but understood that life was good and that one should not throw it away foolishly. In comparison, what did the Swiss have to look forward to at the end of a campaign? Switzerland was cold, the fields could not grow grapes for good wine, and local warfare was discouraged. No wonder the Swiss were willing to fight with all their heart – the characteristic that made them the 'gold standard' of mercenaries. Naturally, they preferred to be paid in gold.

The Swiss Confederation was an unlikely nation – most cantons spoke dialects of German, others French; some cantons were urban, others rural; some were mountainous and others had flat lands, but none possessed resources significantly more valuable than tolls levied on merchandise carried over the mountain passes. They had been brought together by resistance to Habsburg tax collectors, but their unity consisted mainly of an agreement to leave one another alone; this became even more important after the Reformation divided them along confessional lines. Even then Swiss Protestants refused to copy German models, but created their own democratic Swiss church. They did not like each other much, but they put aside local disputes for profitable employment as mercenaries; gaining loot from their neighbours was an attractive bonus.

Military service was often the only hope that many Swiss males had for acquiring sufficient capital for an independent future. Whenever they took employment, they worried that their unit would be pitted against one from another canton; since Swiss rarely retreated, a confrontation would be unbelievably bloody. Therefore, opposing units would be likely just to sit down. Fighting German landsknechts, however – that was different!

Swiss mercenaries first entered Italy in large numbers in the service of Charles VIII in 1494, attracting such attention for their ferocity and loyalty that Pope Sixtus IV opened negotiations with the Swiss Confederation three years later, going so far as to build a barracks near the Vatican and designate the church of St Pellegrino for their use. Still, it was not until 1506 that the first 150 guards entered papal service, marching through the Porta del Popolo to be reviewed and blessed by Pope Julius II. They performed so well that only six years later he gave them the honorary title of 'defenders of the Church's freedom'. Probably they would have preferred a raise, but every employer knows (or should know) that a little praise now and then can ward off other employee complaints.

The Swiss were ferocious warriors. However, they did not shed blood unnecessarily. They would not disperse to pursue anyone who had thrown down his weapons and fled, because they did not want to incur casualties from chasing desperate men, though they slaughtered those brave enough, or foolish enough, to continue fighting. Swiss ranks rarely broke even when beaten, making opposing troops wonder if killing the last of them was really worth the price. Discipline thus gave victory to mountaineers who had few weapons except a long pike and the dagger or knife that every male wore on his person.

The major Swiss weakness was in siege operations, where discipline counted for less and engineering skills were needed. Still, their reputation of never giving way, of killing everyone who resisted, but not pursuing those who fled, worked as it had for the ancient Spartans, opposing armies often melting away as soon as they caught sight of their foe marching swiftly and enthusiastically into battle. This was not true of the two new enemies who challenged them on Italian battlefields – Spaniards and Germans.

The Spaniards were swordsmen, skilled at slipping beneath the mass of spear points to close with the pikemen, although this tactic did not always work. The Swiss found the Germans much more dangerous opponents.

After Maximilian had been defeated by the Swiss at Dornach in 1499, he encouraged southern Germans to emulate their tactics – that is, to create more landsknechts. These warriors were less attack-oriented than the Swiss, and more willing to fight in combination with cavalry and other infantry forces; most importantly, they were willing to serve as a screen for musketeers, whose firepower could be effective only if attacking pikemen and cavalry could be prevented from closing with them. The landsknechts, whose spectacular dress uniforms lent prestige to their profession, were already employed across Germany and even in distant Livonia, but they rarely won battles alone. Musketeers may not have been able to hit an individual target consistently, but they could hardly miss a closely packed body of stationary infantry if they felt confident enough to aim steadily. And cavalrymen appreciated their quickness and steadiness in providing them shelter behind which they could rally.

A screen of landsknechts could give musketeers and cannon time to shatter opposing formations, after which the pikemen would advance to sweep the enemy from the field. No musketeer wanted to advance into a mêlée, since an unloaded weapon was useful only as a club; and the crews of cannon had no desire to face cold steel unarmed. For this reason, pikemen earned double pay.

Swiss and Germans generally hated each other, especially those from neighbouring regions who shared a common written language but found the other's dialects nearly incomprehensible. The Swiss had a long tradition of resistance to Habsburg ambitions on their lands, and Germans had formed those invading armies. There were also religious differences, which seem as small to us today as they were large to them in their time. And while Germans perceived themselves as culturally superior and historically more important, the Swiss were proud of their local traditions, their self-government and their warlike prowess. Their encounters were unbelievably bloody.

New Armies

By 1500 hiring mercenaries was popular not only with rulers, but also with vassals and citizens who no longer had to perform military service for long periods, far away from home – and northern Italy, the strategic centre of European warfare, was usually far from home. A mercenary army also allowed a ruler to exploit opportunities to make war without negotiating with parliaments, or breaking off campaigns just short of victory because feudal contracts had reached their limits. A mercenary army required changes in the way that money was raised, decisions were reached, and the kind of troops employed, but these were no more complex than traditional negotiations. Proposals for military reform were discussed by every political figure of importance, but it took more than half a century to work them out in practice. The most important of the immediate innovations was less reliance on cavalry and more on infantry. This came as an unpleasant surprise to the established order.

Cavalry had long been the dominant arm on European battlefields. Many medieval mercenary armies had horsemen at their core – usually knights and men-at-arms. Not only were cavalry more mobile, but command of foot soldiers was easier from horseback than on foot. Still, for those willing to adapt, by the early fifteenth century various forms of infantry – English archers, Genoese crossbowmen, Bohemians hauling primitive guns on wagons – had already proven their effectiveness. Still, because these units had specialised in decimating oncoming cavalry with missile weapons or firepower, followed by a decisive cavalry charge, the lesson was easy to miss. Not so by the late fifteenth century, when Swiss fighting in serried ranks temporarily swept all opponents from the battlefield.

Fighting in tight formations with pikes held high until about to collide with the enemy was a regional speciality, mostly from contiguous regions in Switzerland and southern Germany.[7] They divided all plunder according to democratically agreed rules, thereby reducing the incentive to disperse and grab whatever loot was at hand. Such social cohesion was rare. Like the English archers of patriotic legend, only free men made effective pikemen and landsknechts. Most European peasants, being either serfs or deprived of anything more than nominal freedom, saw little point to fighting except in defence of their hovels and families – and were usually ineffective then.

However, that was not the only reason that rulers avoided arming them. As William McNeill pointed out in *The Pursuit of Power*, when commoners realised that they were as important as their betters, they turned into independent-minded democrats; the Habsburgs' inability to crush Swiss independence and tiny Dithmarschen's successful resistance to Danish aggression were warnings against allowing subjects to own weapons.[8]

Rulers avoided being confronted by the domestic equivalent of the Swiss by disarming their subjects as much as possible, then hiring foreigners who had little in common with them – perhaps not even being able to speak their language – as soldiers. This would have the secondary benefit of sparing from slaughter those workers whose products and taxes made possible both civil peace and military adventures. In addition, rulers could round up the riff-raff that every community seems to produce and forcibly turn them into soldiers. After years of service, those threats to local law and order would have even less in common with the people they had grown up among; and, once discharged, would have no occupations to fall back on. Thus, ex-soldiers would languish in the poorhouses and jails until there was another call to arms, to which they would spring as rapidly as their unpractised muscles allowed – to the great relief of neighbours and local budgets.

The only way to replace natural social cohesion was by artificial ties – group solidarity created by training, by living and fighting together, and by having a common enemy. The Spanish military machine sent Castilians from different provinces to Italy for training and to serve as garrisons of important cities until they were ready for combat. Such moulding of civilians into soldiers was a vision of things to come, but it was a model that could only be copied by wealthy rulers.

This being the age of Shakespeare, it is appropriate to imagine that the stage was being set for the great contest for European hegemony that would last past the end of the seventeenth century. When that contest began, the essential characteristics of the mercenary were well developed, and within a few years the mercenary armies had changed European warfare forever.

European Armies in the 1600s

The Thirty Years War (1618–48) marks a watershed in European military practices. In this great conflict regiments may have originally reflected the region of their origin, except that each was supposed to understand the employer's language of command. However, the replacement of even normal 'wastage' required recruiting in the areas where units served. Uniforms varied widely. With so many soldiers moving from army to army, while continuing to wear the clothing they bore at the time of enlistment, it was more practical to employ some distinguishing mark – such as a feather or sash, the Habsburg troops having a red symbol, the Swedes a blue and yellow hat band – than providing new clothes. It was customary to give an enlistment bonus, which could be left with the soldier's family, perhaps new clothes, certainly a promise of regular pay and hope for occasional opportunities to loot and plunder.

Most of the soldiers were members of the employer's church – broadly defined, in the case of Protestants, but certainly obligatory attendance at religious services guaranteed outward conformity in all cases. The Beatitudes do not seem to have been stressed. Protestants understood what religious persecution meant, having had first-hand experience with Roman Catholic excesses. When it was their turn, they burned churches and mistreated those who wept at the sight. There were also exiles or volunteers from the British Isles, especially from Scotland. Robert Munro explained in his famous memoir that he had originally joined to fight for the Bohemian cause, but after that had failed he found the Swedish service attractive. As Geoffrey Parker warns us, in *The Thirty Years War*, mercenaries were not 'craven economic determinists', enlisting only for the money.

Maintaining an army was more expensive than simply passing out pay at regular intervals. Commanders had to provide for the soldiers and also – directly or indirectly – for the larger army of women and children and civilian employees that accompanied them.[9] Illness was a problem, with perhaps 10 per cent of the troops sick at any given moment, and many more during epidemics. Plague and typhus were the most deadly, but what we consider treatable childhood diseases were often fatal, too.

Because supplies could not be provided regularly, soldiers had to forage for food and fodder. The line between foraging and plundering was indistinct – and for the peasants it was largely non-existent. When soldiers met resistance, they used force; when they encountered armed resistance, especially guerrilla tactics, they retaliated brutally. This probably discouraged desertion, since fleeing soldiers would have had to seek the aid of local farmers for food, shelter and clothing, and farmers would have properly suspected them of intending to rob them. Undoubtedly, many a deserter ended up buried behind the barn, his money and clothing reckoned as a partial repayment for requisitions and taxes. The events of the war would become a part of national folklore, reminding people of the need for a strong ruler who could keep foreign armies away.

Later, most mercenaries would have started their careers as poor boys or men who saw military service as a way to earn money – this was especially true in hard times. (The root of the word soldier is *Sold*, the German word for money.) Others wanted to get away from home, from strict fathers and unhappy marriages, or just to see the world. German recruiters preferred country boys over less sturdy fellows from the city. Whenever units were stationed near home, boys raised on farms would help the economy, because it was a common practice to furlough soldiers for planting and harvesting. This created problems for soldiers recruited from nearby states, in that officials who learned that they were helping relatives bring in the crops might forcibly induct them into their own army. City boys were useless for planting or harvesting, and going home was not a good idea, because burghers would complain about them being worthless riff-raff – unemployable troublemakers. Commanders suspected that many might well have been criminals to begin with – they began to give criminals a choice between punishment, leaving the country and enlisting in the lord's army. In an era when jails were few and the state had little money for feeding prisoners, it made sense to use whippings rather than incarceration. Understandably some felons became tramps, and others became soldiers.

In time of war every country emptied its jails and poorhouses, not just to remove menaces to peace and order, but because that is where unemployed soldiers were to be found. After a few years in any army, the average soldier was not likely to return to civilian life with either a useable trade or improved morals.

A second class of mercenary was composed of nobles who either saw no future at home or who were in exile. On the Continent, these exiles tended to be Protestants; in Ireland they were Catholics.

A third class of mercenary – more common in the seventeenth century – was made up of rulers of minor states. Since armies were expensive, a lord could cover the costs of equipping, housing and feeding his men by renting them out to a rich ally. He rarely provided his enemies, political or religious, with his ready-made forces, but as long as he saw no harm coming to his own short- and long-term interests, he was quite willing to take money in the form of a subsidy – to keep his army available in case of an emergency – or a straight-forward rental agreement. The price depended on how serious the ally perceived the potential crisis to be.

In the case of German princes contributing to armies fighting the Ottoman Turks or the French, the arrangement might have begun as a patriotic obligation, the service required of each 'circle' (geographic district) of the Holy Roman Empire, but which later evolved into a business arrangement.

Each ruler sought to protect his local economy from losing its work-force. Rather than drafting his own subjects, he sent recruiters to other states; although he tried to forbid foreign recruiters from operating in his lands, young fellows who thought a career (or a few years of service) as a mercenary was better than staying at home usually managed to enlist where the wages were highest. Every description of soldiers – and we wish we had more – remarks on the diverse origins of the troops. Thus it was that even armies we think of as national contained a good number of foreign mercenaries, sometimes a majority.

Money to hire these men came from taxes and tariffs. There were also special exactions on towns where troops were stationed – justified by pointing out that the troops would be spending their money there; thus, a tax on beer would result in the mercenaries helping to support themselves. In wartime money could be saved by allowing the troops to live off the land; this was also a means of wearing down the enemy economically. No doubt some mercenaries looked forward to night-time looting as much as they did pay day.

Thus it was that the term 'soldier of fortune' has to be said with a tone of irony. Chance often determined what army an individual joined, whether he lived long or not, and whether he managed to accumulate anything that could be called a 'fortune'. To increase the odds of both steady employment and enrichment, he usually had to travel far from home, to places where men of means hesitated to trust their fortune.

CHAPTER THREE

Technology, Weapons and Fortresses, and the Growth of Empires

New Weapons

After 1500 the number of mercenaries increased steadily and significantly. German landsknechts and Swiss pikemen seemed unbeatable until the Spanish *tercio* appeared. This flexible formation, composed of a centre and two wings, allowed commanders to employ the first portable firearm (the arquebus), more swordsmen (a better weapon once a battle broke down into a mêlée) and a front wall of pikemen; it also allowed artillery and cavalry to fit into spaces between formations. This evolution was not uniform and it did not change the basic facts of politics: if a ruler could not defend his lands with the troops on hand, he had to either make an alliance with a powerful ruler – a potentially dangerous step that might compromise his future independence – or hire professional officers and soldiers. Machiavelli denounced both choices, proposing instead a civic militia that military professionals dismissed as laughably ineffective; moreover, rulers sensed that a self-consciously powerful citizenry would eventually dispense with their services. Machiavelli's programme was, in any case, a long-term solution to immediate problems; and since short-term security usually trumped long-term interests, most territorial lords chose to hire experienced and competent professionals.

Landsknechts were often asked to play a defensive role, to nullify the enemy's superior cavalry. When they moved forward against infantry, their weight was usually decisive, but if they could be brought to a standstill either by cavalry or field fortifications, they could be cut to pieces by muskets and cannon. When commanders ordered their men to 'dig in', their troops were not always as thorough as the Romans whose histories they read, but any defensive works made musketeers much more deadly.

Archery was disappearing quickly. This was not because arrows were ineffective at inflicting casualties – a trained archer could fire faster than a musketeer and almost as far – but good archers, whether employing longbows or crossbows, could not be trained as quickly as musketeers. Good bowmen were regional specialities – and rare.[1] Moreover, firearms, while not easy to master, produced loud explosions that assured the men firing the weapons and intimidated those on the receiving end –who could not see the missiles coming at them to judge whether they were truly in danger or not.

This led to what scholars have called the 'gunpowder revolution'. Gunpowder was composed of naturally formed materials, each of which had its uses in medicine or alchemy (practical chemistry that developed out of a combination of experience and curiosity). Sulphur provided the ignition, making the charcoal flame up instantly and causing the nitrogen-rich saltpetre to explode. The process of discovery was so simple that any state with alchemists would have stumbled onto it eventually, but it was China and India that led the way – a reflection of how much more developed their societies were between the tenth and twelfth centuries. A logical progression led from fireworks and rockets to mining, then to containing the explosion in a bronze or iron tube. Military exploitation was limited by metallurgy – the only expertise in pouring bronze and iron was that of bell-makers – and the rarity of saltpetre. Although saltpetre can be found wherever human or animal waste accumulates, scraping it off heaps of manure was slow work; significant amounts are generally found in warm and moist climates. Since three-quarters of gunpowder was saltpetre, it was more essential than the processed charcoal and sulphur. Any region with naturally occurring saltpetre was visited by merchants, whose interest was noticed by rulers who then sought to establish a monopoly of the product for themselves or to offer it for sale at high prices. However, that happened only after metal-workers could produce cannon barrels that could contain the explosion. After that it was only a short time before they produced smaller barrels that could be attached to a wooden stock and carried by an infantryman.

All early firearms were smoothbores and, therefore, inaccurate except at close range. Cannon smaller than siege weapons could be mounted on carts or wagons, which could then serve as a barrier against cavalry attack, but they were most effective when placed in field fortifications with a prepared field of fire. Like siege guns (bombards), the closer the target, the more deadly they were – luring an enemy into a killing zone, then fixing them there, was essential to using firearms effectively.

Musketeers were recruited from militia units and from regions where hunting was common. The former had trained to defend city walls – in Germany shooting societies known as *Schützenvereine* became very popular – and strove for accurate marksmanship (without actually achieving much until the development of the rifle); many militias still relied on crossbowmen such as the famed Swiss archer, William Tell, but that weapon was already old-fashioned. Recruiters persuaded listeners that it was easy to fight in the open and to fire in volleys, an argument that was plausible after landsknechts had demonstrated their ability to protect the men wielding firearms.

The arquebus could be easily carried by an infantryman, whereas the early musket was so heavy that few men could level it without a Y-shape brace to hold it steady. Even so, since the small ball of the arquebus could not penetrate armour, the musket became the preferred weapon.[2] (This meant that musketeers had to be larger and stronger than the average man; not surprisingly, they earned as much as double what men with lighter weapons were paid.) At the same time cavalrymen began to abandon armour because it exhausted man and mount without providing much protection. So, when the heavier ball was no longer needed to shoot down armour-clad horsemen, infantrymen were equipped with lighter and lighter muskets until the weapon resembled the earlier firearm. By that time, all long-barrelled infantry weapons were called muskets.

Most muskets were simple matchlocks, a trigger releasing a spring to touch a lit fuse to a primed firing pan.[3] The wheel-lock that was introduced around mid-century rotated a toothed steel wheel against pyrites (not a flint, which would wear away the steel) to send sparks into a nearly enclosed pan; though less likely to go off by accident and more dependable in damp conditions, the mechanism was too complicated and expensive to use for muskets, but it was highly suitable for cavalry pistols, where a burning fuse was not practical – and nobles had the money, or could borrow it, to equip themselves properly. Commoners had to make do with matchlocks, which took up to a minute to load and to adjust the fuse. That was a long time if an enemy was charging at a run and the weapon's effective range was only fifty metres. Soldiers had to also look for their commander's signal to fire – voices were often drowned out by the sound of battle – lest the volley be too early or too ragged.

Though our sources hardly document motivations, we see that strong commanders would fight a long war of attrition, while weak ones would risk everything on one battle; commanders with many firearms would avoid combat in wet weather, while one whose troops had only broadswords would welcome a downpour. Although early firearms were changing warfare, new weaponry was expensive, and new tactical formations were often not much better than old ones had been. With troops objecting to anyone experimenting with their lives, it comes as no surprise that commanders often fell back on tried and tested methods.

Change was ongoing, but not consistent. Charles VIII had relied on heavy cavalry and forty siege guns, but he had brought too few infantry to spare many as garrisons for captured cities; as a result, he lost his gains almost as quickly as he had won them. Heavy cavalry remained useful in the field, especially when acting on the defensive, making decisive counter-strokes, but headlong charges into infantry formations defended by massed spears and perhaps hidden spikes buried in the ground became rare except by inexperienced warriors. Spanish cavalry, lighter and swifter than French or Italian horsemen – perhaps a reflection of Spanish climate and geography as well as tradition – proved equally ineffective against firearms protected by landsknechts.[4]

A combination of musketeers, pikemen, cavalry and artillery became the norm for all European armies. Even so, weather, disease, terrain, reconnaissance, poor judgement and luck probably decided more campaigns than the particular mix of weaponry. Troops willing to fight often defeated men who were better armed but reluctant to risk death. Old-fashioned armies became ineffective at the same time that cities and castles seemed unable to withstand sieges, but the cost of new weapons and new fortresses made rulers hesitate to spend the money – if they had it. Military minds desperately tried to make sense of the changed circumstances.

Although battles could rarely be won without attacking, everything worked towards standing on the defensive, either behind a fortification, on a hill or across a river. This strategy was emphasised by a new geometric form of fortification known as the *trace italienne*, developed during the time of Michelangelo, who designed fortifications for Florence: castles, which in 1494 proved to be traps for the garrisons inside them – awestruck by the firepower, the walls collapsing under them, and unable to escape – were evolving into earth-reinforced fortresses that could not be captured without employing large numbers of infantry. Such a geometric fortress, often located on a steep promontory or partially sheltered by a river, presented little profile to artillery, but its concealed cannon could slaughter infantry that ventured into its deep dry moats. Therefore, attackers had to fill the moats with the rubble of walls and bastions or by carrying in baskets of dirt; destroying the fortifications by cannon fire or exploding a mine underneath them was so time-consuming that fortresses could often hold out until the besieging army ran out of ammunition and supplies, began to die off from bad food and water, or until a relief army arrived.[5]

Therefore, though a fortress was expensive, it was still cheaper than maintaining a standing army. It was essential that each ruler erect a fortress in his capital to cow his unruly subjects, but only very rich ones could afford to build them on the borders where they were needed to prevent invaders from destroying the regional economy – a frontier garrison might be small, but it could fall on an invader's supply lines and its cannon could dominate strategic river crossings and passes; moreover, since it was not usually possible to hire a suitable force of mercenaries at the last minute, the larger size of enemy armies and their greater speed made fortresses good investments.[6]

A second reason for building fortresses is that mercenaries in the field were liable to demand more pay once an enemy force appeared. This was especially true if the enemy appeared to be larger or better equipped. What was a wise prince to do? The importance of Machiavelli, the Florentine politician/writer/Italian nationalist, in forming modern opinions about mercenaries cannot be ignored. He denounced them for their reluctance to risk casualties, their willingness to change sides and their expense. Nevertheless, while his observations seem persuasive today, contemporaries were alert to the practical shortcomings of citizen armies. As a result, although everyone interested in statecraft had probably heard of Machiavelli, military officers were reading Caesar's *Gallic Wars* rather than *The Prince* or *The Discourses* – they appreciated the discipline and organisation of imperial armies, and saw through the pretence that late Republican troops were motivated by patriotism and concern for the public welfare. Machiavelli's ideas spread to Germany partly through translations, partly through denunciations of his cold analysis of statecraft,[7] but also through a 1578 book by Lazarus von Schwendi, *Kurtzer Begriff eines gantzen Kriegswesen* (A Short Account of a Way of Making War Better). There were calls for a German national army, but that was an idea that could not be realised for generations.

Military theorists such as Maurice of Nassau (1567–1625), the son of William the Silent (1533–84) of Holland and prince of Orange, were more interested in what worked in practice than in revolutionary ideas. Maurice organised the defence of Holland against armies coming out of the Spanish Netherlands and trained the next generation of Protestant generals in the principles of war, but he was always utterly practical – if flooding fields to hinder the construction of siege works was unconventional, so be it. Honour does not wear well at the end of a rope, and a head held too high might end up on the block. Experts who understood war from the perspective of the saddle always relied more on experience than theory, whereas those who observed from armchairs did the reverse. Maurice also dotted the Dutch frontier with numerous artillery-resistant fortresses. This would alter warfare significantly – part of changes so profound that they have been called the Military Revolution.

A revolution usually has little connection to the origin of the word, which implies turning around, but rather an overthrow of the existing order – a radical speeding up of the process of change, often accompanied by violence. The Military Revolution, which occurred between 1560 and 1660 (according to Michael Roberts) or between 1660 and 1710 (Jeremy Black), is one of those changes that mark the evolution of warfare into recognisably modern forms, but, awkwardly, this evolution occurred so unevenly and over so many decades, that the debate over its inception has been fierce. Given the wide geographical range of the examples and the long expanse of time during which this revolution occurred, it is unlikely that there will ever be universal agreement on it.

Still, there is some consensus that some aspects of the Military Revolution were in place well before 1618. However, once the Thirty Years War began, the process of change speeded up: previous army organisation, tactics and strategy soon became passé, as educated people were soon wont to say. Not only did equipment improve, and firepower become more deadly, but the size of armies swelled. At the onset of the war, a force of twenty thousand men was considered large; within a decade one hundred thousand would be under one commander. Such an army could not be brought together on one battlefield – command and control was too great a problem, and food, fodder and good water could not be provided for so many men and the many women, boys and children who accompanied them – but as the conflict spread out, not over battlefields, but entire provinces, the scale of war became greater than ever imagined.

Finding fodder for the animals was perhaps the greatest challenge. In the summer there were always pastures (though these could be quickly overgrazed by a cavalry unit), but in winter the army had to find barns with hay; the soldiers and their women would be quartered on the civilian population, filling the small houses with a combination of tobacco smoke and foul oaths, taking the choice seats closest to the hearth and presumably monopolising the featherbeds. Meanwhile, the harshest treatment would be meted out to those who did not share the soldiers' faith; imperial forces were very successful at using this strategy. It was not quite the same as a forced conversion, which had successfully returned entire regions to the Church, but merely giving them a choice – to accept abuse, expense, robbery, seduction and rape, or to return to Catholicism – would have done the trick.[8] Protestants seldom thought of imposing their beliefs on Catholics, but their treatment of Catholic townsfolk and villagers was rarely gentle, and they burned churches. Germans, Czechs and Poles remember ruefully the misdeeds of Swedish occupiers, but they were not alone. In the Thirty Years War all sides provided examples of military tyranny.

Raising these armies was the task of semi-private entrepreneurs – both at the highest levels of command and at the head of regiments – but the commissions were now awarded to officers by a territorial ruler, who thereby avoided some of the problems inherent in the earlier contract armies. The colonels of regiments were, to a certain extent, businessmen, perhaps as much intent on making a profit as gaining fame and honour; they also cheated, carrying more men on their rolls than were actually in arms, not delivering to the troops the supplies and equipment they promised, and taking their share (or a bit more) of the plunder. There were reasons for all this, sometimes good reasons, but the practices stand in sharp contrast to those of good modern armies.

The men often brought their own weapons, even their own uniforms; replacements were recruited on the march, diluting whatever original identity existed when the regiments were created. Troops spent far less time on drills than in gathering and preparing food, and many men were so ill, ill-fed and ill-clothed that every unit became smaller month by month, whether or not it was in combat.

One way to moderate this trend was to have a second army almost as numerous as the first, an army composed of women and boys.[9] Of course, there were commanders who saw these women and their families as more trouble than assistance, but for every one who worried that the soldiers would be overly concerned about the safety of their improvised families, there was another who worried that men would desert to join their wives back home. Germans tended to have more women in their armies than other Europeans, but that may reflect the fact that so many wars were fought in Germany.

Napoleon observed that an army travelled on its stomach; that was true of these armies, but the soldiers required more than food and shelter – they demanded pay. And so far the Habsburgs had been able to offer better wages than any of their opponents, and they were more likely to pay their troops on time. The need for hard cash eventually led to the formation of that economic theory called mercantilism (at this time perhaps more accurately called bullionism), which promoted economic policies that would keep gold and silver inside the state. In the 1600s rulers and their advisers might sense the wisdom of having cash on hand, but they had no theory to base policies on. (And in any case, there were always good reasons for spending money, even if the money had to be borrowed.)

Meanwhile, there were significant, though expensive, improvements underway in the art of killing. As armies became better organised, better led and larger, formations changed: the looser Swedish line slowly replacing the Spanish *tercio*, more mobile artillery came onto the battlefield and better firearms appeared in larger numbers.[10] While commanders were reluctant to risk their livelihoods on unproven theories and untested equipment, changes did occur; improvements, when adopted, entailed adjustments.

One was a lessened reliance on the lance and pike. As cavalrymen relied more on their pistols than lances, it was less important to have men bearing pikes to protect musketeers from them. Pikemen remained essential for assailing enemy positions, but awkwardly improvised bayonets gave soldiers an effective stabbing weapon to use against them. Another change was in volley fire. Since not even the best marksmen could hit a target predictably, it was necessary to shoot as many balls as possible in the direction of the enemy as quickly as possible. This meant that although a close formation was a good target, the more musketeers standing shoulder to shoulder, the better; also the faster they could fire, the better. Since a matchlock could easily set off another's weapon, soldiers practised to avoid that problem – knowing that in combat, soldiers would be falling dead and wounded and that orders might come to step over their writhing bodies to move to a new firing position. One has to admire the courage of the soldiers and the competence of the officers, to keep fighting after a third or more of their number could have been shot in only a few minutes. No wonder victors often massacred defeated foes – revenge was not a dish they wished to eat cold, but while their choler was up.

By the end of the century – as we shall see – warfare had evolved so far that European armies could compete with Turkish ones. That was a major shift in the balance of power. Whereas once Europeans had to count on distance from the Turkish heartland for protection, by 1700 they were able to carry the war deep into the Turkish borderlands and even to dream of driving the Turks from Europe altogether.

That was the result of the Military Revolution.

Nowhere was this more noticeable than in the effect that European weaponry and tactics had in the encounters with peoples who had previously been militarily superior. This has often been attributed to advances in technology, perhaps exaggeratedly, although the development of new ships, greater confidence in sailing on the high seas, and the financial and moral support of powerful rulers must also have been contributing factors.

The Ottoman Turks at Vienna

When the Ottoman sultan, Suleiman the Magnificent, marched up the Danube to Vienna in 1529, Charles V was still trying to sort out the confusion in Italy. Consequently, he could give his brother Ferdinand, the archduke of Austria, very little assistance; and the pope could give even less.

The Habsburgs had feared an attack on Vienna ever since the battle of Mohács in 1526, a disaster that many historians attribute to the Hungarians having disbanded the splendid mercenaries of Matthias Corvinus. That famous Black Army had defended the frontiers effectively until the king died in 1490, but Matthias's successor listened too carefully to his peasants complaining about heavy taxes and nobles fretting over their loss of influence. When he dismissed the troops, they went on such a rampage that it was impossible to hire a mercenary army again. Thus, in 1526 young King Louis II (1506–26) had to defend his land with only his feudal army of four thousand knights and volunteers from Austria, Bohemia and Poland – in all, only twenty-five thousand men of diverse training and expertise. He had little chance against four times that many well-disciplined and well-led Turks, with their contingents from subject peoples and allies. He made matters worse by refusing to wait for approaching reinforcements – his cavalry army was so beautiful that he easily imagined its charge sweeping the Turks away and even recovering Belgrade, the border fortress lost five years earlier. However, dreams are dreams, and the reality was something else.

The Turkish sultan had a more modern army than Louis II, and he had better generals – Mohács was not an even contest. The Hungarian knights charged into a deadly crossfire of muskets and cannon.[11]

It did not have to have been so, but five years earlier Louis's nobles had provoked the peasants into an uprising, then repressed them so savagely that one cannot imagine commoners wanting the nobles – in their gorgeous costumes, bearing outdated weapons, mounted on prancing horses – to prevail. The king was young and chivalrous, the nobles proud and impractical – a perfect combination for falling into an Ottoman trap.

The king's death without children allowed Ferdinand of Habsburg to claim the inheritance for his wife, Louis's sister; he seized Bohemia, Moravia, Silesia and parts of Hungary before Sigismund the Old of

Poland (1467–1548) could persuade his nobles and clergy that enlarging the Polish–Lithuanian Commonwealth was in the national interest. Possession of those lands – that famous nine-tenths of the law – belonged to Ferdinand, and he would not surrender them. Nine-tenths of Hungary, however, belonged to Suleiman. Luckily, the Habsburg tenth contained silver mines, which later allowed Ferdinand to fortify his new frontier and hire mercenaries to serve in the garrisons.

Ferdinand needed the new fortresses, because as long as there had been a Christian Hungarian kingdom, the Turks had been held far to the south, beyond the eastward bend of the Danube. After 1526 Austria was attacked almost annually by raiders dispatched by the Ottoman governor at Buda (Ofen), the high fortress looking down on the Danube, with the commercial centre at Pest on the opposite bank. Ferdinand had tried to push the Turks back early in 1529, capturing Buda. However, when the sultan's gigantic army came north, it was delayed only by the need to cross the great river's many tributaries; therefore, the Turks recaptured Buda and arrived before the walls of Vienna without having suffered much from the usual problems of disease and exhaustion.

The imperial marshal, Wilhelm von Roggendorf, took command of Vienna's defences, and an ageing mercenary, Nicholas von Salm, brought reinforcements in the form of landsknechts and Spanish musketeers.[12] In the end, inclement weather – snow – was more responsible for the Turkish retreat than the defenders' resistance; this happened again in 1532, when the slow march north left insufficient time for siege operations. Suleiman could do nothing except permit his horsemen to ravage Croatia, Slovenia and Royal Hungary, then lead them home. Afterwards Ottoman military leaders were cautious about attacking Austria. Autumn rains could slow the retreat down so much that cold, hunger and exhaustion would result in massive losses of men and animals.

The better choice was for the sultan to leave military operations in Hungary to his governor in Buda, much as the Habsburgs would come to rely on powerful local families in the borderlands.[13] Here as well as elsewhere, Ottoman diplomacy was as important as armed incursions for achieving Suleiman's goals; alliances with various Christian princes who were fearful of Habsburg ambitions made the sultan's defence of his Hungarian province relatively easy.

The siege of Vienna had come three years after Charles signed the peace treaty with Francis, who obtained his liberty by paying a huge indemnity and contracting to marry the emperor's sister – the widow of King Louis of Hungary – while Pope Clement VII agreed to crown Charles as Holy Roman emperor. That had freed Charles to take the war to the Ottomans by sea, occupying important cities in Africa and making local Muslim rulers his dependants.[14] The challenge provoked an energetic response from the Ottoman sultan.

Suleiman understood that he could conduct a war in the Mediterranean more effectively only if he limited his commitments elsewhere. Therefore, he refrained from actions in the Balkans that might be interpreted as a religious war, actions that might unify Christendom in another crusade. This gave Ferdinand an opportunity to organise his Austrian domains as an effective base for future ambitions. The sultan's last northern campaign, many decades later, was delayed for a month by the heroic defence of a border fortress by Nikola Šubić Zriny (c.1508–1566), the governor of Croatia. Not knowing that Suleiman had died in his camp of natural causes, Zriny led a desperate sortie from his beleaguered citadel. The attack failed, but Zriny became a national martyr.

Between 1529 and 1566, Christendom was a difficult concept for Europeans: Roman Catholicism was under stress from the Valois–Habsburg rivalry; the pope was fearful of imperial domination and the French king refused to co-operate in wars against Muslims; and Germans were demanding religious reforms, a call that was echoed in towns and valleys across Italy and France. As one state after another became Protestant, the excesses of peasant rebels and radical extremists threatened to overthrow the social order. This led fearful Catholics to strike out at anything smacking of 'heresy'. Later, when the reforms of the Council of Trent (1545–63) eliminated the grossest abuses in the Catholic Church, other issues that offended Protestants became even more deeply entrenched. Protestants quarrelled over theological minutiae, agreeing only that the pope and Catholic traditions were dangerous errors that refused to go away. With western Christians watching each other suspiciously, believing (sometimes correctly) that the others were plotting their destruction, conformism and paranoia became more evident than loving one's enemies and respecting their traditions.

Russians, taking their lead from Orthodox churchmen trained in Byzantine traditions, also saw the pope as a dangerous heretic. Believing themselves the last 'true believers', Russians felt beleaguered by Muslim Tatars and Turks, by Catholic Poles, and later by Protestant Swedes. The 'Tatar Yoke', the long domination of Russia by the tax collectors and slave raiders of the Golden Horde, remained a powerful memory, and recovering lost lands became a national obsession. This enterprise would take much of the next century and would involve western mercenaries, many drawn from Germany.

Mercenaries Here, There and Everywhere

Sometimes a smaller theatre of war provides greater insights. Thus, Scandinavia shows us how mercenaries, both cavalrymen and landsknechts, were employed to create regional empires, with Danes and Swedes ruling over large numbers of Germans, Poles, Livonians and Finns.

Denmark had long been more advanced in the military arts than the Swedes. The king of Denmark had both a feudal nobility and the resources to hire mercenaries. In less populous and poorer Sweden neither the handful of nobles nor the peasant militias could be easily compelled to adopt new weapons, to train regularly or to serve abroad.

This began to change after Gustavus Vasa (1496–1560) made himself king of Sweden in 1523. He won independence from Denmark with mercenaries, suppressed insurrections with mercenaries and intimidated his nobles with mercenaries, but he found that he could neither afford to maintain his foreign soldiers in peacetime nor control them. A compromise with the parliament (*riksdag*) in 1544 gave him a draft army of native Swedes. It was not an elegant solution – he had to allow some of these new soldiers to return home to help on the farms, and equipment was inadequate.[15] When King Erik XIV (1533–77) entered the Livonian war,[16] he equipped his men with the usual pikes and muskets and allowed the cavalry to experiment with the caracole – riding up to the infantry, firing their pistols, then circling back to the rear to reload. This use of small arms broke up formations of pikemen without the necessity of charging into them. Of course, it did not work as well against formations with firearms or archers, or on-coming heavy cavalry.

It would be too much to say that the Swedish successes against larger Russian armies were due to such new weapons and tactics: one could easily make the argument that the poor leadership of tsarist forces was more important than western skills; or that Ivan IV (the Terrible, 1530–84) had simply taken on too many enemies at once to respond effectively to any of them. Nevertheless, the tsar was so impressed by the technological and organisational efficiency of the armies opposed to his that he hurried to hire similar forces and to equip them properly. However, he and his successors, operating reactively rather than innovating, were always one step behind.

When Johan III (1537–92) became king of Sweden in 1568, he appointed mercenary generals such as Pontus de la Gardie (1520–85), who drove back Ivan's armies and made Estonia into a Swedish province. After Johan's son Sigismund III (1566–1632) united the crowns of Poland and Sweden, he should have been able to occupy all Russian lands to which he had an historic claim, and more besides, but his insistence on autocratic rights and on all his subjects accepting Roman Catholicism caused a Swedish revolt in 1599. He was not alone, however, in combining political foolishness with religious bigotry: he similarly offended his many Orthodox subjects. In 1595–6 he had persuaded churchmen from Kiev to join the Union of Brest, by which Russians recognised the primacy of the pope but kept many of their eastern practices and Russian language services. This 'Greek Catholic' or 'Uniate' Church seemed a reasonable compromise for an insoluble problem, but it only made matters worse. Many Orthodox Russians henceforth looked to Moscow, not Kiev, for leadership. Counter-Reformation piety and fanaticism had sharpened the religious division, not healed it.

Sigismund's efforts to recover Sweden militarily failed miserably. The Swedish regent, then king, Charles IX (Karl, 1550–1611), defended Livonia by hiring mercenaries from Scotland. However, that was no remedy. His commander, Munro, noted that cavalrymen were discarding their armour – it limited their mobility when fighting Russian and Tatar cavalry – and infantrymen employed fewer pikes, as the cavalry were using the caracole and the infantry were arming themselves with matchlocks. This left both at a great disadvantage against Polish heavy cavalry – the hussars charging at a gallop and scattering the lightly armed Swedes, who could get off no more than one volley before being ridden down. The result was a stalemate in Livonia and an almost permanent state of war between the two kingdoms.

Scots became prominent among mercenaries in these wars – they were already going abroad for money, some for religious reasons, some banished for crimes and some for having offended powerful clansmen and neighbours. Holland was their 'university', but Scandinavia provided their favourite employers. Climate may have been important in this choice, since few Scots made their way to warmer countries. Also, hot summers were generally associated with Roman Catholicism and most Scots were enthusiastic Protestants, many of them Calvinists.

Catholic Scots tended to join the French king's Garde Écossais, and Henry II, famously perishing in a 1559 jousting accident, had as his chivalrous opponent the count of Montgomery, the captain of his Scots Guard. The connection to Mary, Queen of Scots, made authorities in their homeland nervous, and rhetoric about undermining the Protestant establishment made their exile permanent. In time the numbers of Scots in royal employ diminished, until there were few Scots at all in the Scots Guards. This was not surprising, since every regiment recruited locally wherever it was stationed or fighting, and often enrolled captured foes.

Most Protestant Scots went to Sweden, to fight in the wars against Denmark and Russia. In 1573 between 1,500 and 3,500 appeared in Swedish employ in Estonia, making themselves locally unpopular for thievery, religious fanaticism and quarrelling. Unwisely fighting with German mercenaries in Reval, most of them were massacred.[17] The next largest number of Scots served in Poland, where the chaos of war reached its highest (or lowest) possible level in the early 1600s.

When rulers raising armies to fight in the Thirty Years War looked for experienced officers and soldiers, they hoped to recruit Scots, whose valour and discipline had become legendary. It may be that as many as one adult Scottish male in five served in a European army. Many were musketeers, mastering quickly the complicated instructions for firing their matchlocks in volleys and the even more complicated drills necessary to bring their formations into the most advantageous positions, though their greatest skill was in using the pike, a weapon that required great strength. Pay was generally good – clothing, equipment, food and pay (always difficult to calculate and compare) were better than semi-employed men could get at home. Scotland was poor, and prospects for uneducated men without land were even poorer. There was always the prospect of plunder – if not from enemy lands, then from whatever people were at hand.

As European wars became great multi-generational struggles, with battlefields in the far corners of the world, European rulers could fight them only by enlisting mercenaries. If there was ever a case of the rich exploiting the poor, this was it. But the poor sometimes saw it the other way around. When before had the prospects for employment or the opportunities for travel been so good? There was Asia, the Americas, and even Africa.

Recent European innovations in ship design had made long voyages possible, and cannon were much improved, too. Cannon rarely exploded now, and 'corned' gunpowder was more powerful and more dependable. Consequently, when Europeans reached Africa and Asia, they possessed military capabilities that no previous generation had enjoyed.

War in Sub-Saharan Africa

The immensity of Africa is such that many can grasp it only by looking at a globe. The continent is so large that the borders of some nations there could easily swallow several European states, yet what we understand about them is often little more than vague and often inaccurate stereotypes. Our impressions are, after all, formed on information from between 1500 and 1700, when disciplined European soldiers and seamen encountered African 'crowd armies' and explained their opponents' very different military systems as a reflection of tribal chaos.

European explorers, adventurers and imperialists did not take seriously the coastal African kings who became their trading partners, and dealt with their unfamiliar political systems by disdaining them. Modern scholars have often done the same.

It has not been easy to write about African military history. Researchers had not seen the early modern period as particularly important except in connection with the slave trade, and publishers saw little reason to print books that the public would not buy. More recently, devotees of political correctness have been antagonistic to 'the military' (as if that was a uniform and uniformly negative institution). Nationalist-minded historians in newly independent African nations subsequently replicated many of the achievements and failures of their nationalistic European predecessors, often focusing on Marxist interpretations of colonialism; some repeated Franz Fanon's call for violence and blamed neo-colonialism for every problem that could not be attributed to the colonial past. While this new generation of historians has produced fruitful insights into Africa's past, the effort to blame the West for every problem that Africa had experienced made it seem that Africans were merely onlookers in their own stories.

This began to change when oral history and archaeology began to undermine narratives based on Western sources.[18] Still, the traditional interpretation dominates our understanding of the era: that is, that the trade in human beings enriched African coastal chiefs sufficiently to oppose and even defeat the dominant inland states that had formerly exploited them and carried off their people across the Sahara for sale. The collapse of the long-established inland states was thus partly because European traders changed the balance of power.

There is much that recent military historians have contributed to our understanding of African warfare. For example, the loose formation of warriors constantly moving and shouting was an effective way to deal with a barrage of spears and arrows; it allowed warriors literally to dance out of the way of incoming missiles. This could not be done if they had fought in closely packed masses. This formation was a disadvantage when faced suddenly by Europeans using a close formation, moving rapidly towards them with pikes and firing bullets that no one could see. The psychological impact of firearms, however, did not last. Africans withdrew into terrain where cannon could not be employed effectively, nor even horses, and Europeans could not supply themselves easily with food and safe water. Once African warriors saw how inaccurate the musket and handgun were, and compared their own numbers to the small forces that Europeans could afford to send against them, it was impossible for Europeans to do more than hold coastal forts and forge alliances with nearby native kings – if ever they had wished to do more. Such minimal commitments made it possible for European colonial powers to curtail expenses and so maximise their profits.

This was important to European military history because incomes from taxes and monopolies gave Portuguese, Spanish, French, Dutch and English monarchs the money needed to pay for armies and navies; colonial experience trained men and officers in war, administration and national identity. Arabs, Turks and Moors profited, too, to varying degrees, and sub-Saharan Africans found trade to their benefit as well.

Portugal's Colonial Era Begins

The Portuguese were the first sailors since the Phoenicians to reach all shores of the immense African continent. Their small trading posts sold European cloth, weapons, food and alcoholic beverages in exchange for gold, ivory and human beings. The latter commodity occupies our attention today, though at the beginning of the colonial era, slaves were not that important a part of trade.

The first Portuguese conquests were in Morocco, paralleling the Spanish *Reconquista*, which was the recovery of Iberian lands long in Moorish hands. For the next century Portuguese kings occupied coastal enclaves, profiting from the trade and taxes that the feuding Moroccan sheiks preferred to share with the Christians rather than have them fall into the hands of rivals. When the king put the resources of the Order of Christ into the hands of the younger brother, who became known as Henry the Navigator, ship after ship sailed south along the African coast, each as interested in finding a current that would carry him home as in establishing trade with the native peoples.[19] While the trade with Morocco was valuable – especially in saltpetre, the most difficult of the components of gunpowder to find – it was when the Portuguese merchants were able to deal directly with Black Africa, cutting out the Muslim middlemen, that the profits became truly substantial. Later, shortly after 1500, when Portuguese explorers reached India, the profits became spectacular.

The first employment of white soldiers in Black African conflicts may have been in 1491, when Portuguese explorers assisted a Congolese ruler to put down a revolt in return for the king undergoing baptism.[20] Such arrangements were important in the swift expansion of the Portuguese trading empire.

The Portuguese had already been given slaves in exchange for releasing some Moroccan prisoners; employing these slaves on estates in the Azores and other islands, they developed the practices that were later extended to the New World. Once the Portuguese had reached Black Africa directly, it was easy to purchase individuals who had been captured in war or condemned for various crimes. This became important in Brazil and the West Indies, because slaves were needed to grow sugar and other tropical products. Efforts to supply labourers from home had failed – Irish, Scots and Frenchmen succumbed too quickly to heat and disease to produce a profit.

Another place where whites made an impact was in the Nile Valley. This was not because whites were racially superior, but because they were slaves.

Egypt

The Mamluks ruled Egypt on and off from the tenth to the sixteenth century, then recovered power in the eighteenth. Prefiguring the Ottoman janissaries, they were also more important – they did not just dominate the sultans, but supplanted them; when the caliph fled to them from Baghdad, they kept him in Cairo as an honoured prisoner. The first Mamluks had been slaves of Turkish origin, but from the late fourteenth century onwards most were Circassians – natives of Russia, Poland or the Caucasus regions. Some were from Black African and Turkish regions, but the warriors in the prestigious Cairo garrison were mostly Circassians. Although technically all were slaves, there were no masters and none of them was servile. Still, many remained loyal to their original owner/trainer and supported him against all rivals, a practice that was disruptive whenever there was an election for a new sultan. Married Mamluks sought to have their sons join their units, but these efforts were always resisted by traditionalists who pointed out that, as sons of Muslims, the children were Muslim and could not be enslaved. Mamluk officers and soldiers therefore had to make provisions for their children in civilian society. Efforts by sultans to make exceptions for their own sons usually provoked rebellions by commanders who saw themselves as strong candidates to be his successor.

Mamluk strength lay in their military discipline. Proud of their ability to fight from horseback with bow and arrow, or spear and sword, they were reluctant to use firearms, except cannon in sieges. The Royal Mamluks, the servants of the present and former sultans, were stationed in the major cities; ordinary Mamluks stationed on the frontiers had inferior weapons and mounts, but were more experienced in combat. Freeborn cavalry and native auxiliaries rounded out the cavalry corps. Their thundering charges brought them victories for 250 years, so that only at the very end of their era of greatness did they see any necessity to employ musketeers and field artillery.[21]

They were not particularly aggressive towards their neighbours, perhaps because in their system of government no sultan was connected biologically to his predecessor or his successor; if new lands were ruled by governors who were likely to become rivals, it was wise to refrain from making conquests that would enhance the governors' power. Financial problems were met by the temporary expedient of inflation. Luxury and frivolity made Cairo into a faithful copy of the *One Thousand and One Nights*, appropriately so since the story's setting in Baghdad was a fictional device to deflect criticism from the author.

As military discipline inevitably disintegrated, the military virtues were replaced by civilian vices. A civilian society can approve of students appreciating scholarship and disliking war, but when a self-perpetuating military machine does it regarding its troops, its very reason for existence is brought into question.[22] This internal contradiction became apparent when foreign challengers appeared – Ottomans to the north and Portuguese to the south. It was the latter who were dangerous first, taking over much of the trade with India shortly after 1500.

The Mamluks and Ottomans did not immediately sense the importance of this Christian intrusion, their attention being more drawn to Shah Ismail of Persia (1486–1524), an upstart Shiite champion from Azerbaijan; the Portuguese were merely a few cursed infidels in a handful of small vessels. Still, after Persian and Indian deputations came to the Mamluks to ask for help against the Christians, the sultan realised that something had to be done to reopen the trade lines. However, because Mamluk warriors would only fight on horseback, to build a fleet the sultan needed Ottoman and Venetian help, and to man the ships he had to hire soldiers and sailors from the Mediterranean coast, from Black Africa and the Turkish states.

When Egyptian fleets were annihilated by Portuguese ones in battles off the Indian coast, Islamic trade with the Orient diminished significantly. Henceforth Europeans travelled less frequently to Egyptian ports for spices and Asian luxury goods, and bought them from Portuguese merchants instead; Mamluk incomes declined.

Therefore there was less money for new weapons, though that seemed to matter little to the Mamluks because they considered firearms cowardly, and they had become accustomed to financial troubles for decades. To pay for what they needed, they debased the currency and froze prices; to augment their declining incomes, they resorted to corruption – to keep their subjects in line, they tortured rebels to death and sold their families into slavery. More importantly, dangerous rivals could be intimidated by the Mamluks' magnificent swords and spears, and their fiery warhorses.

Shah Ismail, understanding that the naval disaster had weakened the Mamluk sultan, began to make demands on him; this led the Mamluk sultan to ally himself with Selim, the Ottoman sultan. As it happened, the Turks bore the great share of the fighting, which soon deteriorated into mutual Sunni–Shiite massacres. Selim's 1514 march into Azerbaijan was hindered by Ismail's scorched-earth tactics, although he had not brought many cavalry into that rugged countryside anyway. In 1512, at the battle of Chaldiran, he sheltered his janissaries behind carts, where they could not be reached by Ismail's light cavalry. The battle ended as a great victory for the Ottoman forces, but not a decisive one. When Selim's troops refused to advance farther into Persia, he made peace.

Subsequently, Shah Ismail changed in personality, dropping every characteristic of the warlord to concentrate on poetry and religion; withdrawing into his harem, he left governmental affairs to his ministers. It is said that he died of heartbreak from having his favourite wife captured at Chaldiran and not being able to obtain her release. Without much doubt, Selim kept her captive to ensure Ismail's good behaviour during the Ottoman campaign into Egypt that followed the peace treaty. Shah Ismail's successors, the Safavid dynasty, became famous for its encouragement of architecture and the arts, including the carpet industry. As poetry, philosophy and religious thought flourished, Persian became the international language of the era, so attractive that even Selim I wrote poetry in it.

The Mamluks had not celebrated their ally's victory, for it was obvious that their own Syrian territories were next on Selim's list. When Mamluk reinforcements went north, the result was not a stronger army, but a civil war, the two groups of slave warriors fighting one another rather than facing the common enemy. Selim took advantage of the disorder in 1516. His army was far stronger – perhaps two hundred thousand men – but Mamluks were accustomed to prevailing over great odds. A wild Mamluk cavalry charge almost swept the Ottoman army away, so that for a few hours it appeared that Selim had been beaten, but the Turkish sultan managed to restore order. At length one wing of the Mamluk army came over to him and another formation, one of young Mamluks, refused to join the combat. When the Mamluk sultan saw his army coming apart, he fell from his horse, presumably dying of a stroke. His body was never found, lost among the corpses of his best horsemen, who were mercilessly slaughtered. The next year the Ottomans invaded Egypt. Too late the Mamluks adopted Ottoman practices – musketeers behind wagons and lines of wooden shields – but they now lacked sufficient cavalry to prevent their positions from being flanked.

The Ottomans took Cairo easily, but found it difficult to finish off the last Mamluk cavalry units. Still, Egypt did not offer horsemen much room to manoeuvre against an army of infantry supported by ships. After an orgy of mutual beheadings, Selim's men prevailed.

Afterwards, some Mamluks – those who had betrayed the last two sultans – served as Ottoman governors in the endangered provinces of the south. In 1769 Ali Bey al-Kabir (1728–73) overthrew the Ottoman governor and tried to restore Mamluk independence. The son of a Georgian monk, kidnapped at age thirteen, he had risen to the top of the Ottoman administration by sheer ability. He died in battle against an Ottoman army, but the sultans thereafter resigned themselves to Mamluk governors being essentially independent rulers. Not long afterwards Napoleon put an end to the Mamluks' long and glorious reign.

In the meantime, taxes from Egypt greatly augmented Ottoman revenues, making it easier to finance Suleiman's land wars against the Austrians, Russians and Persians, and to support his naval ambitions. After the epic siege at Rhodes had ended victoriously in 1522, the sultan looked westwards. There he found pirates preying upon the Christian coasts of the Mediterranean: these 'Barbary pirates' were aided by Moors expelled from Spain who knew the Spanish coasts well.[23] Their raids on unprotected coastal villages and towns helped distract Charles V from opposing the Ottoman sultan directly; later, their descents on the Italian coasts – aided by Francis I providing ships, harbours and supplies – prevented Charles from dealing with his problems to the north. The desperately fought sieges of Malta (1565) and Cyprus (1570), then the battle of Lepanto (1571) illustrate both how important the naval war was and how difficult it was for the Christians to fight it effectively.[24] Divided by religious quarrels, dynastic ambitions, and national interests, Christendom could not concentrate its efforts nearly as effectively as could the Ottoman Empire.

Meanwhile more Europeans went into Muslim slavery than Muslims or Africans into European servitude; and those who found themselves chained to an oar in a large war galley had cause to envy those whose fate was agricultural labour.

East Africa and India

Slaves had long been taken from many parts of Africa by Muslims. Scholars disagree as to how many slaves there were and how long the institution had existed, but clearly the European slave trade on the Atlantic coast began after the Arab slave trade along the Indian Ocean coast and across the Sahara desert. In the sixteenth century white slaves in Africa outnumbered black ones elsewhere – a political and social reality changed only much later by the suppression of piracy and the introduction of sugar production in the West Indies and Brazil.

It is understandable that slaves would convert eagerly to Islam, since that was a step towards freedom. However, until recently we knew little about African slavery except from stories told by Europeans. There were no Muslim organisations to campaign against slavery, telling of its horrors, as occurred later in Christian Europe. What is not in doubt is the prosperity of the commerce in African products, including human beings. Ports such as Zanzibar were part-Arab and part-African in population and culture. Although their trade was based more on ivory, iron and gold than human beings, there was – in the Muslim world, as in Europe – a demand for exotic servants and cheap labour.

The daring of the first Portuguese captains to make their way to India is difficult for us to comprehend, partly because our familiar Mercator projection maps were drawn to make the print identifying important places in the northern hemisphere easier to read – the result is that Africa and the Indian Ocean appear smaller than they are. In 1500 there were few maps – and those were inaccurate; moreover, the captains had only vague ideas about the coastlines, shoals, native peoples, established trade routes, prevailing winds and currents, and certainly nothing about the monsoons.[25]

Portuguese vessels were superior to Arab ones, but they were nevertheless still small and frail, and their crews were hardly confident of their ability to conquer the relatively unknown worlds they were encountering. We know something about their officers – they were for the most part noble and wealthy (or soon would be) and they left us their logs and correspondence; a few were Italians, such as Christopher Columbus – the Genoese were close trading partners, while the Venetians had close ties to the Ottoman world. Had the Portuguese king believed Columbus's assertion that the world was actually smaller than it was, he would have financed his voyage, expecting to find India roughly where Columbus actually found 'Indians'. On the advice of learned counsellors, however, the king declined to finance the voyage, after which Columbus famously went to Ferdinand and Isabella, thus providing them with the immense empire in the Americas that they might not have even thought about until 1500, when rumours came from Portugal that Pedro Cabral (1467–1520), swinging far to the west to clear a dangerous part of the African coast, had encountered land. That was Brazil.

The crews were divided into three groups. First the sailors, who could perform the complicated tasks of navigating dangerous waters in all kinds of weather; most of these men were probably Portuguese. Second came the gunners, who manned the weapons that delivered devastating broadsides once the captain and sailors had brought the vessel into an advantageous position – usually manoeuvring upwind of the enemy, then descending on one isolated part of his fleet (usually the strongest) and destroying it completely. Third came the men-at-arms, who would storm onto enemy ships or repel boarders. Wearing armour, using firearms and wielding swords, they knew that anyone falling overboard would go straight to the bottom.

The gunners and men-at-arms were seldom gentlemen, though their officers might have considered themselves such. The crews were rough and ready men, much like their counterparts in any European vessel of the era – ready for a fight, eager to get enough money together that they could retire from the sea to some farm or tavern (though it is unlikely that many were able to save much of whatever they acquired). Some were undoubtedly criminals given an early release, some were bankrupts, and some were foreign mercenaries. All lived in close quarters, with bad food, no facilities for bathing and washing, and no female companionship. Chivalry meant little to any of them except a handful of officers – that was a concept at odds with seizing wealth, laughing at pleas for mercy and exacting revenge. When the opportunity came to board an enemy vessel or sack a city, they were formidable warriors – and their terrified enemies knew it.

The Portuguese Reach India

When Vasco da Gama (1469–1524) reached Calicut (in modern Kerala) in 1498, the fact that he was actually there far outweighed the small size of his fleet. The local ruler was friendly – he obviously understood that more competition meant that he could negotiate more profitably with foreign merchants. His Arab and Asian trading partners, of course, were not pleased to see the Portuguese; they warned the Christian newcomers to leave. Da Gama managed to extricate his men, then sailed down the coast, where he was able both to trade and to learn how unstable the political situation was. If one ruler was hostile or unwilling to protect Portuguese merchants, there was always another who would welcome them. He also learned everything he needed about wind patterns for the next fleet to make the long journey more quickly.

In 1500 a stronger fleet was brought to India by Pedro Cabral. Although the ruler of Calicut allowed him to establish a trading station, after a few months Arab rioters killed all sixty merchants there. Since the local ruler did nothing to protect the merchants, Cabral retaliated by sinking all the Arab vessels in the harbour – a feat that the Arabs had not believed possible, given their overwhelming numbers and the few guns on the Christian vessels – then destroyed the city in two days of murderous bombardment.

The Portuguese fleet of 1502 consisted of twelve relatively large ships and half a dozen caravels. Led by Vasco da Gama, it destroyed Calicut a second time. Only afterwards did da Gama learn why there were no Arab ships in the harbour at the time – they had been ordered to join a vast armada that was now on its way to attack him. Because the Muslim commander assumed that da Gama would flee rather than face such odds, he made towards the open sea to cut off escape. That was a mistake. Da Gama, taking advantage of the shore breeze, brought his caravels close enough to the enemy dhows for his guns to do maximum damage to their sails, after which the Muslims could not close with his vessels to board them. Da Gama let the damaged vessels drift into the paths of the following Muslim vessels until the Arab-

Indian fleet became hopelessly tangled, then he destroyed the smaller ships one by one. The sea was soon a mass of sinking ships and drowning men. A following Muslim fleet of galleys was still dangerous, since it could attack the Portuguese even against the wind, but the rowers could only keep up ramming speed for a few minutes; the breeze kept the Portuguese vessels a consistent distance ahead until the captains chose to deliver horrendous broadsides against the leading galleys, then sailed on.

This cleared the way for the Portuguese to establish a monopoly on trade in East Africa, which they did with spectacular brutality.[26] This was not unexpected, since the sailors and marines had been told they could enrich themselves with booty, and the policy of terror was designed to intimidate anyone who thought of resisting later. When the inhabitants of coastal towns fled inland, the Portuguese occupied their ports as trading centres.

In 1507 a fleet commanded by Francisco de Almeida (1450–1510) penetrated right into the Red Sea and Persian (Arabian) Gulf. Almeida had left Portugal with twenty-two ships, a force sufficiently powerful to capture Arab trading posts along the East African coast, including Zanzibar. He gave command of one squadron to his son, Lorenzo, to capture whatever Arab vessels ventured to sea, while he sailed on to Bombay.

Unwilling to accept a permanent Christian presence in India, the Mamluks of Egypt and the Ottomans combined their resources, and the Muslim ruler of Gujarat in India provided more men and ships. Having learned from the earlier combats that their bulky dhows, while excellently built for peaceful trade, were not suitable as war vessels, and that their archers were no match for Portuguese cannon, they hired sailors and gunners from Venice and Ragusa (modern Dubrovnik), cities with commercial and military ties to the Ottoman sultan. These mercenaries were fine warriors on the open seas, and the artisans were expert in constructing galleys like those that had been so effective on the Mediterranean Sea. The Ottomans purchased the finest bronze cannon and even Dalmatian oak to construct four galleys.

Galleys had one major drawback compared to sailing vessels – the ranks of oars and the narrow width of the vessels made it impossible to mount cannon along the sides. On the other hand, they were not dependent on the wind, but could row directly at motionless ships, using their heavy fore and aft cannon to deadly effect. In addition, the Muslim allies equipped eight large sailing vessels for war, and acquired dozens of smaller ships.

The Muslim fleet arrived at the Indian port of Chaul in 1508, catching unawares three Portuguese warships and six caravels in the river there, about sixty miles south of Bombay. The Muslim commander decided against using his guns. If he could board the Christian vessels, which had no room to manoeuvre, he could capture them intact, then employ them against a future Portuguese fleet. If the Portuguese could have managed to get to sea, even a light breeze would have allowed them to escape the rowing vessels, but in hand-to-hand fighting their only advantage was having musketeers protected by armour. The first day's fighting was desperate, coming to an end only as night fell.

In the morning the Portuguese commander, Lorenzo Almeida, took advantage of the tide to fall quickly on the two largest galleys. After capturing them, he set them ablaze, to drift down onto the rest of the Muslim fleet. The tactic did not work, and that day's fighting ended only when the flood tide carried both fleets back into the river. There the shallower draught of the Christian vessels proved their salvation. On the third day the Muslims concentrated on Lorenzo's flagship, ultimately taking it, but the rest of the Portuguese fleet escaped in the confusion. Technically, it was a Muslim victory, but it had been so hard-won that the Muslim commander sailed away without attempting to take any of the Portuguese posts.

This was a mistake. Control of ports was essential to any naval power that wanted to control trade. Subsequently the Portuguese sold licences to Muslim traders, using the gold to buy spices that then sold for extraordinary prices in Europe; and while European products were almost worthless in India, they were valued in Africa, being exchanged for gold that could be transported to Asia. If a Portuguese warship, which was almost always swifter than a heavily laden merchantman, captured a Muslim ship without a licence, the ship, cargo and crew were all forfeit. Moreover, while it was impossible for the Christians to catch every Muslim vessel that ventured to sea – or perhaps even many of them – unless the Muslim captains had some place to sell their cargoes, all they could do was turn to piracy. After the Portuguese seized the ports in the sparsely populated East Indies, they made a fortune in the spice trade. But they could not have secured that monopoly without bases in India.

In 1509 Francisco de Almeida received reinforcements that allowed him to return to India. Arriving at the trading centre at Diu when most of the galley crews were on land, he immediately headed for the stationary vessels anchored under the protective guns of the castle. As it happened, the castle's guns remained silent. (This was perhaps a reflection of the Hindu ruler's secret wish to trade with the Christians – especially in horses, which did not thrive in the southern climate, but were essential for fighting Muslim adversaries.) Almeida destroyed or captured the larger vessels, then turned to deal with the small ships that had managed to get under way. Although these Muslim ships swarmed around the nineteen Christian vessels, their sides were too low for their crews to board, while Almedia's men could fire down on them with devastating effect.

After the Portuguese had routed their foes, they slaughtered most of the prisoners – both in revenge for the losses of their men the previous year (especially Almeida's son) and as a warning not to sail again upon the Indian Ocean. These seas were henceforth Portuguese, ruled from the strong base at Goa that was acquired the following year. Although the small Portuguese navy could not patrol every coast, it destroyed commercial competition almost entirely and did not even spare pilgrims en route to Mecca. The conflict, of intertwined religious and economic motives, was fought without mercy, a brutal reflection of the warfare in the Mediterranean. Almeida subsequently died on the return voyage to Portugal, slain by South African tribesmen. This event, together with the dangerous rocks along the Cape, caused the Portuguese to avoid the region. Thus, they failed to establish a base there, though the climate and landscape were more like Europe than almost any part of Africa.

Shortly afterwards the Ottomans overthrew the Mamluk state, making the Turks responsible for assuring trade with India. Instead of this causing the rivalry with Persia to flare up again, however, both Selim and Ismail recognised that expelling the Portuguese was more important than their contest for regional supremacy. Nevertheless, they could not expel the intruders from all their new bases.

The Portuguese achievements resulted not only in an Islamic resurgence, but also attracted Dutch and British competitors. The Portuguese had come to trade, not to conquer Asia; and when the Dutch came, it was to seize the Portuguese mercantile network, not its trading partners. The Portuguese empire lasted a century, collapsing from a lack of men and an even greater inability to change with the times. It was supplanted by a Dutch empire, then a British empire. In between and among these powers were swarms of pirates, European, Arab and Asian.[27] Arabs established enclaves along the African seaboard for trade, often taking human beings in exchange for their products, sometimes selling them to European slavers. Also, Arab pirates used the ports as bases, giving them a significant advantage over European freebooters who had to return to the Atlantic periodically to refit. Still, Western pirate fleets numbering as many as ten vessels prowled the Indian coasts, while Indians, Arabs and Malays robbed everyone in their neighbourhoods.[28]

Too Few Europeans

Once Portugal became subject to Spain in 1580, Portuguese men were fed into Spanish wars and were no longer available for service in the East. What to do? Of necessity, the compromise was to recruit sons of that handful of Portuguese who had settled in the East. This number was inadequate.[29] Moreover, the times had changed – perhaps the bloodthirsty crews of the first generation were replaced by men who were more civilised, or at least less eager to exchange their poverty for greater wealth at any cost; perhaps commanders had learned that a little mercy went a long way in dealing with enemies; and perhaps the enemies had become more formidable. Certainly the Spanish occupation of Portugal diverted resources away from the East.

The Dutch had long stayed out of the Indian Ocean for two reasons. The first was the profitability of the Baltic trade – fish, salt and wine brought great profits because the Danish kings levied low tariffs on Dutch ships passing through the Sound, whereas English vessels were heavily taxed. The second was the Spanish fleet, which declined in significance after 1588, when the Armada failed in its assignment to transport the Spanish army from the Low Countries to England; as Philip II's navy retreated towards home waters, his army became less of a threat. In the seventeenth century the Dutch navy sailed out to snatch up the Portuguese bases along the African coast. The only significant difference from their predecessors was that when the Portuguese passed the Cape of Good Hope, they sailed north, following the line of their outposts up the coast before turning eastward to India, while the Dutch sailed directly northeast, heading for the East Indies.

Dutch entrepreneurs were more flexible and daring than the Portuguese because they were less burdened by unimaginative instructions from the home government. Private enterprises usually thrive better than state ones, and it was no different in this era. The success of individual Dutchmen was improved upon in 1600 by the 'London Merchants trading to the East Indies'. Two years later a similar but much larger joint-stock company, the Dutch East Indian Company, was formed to increase the capital and spread the risk. The first Dutch fleet reached the East in 1607, and by 1645 the Dutch dominated the Indian Ocean and its eastern coasts; by 1660 they had taken most of the Portuguese possessions – which by then were insufficiently profitable to deserve defending.[30]

The Portuguese changed the politics and economies of Africa significantly, but their colonies were less profitable after the union with Spain; income declined after they lost access to the saltpetre production of Morocco and European competitors opened trade directly with Black Africa. While they were unwilling to abandon their outposts in Morocco, their expenses were greater than their income; indeed, it appears that they maintained them more out of tradition and pride than from any logical analysis. Perhaps it was the memory of the glorious victories and defeats of the past – they could lose them in a chivalrous defeat, perhaps, but not just slink away like cowards.

The posts in West and East Africa were necessary for the slave trade (that is, for the production of sugar and other tropical commodities in the New World), but the need to supply garrisons had an impact on the mother country, its sons being drawn off to distant death or assimilation into new societies. For the colonists, their fate was much like that of that first generation of Englishmen in North America – a horrendous death rate, and very little economic return. There were not only Africans to contend with, but other Europeans, and the uncertainty of survival discouraged many from emigrating. One might wonder whether the colonies continued to enjoy royal support, not because they were self-sustaining or essential to national prosperity, but because kings and important groups and individuals in the kingdom profited by them. Let the common taxpayer support failing enterprises, as long as the king profited. Subjects had few effective ways of protesting, and, anyway, they were told they should be proud of what their nation was achieving.

*   *   *

The Roman philosophy Pliny the Elder (23–79) once wrote, 'ex Africa semper aliquid novi' (always something new out of Africa). This is true; even in the study of military history there are still surprises to be had. Our Eurocentric concepts about mercenaries are challenged here – there were white mercenaries in black societies and black ones in Moorish states; sometimes there were eunuchs who carried arms and occasionally there were female soldiers. In Europe it was not always easy for a mercenary to change employers; in Africa it was often impossible.

This brings us to the other end of the historical range of the nomad – far from the West African trade route plied by camels for gold, ivory and slaves were Tatar horsemen who raided Russia for cattle, horses and people.

Englishmen and Others in Russia

Russia was organised for war in ways long forgotten by more commercially oriented Westerners – at the heart of each Russian city was a fortress called a kremlin. With only a few exceptions the marketplace and palatial homes of nobles and commercial classes were outside the walls. The boyars, those powerful lords who insisted on retaining the offices and commands possessed by their ancestors, did not hold their lands by hereditary right, as did western Europeans, but as a grant that could be revoked at any time. Hence, though boyars declared that their duty was to die for their tsar, they never hesitated to resist him if he seemed ready to appoint an unworthy person to office. So important were the books listing each family's rank, that one might say that genealogy was destiny. The boyars also saw accepting money for service as an insult, a suggestion that the recipient was no better than a foreign merchant who bought and sold. They disdained mercenaries as lower-born, foreign, money-grubbing heretics.

The boyars served as cavalry. Infantry and artillery – dirty, sweaty work – were given to the lower classes. This meant that, although the boyars held positions of overall command, they were not interested in leading units of musketeers or overseeing gunners: those positions could be best filled by foreigners. They resisted every suggestion that talented individuals be promoted from the ranks – without leaders, rebellious peasants were nothing more than a rabble. Good officers could make serfs into courageous, if somewhat unimaginative, infantry, and hiring foreign mercenaries for this task – and risking their being shot in wartime – was a concession that boyars made to practicality; but they made it reluctantly.

Decades earlier, before 1500, the grand duke of Moscow, Ivan III (the Great, 1440–1505), had conquered the last independent Russian state, Novgorod, and threatened to take over Livonia as well. Shortly afterwards he was rebuffed in battle outside Pskov. It took Poland and Sweden fighting together to push back his grandson, Ivan the Terrible, from the Baltic Sea. In this latter contest the Swedes had come to dominate Livonia, and they heavily taxed merchant vessels trading with Russia. Englishmen who evaded the tolls by sailing north of Norway and entering Russia through the White Sea were welcomed because Russians mistrusted Roman Catholics – meaning Poles and Austrians – and Protestant Swedes. Englishmen were a different kind of Protestant and came from far away. Thus, a conjunction of interests encouraged a flourishing trade between Russia and England via the dangerous seas of the Arctic Circle.

Queen Elizabeth I (1533–1603) encouraged this trade because she needed friends among the merchant class and the revenues that trade would bring. Surrounded by enemies, her hold on the crown was weak: English Catholics hated her, Irish Catholics called her 'Jezebel', Spain's king wanted alternately to marry her and overthrow her, and France was both unfriendly and filled with regicides. The Dutch wanted her help, but not if it made her merchants more competitive. Elizabeth felt that it was absolutely necessary to open up new markets for English commerce, new opportunities for English adventurers. One area of promise was to the west, in the Americas; another was to the east, in Russia.

Of the two, Russia offered the most immediate returns – commercial centres already existed there, and many of the same products found in America (furs, wood) were readily available and closer. However, Russians hardly seemed more civilised than the 'savages' of North America (whose tribal chiefs she gladly accepted as kings, without knowing how small their domains actually were). Nor was her knowledge of the tsar's realm much different.[31] German visitors were equally amazed, impressed and repelled. Modern Russian historians tend to reject these lurid descriptions as propaganda, but sixteenth-century Russians, secure in their own feelings of superiority, paid little attention to what foreigners said. They had little interest in the Western heresies themselves, but they feared that foreign religious fanatics might infect *Pravoslavie* ('true believers'), as Orthodox Christians referred to themselves.

Germans who entered Russia through Poland–Lithuania were usually on diplomatic missions, and German-speaking merchants from Livonia left few descriptions of life or politics in the lands to their east. Western mercenaries in Russian employ were reticent, too, the tradition of military memoirs being a long way in the future. Therefore, it was not until the seventeenth century that we have more than a handful of good descriptions of the state that was calling itself the 'Third Rome'. The best of those descriptions came from mercenaries and diplomats, all reinforcing the picture of Russia as a backward land filled with primitive peoples, violence and superstition.

Englishmen in America

In no part of the world did European technology and organisation have a greater impact than in the Americas. A relative handful of Spaniards occupied first the Caribbean, then the great Aztec empire in Mexico, then the even larger Incan empire in Peru. North America was more difficult to conquer because it was not unified, not rich, and, like Brazil, was composed largely of almost impenetrable woodlands and swamps. The Spanish explored the interior, then ignored it; the English and French established small colonies, first just outside the effective range of the Spanish navy, then in the Caribbean, where they could raise sugar and other crops that sold well at home.

The English and French were also interested in hindering Catholic Spain's effort to conquer the Low Countries. Pirate attacks so endangered the Spanish lines of communication that the king's advisers chose to send troops to the Low Countries overland via the 'Spanish Road' rather than by sea. Soon these attacks were extended to the heart of the Spanish colonial empire, attacking even Pacific Ocean ports so distant they were thought totally safe – so threatening the sea lanes between Mexico and Spain that the Spanish had to resort to sailing in convoy.

Protestant attacks on Spanish treasure-laden ships and rich cities blurred the lines between privateers and pirates. Englishmen claimed to be able to see the difference; Spaniards could not.

The most serious problem for privateers and pirates was to find bases where crews could rest, where barnacles could be cleaned from hulls, and where food and drink could be purchased (water was not safe, even when available). Recruiting crews, on the other hand, was no problem – life in any peacetime navy and even on trading vessels was unpleasant, almost unpaid and degrading. Piracy offered more freedom, more money and more prestige (or, at least, notoriety). By 1588 Queen Elizabeth's 'sea-dogs' had become so troublesome – along with other complaints about English policy, which included English soldiers fighting alongside the Dutch – that the Spanish king sent the Armada to eliminate them as pests, to stamp out English Protestantism, and end their assistance to the Dutch. However, the combination of bad weather and harassment by more nimble English ships had made it impossible to transport Philip II's splendid army from the Spanish Netherlands to England. Had that army made its way across the Channel, it would most likely have overwhelmed Elizabeth's forces.

Fearful that Philip II would establish another base near her kingdom – this time to the west, in Ireland – Queen Elizabeth encouraged English immigration there. Irish resistance led to an interminable war where English soldiers learned the art of fighting irregular forces. Learning that 'uncivilised' people could not be easily defeated by 'civilised' methods – as if war anywhere in Europe was less than brutal – they applied these strategies and tactics in the New World, where they were more successful because Native Americans lacked resistance to European diseases and each tribe had ancestral enemies willing to become allies of the newcomers.[32]

English settlers, who in 1607 established a fort at Jamestown in Virginia, did not come to dispossess the Indians, but to trade with them – they hoped for gold.[33] Their numbers included artisans capable of manufacturing items believed suitable for trade – glass for jewellery, bottles and plates, and other handicrafts. The businessmen who financed the venture were aware that Indians could be dangerous – hence the fort, hence hiring an experienced mercenary soldier, John Smith (1580–1631), to supervise military affairs. Smith was a charismatic figure – athletic, somewhat flashy, very self-confident, skilled at languages and worldly-wise. Smith had fought in the French army against the Spanish, and he had served the emperor and two Transylvanian princes with distinction. Taken prisoner by the Turks, he was sold into slavery and shipped to the Crimea. There he escaped and made his way across the steppe to Russia, then to Poland–Lithuania. Not surprisingly, the Virginia Company saw in him a person who could lead the settlement's military contingent.

Without Captain Smith's driving personality and his having the authority to bend the colonists to his will, Jamestown would no doubt have perished much as Walter Raleigh's settlement at Roanoke had. As it was, the death rate was astronomical. Disease and starvation swept off most of the early settlers; the Indians accounted for a few more (in 1622 they slew a third of the entire population). The most basic problem, as we have learned in recent years, was weather. The Englishmen arrived at the start of a period of climate change – the worst drought ever experienced there dried up not only their crops, but also those of the Indians, leaving little surplus to sell. English diseases also raced through the Indian settlements, making the native chiefs reluctant to meet face to face with colonists. Lastly, no Englishman was ready for the intense heat and humidity of the Virginia tidelands; woollen clothing was suitable only for the frigid winters.

Smith was the man who kept the sinking enterprise afloat. He bullied more than he cajoled and he exceeded his instructions, but by decreeing that only those who worked would eat, he persuaded ill and recalcitrant men to labour. He visited native settlements, often seeking to buy food; if refused, he would threaten to take it; if still unsuccessful, he would seize what his men needed to survive and re-establish a mutually beneficial trading relationship later. The story that Pocahontas, the king's daughter, saved him from having his brains bashed in may not be true, but he had probably been in mortal danger. Pocahontas married one of Smith's men (the first to plant tobacco and subsequently a wealthy man); she later sailed to England as a great lady and upon her death was buried in Westminster.

Smith's exploration of the Atlantic coast in 1614 failed to encourage the investors of the Virginia Company to pour more money into what seemed a hopeless venture. When the company declared bankruptcy in 1618, John Smith's time was past. His services were no longer necessary – the surviving colonists could manage on their own.

The greatest problem had been to find a product they could sell to both Europeans and Indians – that was tobacco. The Indians, reduced in numbers and fearful of new epidemics, had withdrawn from the coast, and the Spanish threat had proved illusory. The colonists, once left to themselves, brought women from England, purchased the cargo of a Spanish slaver from a Dutch pirate and employed the Africans as indentured servants (slavery came decades later).[34]

Smith's own narrative of his Virginia years established the legend of slothful colonists who wanted only to search for gold (a concept that can be held only by those who have never attempted prospecting), while critics created the myth of his irrationally tyrannical behaviour. Modern scholarship has modified both views, and modern archaeology has demonstrated that Jamestown was a greater success than past historians had believed. One thing above all is clear: without Smith's leadership and his men's military skills, Jamestown would have been another 'lost colony'. As it was, by 1625, when England had sent a hundred thousand people to Ireland, Virginia had only 1,210 settlers (approximately a 20 per cent survival rate). Nevertheless, the best prospects for growth lay not in Ireland, but across the Atlantic.

The Spanish Main

Spain was the leading country in Europe for a century partly because its American and Asian colonies provided money to raise and supply its armies. This prompted other European nations to follow its example. Even tiny Courland in the Baltic established a colony in the Caribbean to produce sugar, and another colony in Africa to provide slaves for its plantations. Denmark and Sweden established colonies in the Americas, too. However, it was England and France that were most successful in finding places where the Spanish and Portuguese lacked the manpower or the will to drive them away.

The West Indies contained islands ideally suited for the production of sugar, but the land was so exclusively used for this one crop that plantation managers had to buy foodstuffs from elsewhere – most importantly fish, wheat and rice from North American colonies. The Americans made some of the sugar into rum, which sold well at home and in Europe, but also in Africa – to buy slaves that could be sold in the West Indies. Trade was going global.

Another important commodity was fur, available in the colder parts of the continent. Colonists in New England, New France and New Amsterdam had already entered into this trade with Native Americans, exchanging for furs products such as woollen clothing, steel knives, iron pots and glass beads. At the same time the Dutch seized Portugal's richest colony (Indonesia), not only gaining direct access to spices, but also establishing commercial ties with the Ottoman Empire.

Each of these enterprises needed soldiers. Given the death rates from tropical diseases, no government found it easy to recruit volunteers for units being sent there. The Spanish king could station troops abroad, in healthier climes, for a fixed period of time, but that had unhappy consequences in that when the soldiers returned home, they had to leave behind their native wives and children.

Other European monarchs lacked that degree of authority. They had to find incentives to recruit men to serve in the Indies. This often involved a suggestion that the men just steal whatever they could from the Spaniards. Englishmen and French Protestants happily did that, and when their rulers were coerced into promising to curtail them, the pirates bribed them to ignore their activities. If the pirates brought back rich booty and shared it with their monarch, they were heroes; if they died, not that much was lost.

Entering America from the opposite direction were Russian explorers who had crossed Siberia. They, too, had technological superiority over the peoples they encountered – except for the Chinese, whom they prudently avoided – and were able to establish trading posts and missions along the Pacific coast.

After European weapons created overseas empires, European fortifications secured them against native attack. European technology produced gold and silver from raw ore, made gunpowder out of local materials, and transported people to settle in their new colonies and brought goods home to sell. Nothing of this scale had ever been seen in human history.

CHAPTER FOUR

The Gunpowder Revolution from Sweden and Germany to Turkey and Beyond

Livonia

Just as eighteenth-century Russians saw St Petersburg as Russia's window on the West, sixteenth-century Germans saw Livonia (modern Estonia and Latvia) as their window on Russia. Though Livonia is often described as a primitive frontier land, the lines between medieval and modern were no more sharply drawn there than in Germany: its towns were much like those belonging to the other cities of the Hanseatic League, its nobles much like those of Germany, its church problems exactly like those of the Holy Roman Empire.

Livonian Germans understood that the feudal knights and militias of their Livonian Confederation could not fend off a Russian attack without being reinforced by landsknechts and more artillery. They relied on the Livonian Order, an autonomous branch of the Teutonic Knights, to delay invaders until these could be procured; only it had trained officers and good castles. The Livonian Order, however, was divided and weak, partly because its knights feared that sometime in the future larger and more centralised national states, such as Russia, would overwhelm chaotic feudal states such as the confederation. Some knights argued for converting their religious order into a secular duchy, based on the Prussian model, then unifying all of Livonia; others saw salvation only in prayers to the Virgin and aid from the Roman Catholic king of Poland–Lithuania and the Holy Roman emperor.

The German-speaking minority of nobles, prelates and burghers who governed the states of the confederation placed their hopes in Russia's internal troubles, in the swamplands that separated the coastal region from the interior, and in having an army so well-trained and well-equipped that it could overcome the Russian advantage in numbers. Of necessity they placed their faith in the Livonian Order's strong fortresses, the first line of which stood behind the rivers and lakes that marked the frontier: the Daugava (Düna, Dvina) River flowed west out of Russia past Riga into the Baltic; and the Narva River flowed north out of Lake Peipus into the Gulf of Finland.

Informed civilians understood as well as military experts that landsknechts supported by artillery and cavalry, and commanded by experienced generals, could rout old-fashioned armies such as the ones that tsars had employed in the past. This was not altogether a comforting thought – the kings of Denmark and Sweden were able to raise larger numbers of these troops than they could, and even the distant ruler of Moscow, Ivan IV, was hiring western mercenaries. Ivan was also buying firearms to equip his army in the most modern fashion, and these new weapons – cannon and muskets – were more worrisome than the mercenaries: they were not always effective in Russian conditions, but when they were, they were decisive.

This 'gunpowder revolution' was occurring everywhere. Cannon and firearms endangered all existing military arrangements – feudal cavalry, burgher militias, peasant levies and high stone walls. In Russia it had ended the independence of ancient regions and proud cities, but since Russia never had the equivalent of feudal nobles, their boyars justified their continued hold on ancestral estates by performing military service. When boyars refused to perform the more sweaty duties associated with engineering, artillery and infantry, the tsars sought out mercenaries – Germans and Poles, mostly, serving under their own officers. Some of these mercenaries may have originally been prisoners of war – stationed far away from the temptation to desert; some were given small plots of land and even married to military widows; others were attracted by the money or desperate to escape poverty or legal difficulties. It was easy to find employment in Russia – a mercenary who presented himself at the border was escorted to Moscow with all expenses paid – but it was next to impossible to leave: employment was for life, and efforts to escape were punished brutally. The

Russian name for these foreigners was *nemici*, that is, those who cannot speak Russian; this eventually became the word for German.

For tiresome frontier service the tsars hired auxiliary units of Cossacks and Tatars, but when it became apparent that they were also effective in northern forests and swamps, the tsars used them all across their empire. These warriors quickly made themselves feared, even beyond expectations from stories told by previous generations. In Livonia they struck absolute terror into the populace.

In the 1550s the Livonians – thanks to their merchants visiting Russia – were well aware of Ivan's growing power, and were discussing means of meeting it. This was not the result of textbook theorising, though there were textbooks aplenty, nor a response to the numerous romances supposedly extolling chivalry (but actually showing its irrelevance). Nevertheless, there was considerable resistance to spending the money needed to update the military forces. Importantly, chivalry had not died – local nobles, reluctant to admit that their central role in warfare was coming to an end, extolled its ideals and reminded themselves of the social and political importance of their knightly class. They justified their existence as defending western Christendom and civilisation against native uprisings and Russian attack, and they copied their erstwhile rivals, the Livonian Order, in pointing out that war against the enemies of the Church and their distant sovereign, the Holy Roman emperor, was their ancient calling, and that cavalry warfare was *ennobling*. However, rather than train for war, many knights and gentry preferred drinking, dancing and hunting; they railed against middle-class critics who wanted a modern military force, a larger voice in the government and a Protestant Church. They disliked guns, leaving it to the Livonian Order, the cities, and the bishops to buy cannon and build castles.[1]

The need to supply these guns with ammunition changed commercial practices. As it happened, Pomerania, on the southern coast of the Baltic Sea, was an early centre of saltpetre production. Thus, this lightly populated stretch of sandy soil became the object of its neighbours' interest. Since the king of Sweden had occupied the region and refused to sell saltpetre to his enemies, the best that neighbouring peoples could do was steal it on the high seas. Because no state had a large standing navy, each hired privateers – nautical mercenaries, in a sense. Even Russia hired privateers – Danes who were eager to fight their ancestral enemies, the Swedes.

The evolution to new military systems also threatened long-established political forms. The Livonian Confederation still pretended that its collection of bishoprics, cities and knightly corporations could defend themselves, but in practice what it hoped for was that the neighbouring states would restrain each other from disturbing the balance of power. Many thought, rightly, that the future belonged to those rulers who could make themselves supreme over their nobles, clerics and burghers, then tax all of them to support projects designed to strengthen the economy in peacetime and the military forces in war. They did not want Livonia to follow the Prussian example, though for some that was an alluring model.

Prussia had belonged to the Teutonic Knights until 1525, when its last grand master, Albrecht von Hohenzollern, had secularised the convents under his control and made himself duke of Prussia. The king of Poland, Sigismund the Old, though a devout Roman Catholic, was pleased to accept Albrecht as a vassal. Arguing on one hand that this would assist in a Protestant reconciliation with Rome, and on the other that ending the likelihood of war with Prussia while he was contending with Russia was wise policy, he established a mutually profitable relationship. Albrecht was more co-operative than the Polish Sejm, the most important body in Poland's complicated parliament, which insisted on his adhering strictly to the law *Nihil novi* (nothing new), which hindered him in pursuing both internal policies and foreign affairs.[2]

To the west and north were the Scandinavian kingdoms of Denmark and Sweden, which had vague historical ties to Livonia. To the east was Ivan IV, who would later be known as Ivan the Terrible. Young Ivan was overcoming the internal problems that had bedevilled Russia throughout his father's reign: he had conquered two major Tatar khanates and fought a third to a draw. The fates of all these states would eventually intertwine. War in Livonia would draw them together.

The Livonian War

Livonia may have been peripheral in terms of European geography, but politics there affected all the neighbouring kingdoms. A great crisis followed the long and slow decline of the Livonian Order, weakened by the success of the Lutheran Reformation in Sweden, Denmark and the north of Germany.

The knights of the order, concerned about their dwindling numbers, could not agree on what should be done to turn the situation around. They divided into two groups, split partly by religious orientation, Catholic versus Protestant, and partly on what type of state they believed would be best for defending the region from Ivan IV. At Ivan's coronation in 1547, he had claimed the ambitious title of 'Tsar of all the Russias'; since White, Black and Red Russia were still the eastern territories of the Polish–Lithuanian Commonwealth (*Rzeczpospolita*), he was declaring his intent to reclaim those lands for himself and the Orthodox Church. Thus, a secular Livonian state tied to Sigismund would become involved in that struggle.

The Catholics in the Livonian Order held to tradition – to keep the Livonian Confederation unchanged; to recruit pious knights from Westphalia, the most northern Roman Catholic region in Germany; to pray to the Virgin and the saints; and to ask the pope and emperor for help. The Protestant knights doubted that this would work – north Germany was no longer Catholic, least of all the cities of the Hanseatic League, whose aid was vital; prayers were less useful than allies; and the pope and emperor had never provided significant assistance. Catholics pointed to the nobles of Livonia, who remained faithful to the Roman Church, and to the Polish king, a Catholic champion. Protestants pointed to the burghers of Livonia and Albrecht of Prussia. In fact, it was Albrecht's example that most frightened the Catholics and encouraged the Protestants. He had become a Lutheran, and he hired mercenaries whenever he needed an army. Realpolitik suggested that unifying Livonia under a Protestant duke who was a vassal to a Catholic king would be an effective means of defending the country and, therefore, appealed to moderates of both parties.[3] However, this was totally unacceptable to fundamentalist Catholics and Protestants alike, and to many clerics and secular knights.

Ivan IV was just twenty in 1550, an age when men are often in a hurry. He was also sly, suspicious and brutal – not surprising given the tumultuous events following his becoming grand duke of Moscow at the age of three. Fear being an important aspect of respect, and unpredictability enhancing fear, Ivan chose to be frightening and erratic. He was also an opportunist, and when he perceived weakness in the poorly conducted civil war among the Livonian Knights, he decided to exploit it.[4] He reminded the Livonians that three and a half centuries earlier several Livonian tribes had paid tribute to Russian princes, and that the German missionaries had begged for permission to preach peacefully among the pagans, then maliciously brought in crusaders to occupy the country. He then noted that payment for the right to harvest honey from bee trees in a border district had not been made for centuries – interpreting this as a tax on each person in all of Livonia, he demanded that it be paid immediately, in full, and for every year since the last payment.

Poles, Danes, Swedes, the emperor, the pope – all responded to the cries for help from the Livonian Confederation with sweet words encouraging resistance, but declined to give any actual money or troops. Partly that was because they did not know how many troops would be needed or for how long; partly it was because Livonia was of marginal importance. There were more pressing issues to deal with – the spread of Protestant ideas into France and the Netherlands, the potential for civil war in England, and 'the Turk'.

The tsar's demand amounted to an incredible amount of money, but the Livonian Confederation might well have paid it if they had believed that he would use it for something other than buying weapons and hiring mercenaries. It would be better, they decided, to spend that money on their own defence. As the old adage had it (and every educated Livonian understood the Latin): *si vis pacem, para bellum* (if you want peace, prepare for war). However, in this case it probably did not matter – Ivan lied, the Livonians lied, and nobody could agree on what the past tribute obligations had been or whether they were even relevant now.

Ivan was infuriated when the Livonian Confederation humbly refused to deliver the money. His efforts at extortion having met with little more than delaying tactics, he sent Tatar raiders across the border in early 1558 as a warning. Seeing how little resistance they encountered, he sent in more troops. These were not very effective, except at terrorising peasants, but the defenders were no better. Herbertstein, an imperial observer of the Russian scene, remarked that Russian attitudes were much like those of the Germans: a defiant attack at the beginning, followed by a collapse of morale – the motto was 'run, or we shall'. Ivan's officers were willing to fight to the death rather than face his wrath, but this same fear prevented them from acting promptly and effectively in ambiguous situations. The Russian army improved significantly as time passed, though once Sweden, Poland–

Lithuania, and the Tatars entered the war, Ivan's resources were stretched too far to be effective on any front.

We have several first-hand accounts of this war, that of the mercenary Heinrich von Staden (1542–after 1582) being the fullest. He had travelled through Germany, Livonia and Estonia, moving from job to job, town to town, and after Ivan IV had conquered much of Livonia, von Staden volunteered to serve in the Russian army. There he impressed the tsar with his steady nerves and willingness to carry out orders; as a minor member of the *Oprichnina* (secret police), he witnessed the terror that gripped Russia when Ivan IV grew paranoid and fearful. After returning to the West, he wrote an account of his adventures in hopes of persuading the emperor or the king of Poland–Lithuania to invade Russia – with himself as a key adviser. Since we have less information about other mercenaries in Russia during this period, we tend to envision them all as being much like von Staden.

Russian Expansion East and South

The steppe was especially fertile in the lands lying between Russia, Poland–Lithuania, the Crimean Tatars and the khans of Kazan and Astrakhan.[5] The Tatars accepted Ivan IV's conquest of Kazan and Astrakhan, but were alarmed by the settlement of the great prairie with Russian and Polish peasants and warriors; they wanted to rob these settlers (or carry them away for sale), but for a while the Tatars were satisfied with the Christians paying tribute. Logically, the more people there were on the steppe, the more money the Tatar khans could collect, but in time they became concerned about what would happen when these peoples – such as the Cossacks – became sufficiently numerous to defend themselves and to refuse to pay tribute. The Tatar khans, not willing to await that day, decided to drive the tsar and his potential subjects back off the steppe.[6]

Caught in the middle of Russian–Polish–Tatar ambitions were the self-governing communities of Cossacks that had grown up beyond the Russian frontier (hence the name Ukraine, Russian for 'over the border'). Originally composed of runaway serfs, outlaws and exiles, the members of this brotherhood were unruly, ill-educated, intolerant and brave beyond belief. They lived in isolated communities, housed in a common barracks until marriage, and survived through a combination of farming and raiding. Their lifestyle made them almost instantly available for military action, and willing to undertake daring raids – even manning small boats to sack Ottoman communities on the southern shores of the Black Sea. They were fanatically Orthodox – hostile to Islam, Roman Catholicism and all Jews. While they prided themselves on having driven the Tatars from much of the steppe, they were willing to work with them against their usual employers, the king of Poland and the tsar of Russia. In a sense, they were the ultimate mercenaries – willing to fight for anyone. In other senses, they were the most difficult mercenaries to employ, because their loyalties were so unpredictable, other than to one another, to their communities and to their leaders.

The most important Cossack group was known as the Zaporozhe brotherhood. Its members lived on the lower Dnieper in a fortified camp on a large island, and were therefore safe against any surprise attack by Tatars. They – like the Don Cossacks farther east – disdained agriculture, which they associated with serfdom; but they allowed recent arrivals to practise it because that was the only skill the newcomers had, and because the Ukrainian steppe was well suited for raising wheat. These runaways were not admitted into full membership, but were called 'unenlisted Cossacks'.

Less able to defend themselves were Polish and Ukrainian villagers not associated with the Cossacks. The Lithuanian and Polish magnates did what they could to protect them, but no frontier community could stand up to a raid by 40,000–80,000 steppe warriors, horsemen armed with bows and arrows, swords and spears, and more formidable than any infantry with firearms to be found on the frontier. Retaliatory raids provided Russians, Poles and Lithuanians with captives who could replace some of the losses, but such persons would be slaves or serfs, not free farmers. Communities deprived of food by raiders survived by stealing from their neighbours. The situation, as terrible as it was, did not lead to every male being castrated, nor every female forced into a harem; ransom was possible, and some slaves were freed after serving a dozen years as agricultural labourers, practices that perhaps persuaded captives to submit and co-operate rather than fight to the death.

These desperate combats reflected the heightened religious feelings of the era. Orthodox and Catholic Christians saw this struggle against militant Islam as a kind of holy war. As Russians and Poles moved south, the

Ottoman sultans came to the aid of their Tatar vassals, but, unable to unify the competing khans, they internationalised the conflict without resolving it.

The first Russian armies to move southwards had discovered that they could not cross the steppe in one great advance, because the Tatars set fire to the summer grass, leaving them without fodder for their horses; later, when the armies carried their own fodder, this required tens of thousands of additional beasts for hauling the supply wagons. Nor did a line of static strong points do much to curb Tatar raids. In the end, the successful strategy was to build successive advanced defensive lines – long, deep moats and earthen walls, cutting down trees to make barriers, with periodic fortified settlements where a mobile army could be based, using foreign officers and troops. This took generations. When one barrier was complete, the next would be begun farther south. This strategy was so effective that the Tatars were able to go around the barriers only when the Cossacks were in rebellion against the Polish king or the tsar. With Tatars carrying away a million people between 1500 and 1644, the tsars should perhaps have given this frontier priority, not Livonia and Poland–Lithuania. However, none of the great powers could control either the Tatars or the Cossacks because each of those steppe peoples had an economy partially based on the sale of prisoners and booty. The Cossacks were a headache to everyone who had to deal with them, but the southern frontier could hardly have been patrolled without them.[7]

The drain that the Livonian War made on Ivan IV's military resources became obvious after the Ottoman Turks entered the war in 1569. Not that Tatars had been an enemy to despise, but once their cavalry was reinforced by janissary infantry and artillery, they could attack fortified towns and castles. The Turks were not invincible, as their campaign to retake Astrakhan demonstrated – that was a disaster that reminded everyone that the steppe could be as dangerous an enemy as steppe warriors, and that infantry armies were not suitable to every occasion – but they did not back down when confronted by strong resistance, whereas Tatars tended to ride off in search of easier victims.

Poland–Lithuania, once drawn into the Livonian War, also found that the cost was heavier and the advantages less obvious than had been anticipated. When the Transylvanian ruler, Stephen Batory (Báthory, 1533–86), was elected king, the war was not going well. Yet it was impossible to abandon the region to Ivan, lest Russians invade Lithuania from the north as well as from the east. Batory knew from experience that feudal levies would be ineffective on the distant frontiers; therefore, he recruited infantry from the peasantry to fight on the border with Russia and hired Cossacks to protect the southern frontier. In 1577 he persuaded the Sejm to give him taxes and permission to recruit an army of mercenaries from Germany and Hungary, then employed them in Livonia. In 1579 he pressed northeast from Lithuania to Polotsk, a city that had once been a jewel in the commonwealth's crown, but had fallen to Ivan IV earlier in the war. The siege was a memorable event, the log-and-earth walls being much stouter than Batory's engineers had expected, but at last the garrison surrendered on the condition that the men either return honourably to Russia or enlist in the Polish army. One assumes that the mercenaries, knowing Ivan's history of torturing defeated officers and men to death, would have changed sides rather than face their employer. The booty in artillery and supplies was welcome to the victors, who quickly advanced on a small fortress that had been heavily reinforced by elite Russian troops planning to recover Polotsk.

According to the chronicler Salomon Henning, the siege was desperately fought. First the Poles filled the place with fireballs, setting it ablaze so thoroughly that almost the entire Russian force burned to death. Perishing with them were several hundred Hungarians and Germans who had forced one of the gates only to be shut in the town when the portcullises were dropped behind them. The Russians fought so bravely that even when their clothes were on fire, they faced their attackers and fought to the end.

The year 1580 was filled with simultaneous sieges, battles and diplomatic talks – including the castle at Padis surrendering to the Swedes for lack of food, where the commander was too weak to come to the gate to hand over the keys. Still, the campaign was going so slowly that Batory came to believe that Ivan was waiting for him to run out of money. In the late summer of 1581 he moved to Pskov, a fortress he knew was so important that Ivan would have to fight for it. Since his thirty thousand men easily outnumbered the garrison, his mercenaries vied to be the first to break into the city, but his artillery failed to make a breach in the walls and the exploded mines did not create sufficient gaps for assaults to succeed. Reluctantly, the Polish–Lithuanian army settled in for a siege, for five months fighting off efforts to break through the lines from within and without, suppressing some mercenaries' demands for pay, and enduring both cold and hunger. Meanwhile, Swedish forces drove the last Russians from Livonia and Lithuanians raided central Russia. In January of 1582 Ivan agreed to peace talks.

A ten-year truce was negotiated by Antonio Possevino (1534–1611), a Jesuit sent by the pope as a special legate. It was Possevino's first experience in the Baltic, but he would be active in Russia for years to come. It is reported that when Possevino dared debate the merits of the Roman Catholic and Orthodox Churches, the tsar attempted to murder him. This made nice bookends to the war – Ivan's mad egotism being highlighted both at the beginning and the end. In between, the Baltic world had changed completely – the last military order in the north had disappeared, Sweden and Poland–Lithuania had each spent too much blood and treasure in Livonia to turn it lightly over to the other, and Russia had been, it seemed, fatally wounded. Poland–Lithuania was hardly better off, even if the king brought captured banners home.

The war against Ivan the Terrible had raised the prospect of a future king using mercenary troops to become a despot. To prevent this, in 1582 the Sejm refused to raise the taxes for another campaign. Peace, even an unsatisfactory one, was at least peace. Batory, who might have overthrown Ivan totally, took his army to the Ottoman front, but died before he could accomplish much.

Future Polish kings, even Sigismund III, who was briefly successful, would find it very difficult to fight wars against the enemies surrounding the Polish–Lithuanian Commonwealth, even defensive wars. As for taking advantage of their eastern neighbour's troubles, they found it easy to disrupt Russia, but very difficult to govern it themselves. Russian resistance was important in this, but so was Polish politics – every potential expansion of royal authority was seen as an expensive danger to noble liberties.

Russia was an obvious example of royal tyranny, but Poles failed to notice the lesson. Ivan's death, however much it should have been welcomed by an exhausted nation, brought not peace, but only a new series of misfortunes. Because Ivan had murdered his eldest son in a drunken rage and his younger son was mentally retarded, a confusing struggle over the succession followed. What Russia needed – and Poland, too – were institutions that made an all-powerful despot unnecessary. But such institutions cost money, and nobody wanted to pay taxes. Yet fearful sums were expended on projects of marginal utility – for example, on the great Russian fortresses, each fantastically expensive, similar to those that had been so effective in the contemporaneous struggle between western Christendom and Islam for control of the Mediterranean.[8] Geoffrey Parker, in *The Military Revolution*, reports that the fortress at Smolensk built between 1595 and 1602 was an example of gigantism – 150 million bricks, 620,000 facing stones and one million loads of sand; it had walls six and a half kilometres long, five metres thick and nineteen metres high. Such fortresses were a palliative, not a cure, for Russia's problems.

Livonia had been a poisoned pill for everyone. Each monarch who had tried to swallow it became ill. Long term, the massive dislocations of peasantry created the Latvian people out of the various regional populations, and Estonians, too, became more homogeneous. People, however, exist in the short term: almost everyone wanted nothing more than peace and quiet, but the obvious weakness of the Russian state was too tempting for the region's new governors.

Ivan's Legacy

Ivan IV (the Terrible) has a very mixed reputation. He had grown up around fiercely ambitious and competitive boyar families whose rivalries had made his state essentially ungovernable. When he came of age he looked for means of restoring central authority. In 1550 he had established a unit of three thousand *streltsy* ('shooters', originally archers) drawn from the gentry class and armed with handguns. Later he hired foreign mercenaries, organised the terrifying *Oprichnina*, and made war on enemies internal and external.[9] Although some victims were undoubtedly dangerous enemies, the corruption of these tsarist henchmen put everyone with money or land at risk.

Russian nationalists see Ivan's policies as rational choices that furthered the nation's destiny – much like a chess player. Westerners emphasise his opportunism, his paranoia, his periodic bouts of depression (and perhaps insanity) and religious fanaticism. Western efforts to understand Russians and Russian culture have been somewhat successful no matter what Churchill said in 1939 about Russia being a riddle wrapped in mystery inside an enigma, but sometimes one feels that the more one knows, the less one understands. The most scholars can agree upon is that by the time Ivan died in 1584, Russia was in a sad shape.

However, over the long term much had been accomplished. Moscow's expansion and the divisions among the steppe peoples had brought many Tatar warriors into the tsars' service. The degree to which these were mercenaries rather than vassals depends somewhat on individual judgement about what it means to accept pay in the form of booty rather than money, and whether the horsemen could say no to demands for their service.

Ivan IV's subjugation of Kazan and Astrakhan had opened the way to Siberia, the source of excellent furs. In 1581 Yermak Timofeyevich and eight hundred Cossacks were hired by a prominent fur merchant in Novgorod to establish trading posts on the other side of the Ural Mountains. The expedition was not a success, though Cossacks reached the distant khanate of Sibir in 1582 – the Tatars were unwilling to give up the rich source of income from Kazakhstan, and, after three years of fighting, wiped out most of these intrepid intruders. Later expeditions were more successful, so that by 1598 the tsar's representatives had made themselves masters of the region. From this base they pushed east, reaching the Pacific in 1639, Alaska shortly afterwards, and eventually the future site of San Francisco.

Such an advance would have been impossible without exploiting local feuds – making former allies into military vassals – and the unintentional spread of disease. As was true on the Atlantic coast of North America, when smallpox came into formerly unexposed populations, the native peoples of Siberia experienced a demographic catastrophe. What resistance remained was crushed brutally, as might well be expected – a small body of mercenaries, motivated by greed and fear, on their own in a vast land and surrounded by hostile peoples, did what they thought necessary to protect themselves and to become rich. Religious conflict was also a problem. Cossacks did not hesitate to dispose of open enemies to Orthodoxy, whether pagan or Muslim, but found ways of coexisting with those who submitted to tsarist rule.

The Time of Troubles

The era of turmoil that followed the death of Ivan the Terrible was best remembered by Russians for the audacious impostors who claimed that they were the tsar's eldest son, Dmitri, whom God had miraculously spared so that he could rescue Russia from anarchy and foreign invasion. The first 'false Dmitri' appeared in 1603, five years after the death of Ivan's son. Three years later that impostor perished in a popular uprising that encompassed the lives of several thousand Poles and Lithuanians; a second false Dmitri appeared, with further foreign intervention. The scandals associated with self-proclaimed heirs, imposters and candidates – Russian, Polish and Swedish – who grasped at the throne almost make one forget the many human tragedies that followed each crisis of legitimacy – famine, peasant uprisings, banditry and assassinations.

Ivan's territorial acquisitions had left his successors, real and imagined, with unresolved wars. Colourful figures abounded. One of the most famous was an upstart (as one considered all unsuccessful contenders for a crown), Boris Godunov (1551–1605), who hired western mercenaries to replace the disintegrating traditional army, but could not forge them quickly enough into a competent fighting force. Another was Vasily Shuisky, who abandoned lands between Finland and Livonia to the Swedish king in return for five thousand troops led by the capable general, Jacob de la Gardie. With fifteen thousand Swedish mercenaries, Shuisky was able to crown himself tsar in 1606; however, without a strong party behind him, he was hardly recognised by anyone beyond the eyesight of his hired troops.[10]

Sigismund III proclaimed Shuisky's use of Swedish troops a violation of the truce and, to prevent Charles IX from becoming too strong, invaded Livonia. With money being spent lavishly, French, English and German mercenaries hurried east.[11] At the decisive battle of Klushino in the summer of 1610, Polish hussars defeated a much larger Russian–Swedish army that included five thousand mercenaries, many of them Scots. First the French mercenaries, then the Germans, went over to the Poles before the battle, then the English sacked the camp. These events demoralised the rest of the mercenaries, who were driven into the woods by the Poles' thundering cavalry charges. Afterwards, most of the mercenaries surrendered, and many took employ in the Polish army. This was fatal to Shuisky's hopes –

he was overthrown by his boyars a month later, to die two years later in a Polish jail.

For a short period Sigismund's army occupied Moscow, bringing with it Jesuits – the personification of the detested Roman Catholic heretics. German, Polish and Swedish mercenaries, having made themselves masters of much of the country, quickly made themselves unpopular. At one point, in 1611, they killed as many as seven thousand rioting citizens in Moscow, then set the city on fire. The mercenaries of the occupying armies hated the immensity of the land, the weather and the hostility of the people; they hated Russian food – mostly turnips, cabbage and dark bread – and there was no beer. Unfamiliar with the country, they relied on informers and torture to learn what they needed to know. Worst off were the mercenaries in Russian employ. A Dutch envoy, Isaac Massa, reported that the Germans, Frenchmen and Scots were all eager to escape – and most did, by sea – though all had known that service in Russia was for life. Their response might have been that they had anticipated life would be longer than seemed likely at that moment – and better.

Sigismund was not particularly ambitious. He had grown up in Sweden and felt more at home there than in Poland, but he was also a committed Roman Catholic – that was his downfall. His friends, most importantly his Jesuit advisers, urged him to intervene decisively in Russia; this was the same advice that had cost him his Swedish crown.[12] However, the Polish king was not stupid. He had moved his capital from Cracow in 1596 to the more centrally located Warsaw, then a small town overlooking the Vistula, roughly half-way between Danzig and Cracow; this allowed him to co-ordinate his military operations better. It appeared that once he had learned caution, as he eventually did, the strength and power of his Polish–Lithuanian state would allow him to prevail on every battlefield.

His 1608 invasion of Russia was intended partly to forestall the magnates of Lithuania – those powerful lords who had taken responsibility for regional defence and maintenance of law and order when he was unable to do either – and partly to protect the Uniate Church: that is, Russian rites but recognising the pope and Western traditions as paramount. In short, Sigismund had acted out of concern for domestic issues, only later proposing that his son, Ladislas (Władysław, 1595–1648), become tsar, then claiming the crown for himself. His lack of success can be attributed to the unco-operative attitude of the Sejm and the more important conflict with Sweden over control of Pomerania and Livonia. Denmark entering the conflict in 1611 made the situation even more confused.

When Charles IX of Sweden began to worry that a combined Polish–Lithuanian–Russian state would overwhelm his forces in Livonia, he proposed a Swedish candidate for the Russian crown to oppose the Polish one – Karl Filip, the king's younger brother. Charles IX easily persuaded the citizens of Novgorod to join him after a third false Dmitri had appeared, plunging the region into anarchy. A second ally seemed to promise substantial aid, but he was murdered by his Cossack followers. Still, by the autumn of 1612, Karl's chances looked good – the Polish garrison in the kremlin had surrendered, and Swedish forces had occupied over two hundred Russian cities. However, Karl Filip had to appear in Moscow for the election, and his mother, quite properly fearing for his life, would not let him go.

The delay was fatal – the assembly chose Michael Romanov (1596–1645), the son of a powerful king-maker who had earlier been forced to take holy orders and was therefore ineligible to become tsar himself. The Romanov family had provided Ivan IV with his first wife and had risen through his patronage to even greater prominence. Michael was only sixteen when he was declared tsar in 1613, but he had his father to advise him for the next two decades.

Soon after Michael Romanov's election, Swedish enthusiasm for the war vanished – the troops mutinied, the commanders retreated. After a two-year siege of Pskov, during which the Swedish army was decimated by epidemics, both sides agreed to negotiate. In February of 1617 a treaty brought an end to the conflict. Northern Livonia went to Sweden, which abandoned its claims on further territories. Both sides praised the fair mediation of the English agent in charge of the Muscovy Company, Sir John Merrick.

The Swedish king as of 1612 was Gustavus Adolphus (1594–1632). Multiple crises had faced him, foremost being the war with Denmark. Fortunately, he had the sympathy of the maritime powers, Holland and England, who knew that if the Danish king prevailed, he would charge their ships heavy tolls to pass through the Sound into the Baltic Sea. King James (1566–1625), who wanted to expand English trade, had two able negotiators trying to keep the Baltic open. The first was James Spens

(1571–1632), a Scot who had gone to Sweden in 1610 with a company of mercenaries, then become the English king's representative in Stockholm. Spens's counterpart in Copenhagen was Robert Anstruther, his father-in-law. Working together, these two men ended the conflict and guaranteed the English right to trade freely.

More difficult was Sigismund's claim to the Swedish throne. Over four hundred Swedish émigrés followed his court, hoping for a war that would return them to power. Since most of those men hated Charles IX personally, but not Gustavus Adolphus, it was possible for the Swedish king to persuade many to return home. As Sigismund's party drifted away, so too did his hopes of returning to Stockholm in triumph.

This was all well and good, except that when law and order in Sweden broke down, Gustavus Adolphus did not have enough mercenaries to repress the rebels, and those already in his employ were plundering communities around their posts. In a situation where the king could not even pay his tailor, where counterfeit coins were common and taxes could not be collected, he survived only by borrowing. Jacob de la Gardie and his own mother were principal contributors, at hefty rates of interest.

When the production of Swedish copper allowed Gustavus Adolphus to pay his troops in copper coins rather than debased silver, he regained control of his mercenaries. Such was the demand for copper in Europe at that moment that his soldiers could exchange the coins easily for silver ones. Also, as the Thirty Years War was destroying the German economy, impoverished men were willing to enlist for little more than subsistence pay. Recruiting agents, in contrast, could do well.[13]

When war with Poland broke out again in 1617, the point of contention was Courland, a rich province on the southern bank on the Daugava River. Gottfried Kettler, the last master of the Livonian Knights and the first duke of Courland, had died, leaving his lands to his two sons, Friedrich (1587–1642) and Wilhelm (1574–1640). The young dukes were feuding with their headstrong nobles, who, in typical Livonian fashion, resented any efforts to curb their independence or their mistreatment of their peasants. Sigismund took the side of the nobles – an act that was very popular among the equally independent-minded Polish and Lithuanian lords he was courting.

Duke Wilhelm's foremost supporter was Wolmar Farensbach (1586–1633), the son of the famous Jürgen Farensbach, who had once been governor of Riga; he inherited an estate in central Livonia from his father and claims on lands in Courland from his mother.[14] Wolmar was the kind of man that warriors looked up to – he was all energy and daring, he made good on his boasts and was an exceptional warrior. Also, he was a Protestant who was eager to protect Protestants elsewhere. Earlier he had proposed a joint Swedish–Polish attack on Russia; after Wilhelm's abandonment of his duchy in 1616, leaving young Friedrich in possession of an empty title, Farensbach proposed to assist the Swedish king in making Courland into a vassal state. In 1617 he came into possession of Dünamünde and Treiden in Livonia and Goldingen and Windau in Courland.[15]

Gustavus Adolphus sent a small army to Livonia, but his commander did not strike promptly. Had he done so, he would probably have overrun the whole of Courland, because the Lithuanian commander, Jan Karol Chodkiewicz,[16] had taken most of the troops away for a campaign in Russia and was fully occupied by the Ottoman Turks until the victory at Chocim in 1621, after which he died. Farensbach managed to capture Pernau in Estonia, but not Riga – and Riga was the key to the country.

Farensbach then reassessed his situation. He could not pay his men, and a Polish–Lithuanian army was moving towards him. This army being too large for Farensbach to defeat, he changed sides in 1617, first surrendering Goldingen, then assisting in the capture of Dünamünde and Windau. Had the Poles and Lithuanians pressed north, they might have taken all the towns in Livonia except those on the coast. However, Sigismund signed an armistice in early 1618 so that he could concentrate on the Russian war, and Farensbach vanished from records, reappearing only later in Swedish employ after Gustavus Adolphus captured Riga in 1620. Farensbach could have taken some pride in having persisted so long in defending Courland's right to exist – as Shakespeare says in *Troilus and Cressida*, 'Perseverance ... keeps honour bright.' However, Farensbach's reputation in Germany was that he changed his employer too easily and too often.[17] In the Thirty Years War Farensbach would leave Gustavus Adolphus for the imperial army, then be executed on suspicion of wanting to change back again. Courland did survive, to become a relatively wealthy state by mid-century, which made it a region worth fighting for.

Gustavus Adolphus had not won much in this long conflict, but he had gained a lot of experience that made him rethink the formations and tactics of his troops. Without this, it is unlikely that he would have made the innovations that later proved so effective against the best mercenary armies in Germany. Although in 1624, when he resumed the war with Poland, he probably did not foresee the Thirty Years War spreading as it did so quickly into northern Germany and Denmark; still, he could imagine that imperial expansionism in the name of protecting German lands would endanger his plans to make the Baltic into a Swedish lake.

First, however, he would have to deal with Poland, which was once again at war with Russia. A Polish army of mercenaries from France, England, Germany, Ireland, Scotland and even a few Poles reached Moscow, but failed to breach the walls. According to Isaac Massa, who was well placed to know, the Poles opened negotiations for peace when rumours reported that English and Dutch mercenaries, with ample war materiel and money, were on their way to Michael Romanov.[18]

In sum, mercenaries were important in Russia for the same reasons they were significant elsewhere. First, they were skilled at what they did and were willing to remain on campaign long after boyars and militias were clamouring to go home. Secondly, they were usually foreigners and could be dismissed without offending the noble families which monopolised positions of command. Thirdly, they were mostly infantry, whereas boyars were cavalry. Horsemen were no longer all-important in battle, but they could better display their wealth, their comforts and their pride than any foot soldier. Lastly, if mercenaries were slain in battle or died of hardship and disease, the economic base of the country was not affected: use them, then dispose of them.

Ottoman Turkey

The lessening of tensions in the 1600s in the Balkans worked in favour of the Ottomans. With the outbreak of the Thirty Years War occupying the attention of all Germans, Sultan Murad IV (1612–40) was free to send his army against the Persian shah; at length he took Baghdad despite its defenders being well provided with muskets. After Murad drank himself to death at an early age, his subordinates ignored his instructions to murder his brother, a mistake that had to be corrected later by a coup.[19] Although

Murad's bizarre habits indicated hereditary insanity, he had restored central authority sufficiently that subsequent grand viziers could revive Ottoman military glory, no matter how incompetent the sultan.

The janissaries were the most solid basis of the sultan's authority. Theoretically, these men were slaves who could be dismissed at will, in contrast to the proud warriors of native Turkish stock. The reality was otherwise, in that the janissaries held the most important offices in the state and military; they were well-informed, even well-educated, in ways that the sultan – isolated in his palace – could not be. They had removed sultans in the past, and they could do so again. In 1656 the sultan ordered what turned out to be the last tax of Christian boys. Ceasing this practice was not an act of humanity, but a practical step to limit the janissaries to a number that revenues could support. New janissaries were recruited from the Muslim population – and not always the better part; having married, they hoped to open positions of prestige and power to their sons. As their numbers increased, the janissaries' training and equipment declined. They were still fine warriors, but the old single-minded dedication was gone.[20]

Native Turks were attempting to break into this closed system, usually by working through religious institutions – most importantly the *ulema*, a council of teachers and preachers. They also made their way into the *Divan* (the Council of State, later the Sublime Porte) headed by the grand vizier and including religious leaders, the commander of the navy, the commander of the janissaries, the chancellor and treasurer, the steward and secretary, and the governor-generals of Asia and Europe. The deliberations of state were secret, newspapers did not exist, nor did memoirs, and the writers of history were not very informative. The influence of the harem was considerable, especially in the appointment of government offices; and the courtiers – most importantly the members of the *Divan* – worked on each sultan's suspicions to undermine the grand viziers. As was also true in Christian courts, bribery was central to getting an administrator's ear or an audience with the ruler; and a wife or concubine was well positioned to have a sultan's attention.[21]

Bribery undermined the traditional honesty of Ottoman officials. Since each had to give presents to his superiors – at every level, right up to the sultan – they had to exact money from that part of the population least likely to complain effectively: the Christians. The efficiency and corruption of Turkish tax-collectors was proverbial, and the process angered all subjects, but especially Christians.

Still, when officials had to choose between antagonising Christians and offending the Turkish warrior class, they rarely failed to raise the Christians' taxes. Also, those Turks who provided the cavalry were naturally suspicious of efforts to increase the role of infantry – that is, the janissaries. Many Turkish warriors disliked being sent to fight on distant frontiers, especially when they were unlikely to benefit from the conquest of new lands. They wanted reforms – that is, reforms that returned the Ottoman state to its original form, with less janissary influence, and more offices held by their own *timârli* class.

Awkwardly, many timar land grants remained unfilled. Because these grants belonged to the state, not to the individual holders, in theory, no matter how many *timârli* perished in war, their military roles would be quickly taken up by new appointees. This was not happening. Devastated estates remained without workers or a resident manager.

The opposite policy was creating another serious problem at the top of the Ottoman state. The traditional practice of murdering younger brothers and half-brothers was abandoned in favour of sequestering them in the royal palace. This would have been no problem, not even when the numbers of potential heirs produced by the harem system was considerable, if they could have been sent out as provincial administrators or employed as warriors. However, each sultan was fearful that male relatives would be used as figureheads by conspirators, and their sons would eventually be dangerous, too. When the practice of giving preference to sons, who might be very young, was changed to passing authority to a brother, it brought inexperienced men to power, sometimes relatively elderly men. Such sultans had to rely utterly on their grand viziers for advice.

Contemporaries considered the grand viziers far more important than the sultans. They understood that they had to get through the Sublime Porte to do any business whatsoever. The grand viziers took care of the administrative paper work and sorted through the major problems of their times, then proposed ways to deal with them. This often resulted in plans for reform that unavoidably affected those whose activities were inefficient or obsolete. In military terms, this meant learning from the empire's enemies and copying them as appropriate. Since many of their subordinates were slaves, resistance was less overt than in Western society, but it was still there; and the free warriors grumbled as much as they dared.

Geoffrey Parker says in *The Military Revolution* that the skills of the engineer and artilleryman spread to Muslim lands first from capturing weapons and specialists, then by hiring Westerners. Not surprisingly, many Turks groused that the country needed not Western experts, but a return to the tried-and-true practices of the past. This attitude ran counter to every plan for modernisation, giving rise to discussions that are still relevant today: what is the nature of the good society? The answers led later Muslim intellectuals to ask the same question that Bernard Lewis has more recently posed in the title of a book, *What Went Wrong?* Their answer was that nothing was wrong: it all lay in God's hands, and his will was inscrutable.

If Islam was an 'honour society' and Christianity was a 'material society', the adherents of the latter faith had an advantage in being able to make the kinds of technological and organisational changes we associate with modernisation. Nevertheless, it was not so simple. The Ottoman Empire was so multi-cultural that sultans had to be cautious about offending their diverse subject peoples, most of whom were as suspicious of any change as were the Turks. Many Christians were converting to Islam at this time, most notably Albanians, which meant that ethnic rivalries became central to the debates concerning modernisation.[22]

Alas, other than generalisations, until recently we knew little about the Ottoman military. Suraiya Faroqhi could justly criticise European historians for assuming that the empire was organised solely for war, whereas it is obvious that trade and agriculture provided the wherewithal to raise and sustain armies. Hers was not the usual plaint raised against Orientalists,[23] but an acknowledgement that suitable source materials were rare and the Ottoman archives were not open to scholars.

Contemporaries considered the Ottoman Empire to have been successful both militarily and economically. Successful campaigns from 1640 onwards against Venice, Austria, Poland and Russia demonstrated the vitality of the war machine, and observers at the 1683 siege of Vienna praised the Turkish miners and sappers who had almost brought the walls and bastions to the point of total collapse before the coalition army miraculously came to the rescue. Given the grand vizier's correct understanding of German religious divisions and the impending invasion of the Rhineland by armies of Louis XIV (1638–1715), he had good reason to think that his siege would not be interrupted.

Afterwards, the Ottoman Empire was in decline, though that was not clear until the end of the century. This may have been the case earlier, too, but fear of the future had not led to the grand viziers being more cautious in foreign affairs, but rather their being more ready to take risks – as in besieging Vienna. When business as usual seems headed for inevitable defeat, why not stake everything on one more roll of the dice? Striking at enemies and rebels with extreme brutality was better than placidly awaiting destruction. This undermined the characteristics that had made Ottoman rule tolerable, even preferable, to plausible alternatives – religious tolerance, swift action against anyone who would disturb the peace and encouragement of agriculture and commerce, but most of all responsible and fair government. As for being a peace-loving state, the Ottomans began most of the wars with Europeans during this period.

European Mercenaries in the Ottoman Empire

Europeans living in the Ottoman Empire are among our best sources of information, but few wrote letters or memoirs. Two were English clergymen[24] living in Aleppo, far from Constantinople – though Istanbul was often used by Muslims, the old name for the capital remained in official use until 1923; the slow transition from one to the other was typical of the unhurried pace of Turkish cultural and political evolution. Other Europeans had good reasons for not writing down their impressions. 'Turning Turk' was not uncommon, since that may have been the only way to evade the usual unhappy fates of prisoners of war, or to escape imprisonment or death in Christendom. Some conversions must have been a matter of conviction, but one suspects that self-interest was paramount. Christians trapped by the expansion of the Ottoman Empire may have often welcomed the change of government, but, like the old man in Voltaire's *Candide* said, they never enquired what was going on in Constantinople, but tended their own gardens.

As the Venetian empire was lost, piece by piece, many Christians had to choose between being a second-class citizen and becoming a convert. Most of Crete fell in 1645, though Candia held out for another quarter of a century; and many of the Greek and Italian captives seem to have converted at sword-point (or in order to join the Ottoman army as mercenaries), and many were disillusioned by their apparent abandonment by the rest of Christendom. This had happened at a time when Western ships were becoming clearly superior to Ottoman galleys, so that even relatively little help from Spain or France might have allowed Venice to drive back the sultan's fleets. Considering the tumult inside the Ottoman administration, it would have been difficult for the sultan to have created a larger and better navy.

In the eighteenth century grand viziers who sought to hire Europeans to train Turks in specific military skills were denounced by religious conservatives. Marshall Hodgson, in *The Venture of Islam*, points specifically to Ibrahim Pasha, who governed during the cultural renaissance known as the 'tulip age', 1718–30;[25] he was overthrown following a military disaster in the Persian war. The defenders of absolutism saw a Western-style army as a threat to both their social and their religious power. Kemal Atatürk would demonstrate this in the twentieth century, using his secular army to carry through the reforms necessary to assure the survival of the Turkish state. This would be a *Turkish* state, not an *Ottoman* one.

The Thirty Years War came to an end, officially, in 1648, with the Peace of Westphalia. Dismissing the soldiers took time because many rulers were not sure that their enemies would honour their promises and because almost nobody had enough money to pay their troops off. Most soldiers had seen enlistment as their only reasonable choice – at home they had faced poverty, even starvation, and continued abuse by occupying armies; peasants had been worst off – even if they had a craft, their neighbours had no money to hire them. By enlisting they could at least give their families their bonus. They probably understood that the bonus might be the last pay they would receive for months or even years, but there was always the prospect of pillage. They understood the practice from having been its victims, and they knew that there was some chance of returning home with enough cash to start life anew – or starting life anew somewhere else. Keeping accumulated wealth safe from thieves would be another matter, and victorious troops were likely to torture anyone they suspected of hiding money, but everyone could point to someone who had struck it rich. Better to have a small chance than none at all. Now what were their chances? How would they make a living?

CHAPTER FIVE

National Cultures, Courts
and the Nature of Warfare

There were significant national variations in the practice of war. The most obvious ones are well-known, such as the Swiss mountains lending themselves to masses of pikemen, the steppe to horsemen. The former could not be bypassed easily, the latter allowed for swift and sweeping movement. Personalities had an influence, too, in that charismatic rulers and generals could impose their wishes upon armies. And technology, though often adopted reluctantly, transformed strategies and tactics significantly.

However, culture was important, too. The political culture determined how much authority a ruler could exert, how much money he could raise from taxes, imposts and monopolies, and whom he could select for the offices of government and the command of armies.

Italy
A Nation that Did Not Exist Vanishes

Medieval Italy had been a land of kings, churchmen and city-states, bounded by the seas, divided by mountains and long-standing traditions, yet aware of its common language, literature and customs. After 1550 or so the attachments to familiar political forms and streets began to give way to allegiances to dynastic rulers. Those who chose to serve their French, German and Spanish masters prospered; those who refused, declined.

Connected to this was a Counter-Reformation conformity of belief that discouraged independent thought – or at least voicing it. Galileo admired the simple beauty of Copernicus's heliocentric solar system, but when the Church ordered him to stop talking about the non-Biblical concepts of the northern German-Polish astronomer, he obeyed. Other Italians learned similarly that it was safe, within limits, to paint and sculpt, and almost entirely safe to perform music.[1] It was best not to test the limits.

Many Italians still went to war, and they were considered good warriors, but they were fighting for *stranieri*, and their masters' wars were not a matter of such importance that they should bother to die in them. It was, on the whole, easier to stay at home, to drink some wine in the shade on hot days, to talk with friends. And no place in Europe was more pleasant for such a civilised pastime.

If only the foreigners would stay at home and do the same. But there always seemed to be some king or emperor who wanted their taxes and services, and, of course, their current rulers wanted to keep them for themselves.

Spain
Replacing Diversity with Unity

Spaniards had always been good soldiers. The Romans had considered Iberian warriors valiant men – not steady like legionnaires, but strong and proud, always ready to pounce from mountain lairs or strike by surprise at unwary troops. Through the Middle Ages this ferocity was fed on regional pride and stories of successful wars against culturally superior Moors. Catalan mercenaries had occupied Sicily and Naples in the late thirteenth century, then conquered Athens in 1311 and governed it for the next seventy years. Castilians had been occupied for generations with the *Reconquista* – taking back lands that had been occupied by the Moors since the eighth century. Organising the proud and independent-minded Spanish soldiery into disciplined armies was one of the triumphs of sixteenth-century military reforms.

Such discipline could not, however, be extended to politics. The 1479 marriage of Ferdinand of Aragon (Catalonia) and Isabella of Castile did not quite unite their realms, and although the war against the last independent Moorish state, Granada, gave Catalans and Castilians a common purpose, when Granada fell in 1492, the tensions reappeared. The Catholic monarchs directed overseas the energy and resources generated by the *Reconquista* – Isabella to the New World, Ferdinand to Italy – but the marriage of their daughter Joan (Juana la Loca) to Philip the Handsome,

the son of Maximilian of Austria and Mary of Burgundy, required them
to contribute to the defence of the Low Countries. The heir to these
lands – Austrian and Spanish – would eventually be Charles V. Reared in
Brussels at the brilliant court of his aunt, Margaret (1480–1530), Charles
became acquainted with two problems that would mark his reign – French
aggression and German reluctance to allow any emperor much authority (a
problem that the appearance of Luther made more difficult to resolve). A
third problem grew out of these – how to provide a sufficient number of
men and weapons to defend the Low Countries against the French king.
Charles's military advisers informed him that the people of the region were
suited for commerce and industry, but not for war – he would need to
hire mercenaries. Meanwhile, distant Spanish officials wanted Charles to
concentrate on Turks, Arabs and Berbers, and on the rapidly expanding
overseas empire; they had little interest in his restless northern subjects.

The most important units of Charles's army were Castilian. Honour
and pride made these soldiers formidable, and decades of military success
persuaded them that they were invincible; but these traits were developed
less at home than during training in Italy – good duty, Bert Hall reminds
us. Attachments to the king and to the Catholic Church were important,
but it was poverty that drove young Castilians first to enlist, then training
and experience taught them how to win victories even against great odds.
There were also Catalans, who were employed largely in southern Italy
and Sicily. The rest of the army, perhaps the majority, was composed of
mercenaries of diverse origins who lacked an equivalent unit solidarity;
most were doubtlessly proud to be fighting for the king of Spain, whose
list of titles was impressive even in an era when men took more pride in
what they inherited than in what they accomplished, but they were rarely
as good as purely Spanish units.

Charles V had been able to rely on taxpayers in the Low Countries,
gold and silver from the New World, Africa and Europe, and loans from
bankers to hire soldiers in Spain and Italy, then march them across the
Alps to battlegrounds along the borders of France. Since it was neither
safe nor convenient to send troops by sea, this Spanish Road ran across
the Swiss Confederation into Alsace, then Lorraine, and thence into the
Low Countries. The situation became more dangerous after 1555, when
Charles divided his lands and titles between his son, Philip II, and his

brother, Ferdinand I – the Low Countries and Naples to Spain, northern Italy to Austria. Ferdinand already held Austria, Bohemia, Silesia and part of Hungary; now Holy Roman emperor, he was responsible for defending German territories west of the Rhine from the French king.

Philip II understood that French kings had lusted after the Low Countries for centuries, but he had hoped that his marriage to a Valois princess in 1559 would bring an end to this for at least several years. However, nothing worked out as expected. Outraged by Calvinist zealots storming into churches to destroy statues and paintings, Philip determined to make an example of the vandals. His administrator succeeded in the southern provinces, but not in the northern Dutch-speaking ones.[2] Protestants fled north, organising resistance while proclaiming their loyalty to the distant king – who, as in all such cases, was presumed to be ignorant of what his officials were doing and would set matters straight once he was informed.

Philip's officials were unable to persuade the Protestants either to return to the Church or to remain quiet; by 1567, when the duke of Alba arrived on the scene as governor, the situation was desperate. Most of the Spanish soldiers had been slain, and he had no money to pay those who remained. However, he was an experienced and capable soldier whose career encompassed the battle of Pavia in 1525, Tunis in 1535 and other great Habsburg victories; he knew how to make an army fight.

He imposed a 10 per cent tax to pay the army's expenses. This was highly unpopular even among his Catholic subjects, but he had little choice – one of Philip II's first acts upon becoming king had been to declare bankruptcy. This action, designed to permit the king to use American bullion immediately rather than to pay off past loans, meant that he could not borrow money to pay his troops. The result was the first of the many mutinies (and additional bankruptcies) that marked the coming decades. Alba resolved this by turning his troops loose on the civilian population wherever he met resistance. This 'Spanish fury' may have quieted his mercenaries' demands for pay, but it raised questions in the provincial assembly, which Philip answered by ordering Alba to replace all representational institutions with royal officials; Alba's 'Council of Blood' proceeded to confiscate the estates of rebels and execute any he could arrest. His cruelty and arrogance towards Dutch Protestants so resembled those of the conquistadores in the New World that even Catholics were disgusted.

The French saw profit in complicating Philip's situation, even though they were distracted by a religious war themselves. This made it so difficult for Alba to make headway against the Dutch that Spanish efforts to impose religious and political unity in the northern provinces failed.

It was a different situation in the south (modern Belgium), which had few dikes to cut or rivers to shelter behind. With the most extreme Protestants having fled, the region became arch-Catholic; with trade connections assured, commerce flourished and with prosperity came the great achievements of the Flemish Baroque.

Philip II had money in hand from time to time, but occasionally he had to resort to clever strategies to finance his wars, such as appointing wealthy nobles to command, then requiring them to finance their campaigns until he could reimburse them (an event that rarely happened). Not surprisingly, the commanders allowed the troops to support themselves by stealing from the local population – a policy that stiffened resistance, but allowed the army to make progress. If recruits are attracted to an army on the premise that they would earn their money by plundering the citizens, the results cannot be good.

The prospect of a Spanish victory worried English Protestants. Philip's desires for political and religious uniformity had already raised concerns between 1554 and 1558, years when he was married to Queen Mary Tudor; afterwards, Queen Elizabeth's supporters feared that some Spanish-inspired plot would overthrow her, then restore Catholicism and impose royal despotism. The atmosphere was tense because prominent Protestant nobles and clergymen feared suffering the fate of the French Calvinists (called Huguenots) – already a bloody civil war was tearing France apart, and imaginative partisans could easily believe that it would culminate in a massacre of one party or the other, as happened in 1572, when the St Bartholomew's Day massacre slew many Protestant leaders at a meeting in Paris. There seemed to be no stopping the Catholic juggernaut now that the Spanish king had the silver and gold of the Americas, and increased production in the southern provinces to finance his war machine.

The Dutch position was that they believed that their resistance was justified, that it was Alba who had violated tradition and law; once the king recognised the truth of their cause, they said, they would return to Spanish allegiance. Meanwhile, to organise their army, they chose William the Silent, heir to lands in Orange (southern France) and Nassau (western Germany) and a former confidant of Charles V. He had been associated with the government and defence of the Netherlands against the French until he learned the extent of the persecution that Philip was willing to impose. When he converted to Dutch Calvinism, he put his life and lands at risk. To most outsiders the Protestant cause seemed hopeless, but Calvinism emphasised duty, sacrifice and following God's orders no matter what. To avoid outraging royal opinion everywhere, he took only the modest title of stadtholder – the equivalent of governor.[3]

The English watched with growing concern. According to Brendan Simms in *Three Victories and a Defeat*, the loss of Calais in 1558 was a constant reminder to Englishmen that Mary's popery and incompetence made the island kingdom a potential victim of a more universal power – either France or Spain. It was not a matter of religious bigotry, but fear of domination by whichever European power controlled the Channel coast. The question was which danger to oppose first and how, because France and Spain could not be challenged at the same time.

As it happened, the Spanish king encountered financial problems that no one expected. Whereas previously the problem had been no silver, now it was too much. The flood of bullion made prices unstable and, over the long run, higher. This dislocated the Spanish economy and that in the Low Countries. Meanwhile, the Dutch had learned that by cutting the dikes, flooding the fields surrounding their towns, they could literally bog the Spanish army down. As a result, although Alba had believed in 1569 that he could reduce the Dutch with ten thousand men, he could not; instead, he had to hire many more. Since he was not supplied with hard cash, he found it very difficult to buy supplies or pay his troops.[4]

Then, once France recovered from its internal struggles, Henry III (1551–89) sent his armies into Flanders. No one could imagine peace terms that would be acceptable to all sides, but no one expected the conflict to last long either. Philip II believed that if the leaders of the Protestant movement were removed, the heresy would collapse; then he could concentrate on the defence of Flanders from French attack.

The first assassination attempt on William the Silent was in 1581; the second, two years later, came when he was greeting an experienced Welsh mercenary, Roger Williams (1539–95). The French assassin, Balthasar

Gérard, was motivated by religious zeal, enthusiasm for Philip II and the great reward the king had placed on William's head. William fell, mortally wounded, at the base of the stairway in his home. The assassin almost escaped, but was captured and tortured to death. The event further strengthened Dutch resolve.

However, resolve alone was insufficient – the Dutch needed allies, desperately. So desperately that they had offered to become subject to Henry III of France – who declined at the time, knowing that it would mean war with Spain and earn him the displeasure of the pope; they then turned to Queen Elizabeth. Good Queen Bess, however, was too cautious to challenge King Philip prematurely. She already had to worry about Mary, Queen of Scots, who had close ties to France, where she had once been queen. Elizabeth's situation became more dangerous in 1585 after the Catholic League defeated the Huguenot party in France; Elizabeth did not like the shabby methods used to entrap Mary in treasonable correspondence, but that had helped her realise just how dangerous her prisoner was. When the Spanish army captured the harbour of Sluys, it appeared that Philip's army would soon conquer Holland. Queen Elizabeth, concluding that her own survival was tied to the Dutch tying down Spanish troops, sent English volunteers to Holland, where they were helpful in forestalling the next Spanish offensive. When she turned her 'sea-dogs' loose on the Spanish Main, war was inevitable.

Philip II's response to this was to prepare a great Armada, a fleet that would transfer part of his army from the Low Countries to England. Elizabeth was tempted to bring the troops home from Holland, but understood how unsteady the Dutch situation was. Drake's attack on Cadiz delayed the Armada's departure, then in 1588 the combination of English sailing skill and storms led to the Armada's destruction. Two years later William the Silent's son, Maurice of Nassau, defeated the Spanish army at Breda, after which the Dutch declared themselves a self-governing republic.

Meanwhile, Henry III of France had been assassinated in 1589, bringing an end to the Valois line of kings. Henry had briefly been king of Poland, but had fled that country when he heard that his brother, the king, had died. Henry had been considered a principal instigator of the St Bartholomew's Day massacre, but later had decided that compromise with the Protestants was better than war to the death. This and his sexual ambiguity made him unacceptable to hard-line Catholics. Consequently, it was no surprise that he was murdered by a Catholic fanatic.[5]

Henry IV (1553–1610), the first king of the Bourbon line, came to the throne only in 1594, the five-year interval being filled with a brutal civil war. His humorous *bon mot* of 1593, 'Paris vaut bien une messe' (Paris is well worth a Mass), made some give a cynical smile, but it hardly endeared him to his enemies. His 1598 Edict of Nantes ended the religious wars by granting the Huguenots freedom of worship and the right to maintain military strongholds and refuges. Although Henry reaffirmed Roman Catholicism as the state religion, Roman Catholics believed that he remained a secret Protestant. This led directly to his assassination by François Ravillac, a Catholic fanatic.[6]

The queen mother, Marie de'Medici, struggled to keep the country together for her young son, Louis XIII (1601–44); she barely managed to contain the ambitions of her late husband's cousin, Henry of Bourbon, the prince of Condé (1588–1646), who volunteered repeatedly to bring peace and order back to the kingdom. Marie, understanding the consequences for herself and her son, declined.[7]

In spite of these dreadful events, at the beginning of the seventeenth century it appeared that religious strife might be lessening. In 1601 King Philip III (1578–1621) of Spain appointed his aunt, Isabella Clara Eugenia (1566–1633) and her husband, Albrecht of Austria (1559–1621) to govern the Netherlands. The ensuing decades became famous for prosperity and the artistic achievements of the Flemish baroque.

France
Who Rules? The King or the Courtiers?

Louis XIII had been fortunate to have Cardinal Richelieu (1585–1642) to manage affairs for him after 1624. From childhood he had been aware that royalty was in trouble everywhere – unrest in England, rebellions in Spain, religious conflict in Germany, and the Ottomans seemingly waiting for the Habsburg Empire to collapse. France had been on the verge of dissolution when Louis had become king at the age of eight; consequently, his mother had ruled through favourites until he was sixteen, when he assassinated her lover and exiled her to the provinces.

Intrigue and gossip characterised the court of this odd king. He was an enthusiastic hunter, but avoided the company of women. He had apparently loved (or at least tolerated) his beautiful Spanish wife, but after several children were still-born, sixteen years passed before he slept with her again. Most likely he came to dislike Anne of Austria (1601–66) because she was a female, and the king was suspicious of all women.[8] He also suspected her of treason – when their 1615 marriage was arranged, it provided for his sister marrying the future Philip IV of Spain. It was one of those ideas that sounded good at the time, a means of bringing peace. However, it not only failed to end the contest with the Habsburgs, but added to domestic turmoil. The elder Condé and the Huguenots considered the young king a royal dolt, all the more dangerous because he could be swayed so easily by whichever adviser had his attention at the time – or by his forceful mother; their fears were heightened when he picked Cardinal Richelieu to manage the realm. Long-term planning was Richelieu's domain, short-term affairs the court's – courtiers knew that Louis XIII could be flattered, then ignored, and the queen insulted, then ignored; many of them took affairs seriously only in the realm of sex.

Louis XIII disliked his beautiful wife for many reasons, including her refusal to learn proper French and her rumoured dalliance with a handsome courtier, but one suspects that he hated most of all her being more intelligent than he was. It was in this context that her insistence on corresponding with her brother was so annoying – Philip was commander of the Spanish army in the Netherlands. Louis conceived his elder son in the early winter of 1638 only because bad weather had driven him back to Paris, where it was discovered that his bed had been packed up and sent to Versailles; it was too cold to sleep alone and spending several nights with the no-longer youthful Anne was better than rousting some servant out of his bed or offending some noble. The court and public were so surprised that the middle-aged queen had conceived that they called the son Louis the God-given, then turned their quarrels away from the succession to personalities. Marie de'Medici railed at Richelieu while Anne meddled in politics as much as she dared.

No wonder that contemporaries believed that women ruled the kingdom. In actuality, royal policy was in the capable hands of Cardinal Richelieu, who governed with the help of a large private army that could intimidate the numerous bodyguards of the great lords. The king was free to go off hunting again and the queen to return to her semi-seclusion with a small circle of friends – though not too secluded to have another son.[9]

With Richelieu and Marie de'Medici dying in 1642 and Louis XIII a year later, Anne of Austria became regent; politically inexperienced, she named Cardinal Mazarin prime minister. It was an excellent choice, though many of her courtiers did not think so. Mazarin, quiet and polite with the queen and her party, was disliked as an Italian, a low-born upstart who used his influence to amass a fortune and to marry his nieces into the best families of the kingdom, while holding power that courtiers wanted themselves.[10] His principal problem was how to continue the war against the Habsburgs, keep the Huguenots in check, and humble the great lords who imagined themselves as a better king than the boy, Louis XIV. Mazarin's enemies noted that he was a cardinal, but had never become a priest, and they believed him to be the queen's lover, even the father of her second child. Disputes over status, clothing, slights, love affairs and royal patronage escalated into feuds; duels abounded, and assassinations were common.

As the cliques began to arm, the royal army became less important than the mafia-like private armies that figure so prominently in novels such as *The Man in the Iron Mask* and plays such as *Cyrano de Bergerac*. It would not be amiss to consider most of these gangs mercenaries or close to meeting the definition. Indeed, with so many people considering their allegiance to be to a person rather than to a nation, it is not easy to fit these warriors into modern definitions.

The writings of François de la Rochefoucauld (1613–80) allow us valuable insights into these times. He is widely credited with having provided the first good examples of fine writing in French, but he was more quoted than read – a reflection of the fact that his *Maxims* were short, pithy and clever. He was not a typical figure of the times (good models seldom are), but his exaggerated faults and virtues illustrated how colourless most of his contemporaries were. He was a good warrior, but an indifferent commander. He thought too much, and his thoughts were always cynical. This did not mean that he was wrong, but these were poor qualities for a leader – troops want a decisive commander, not a philosopher. Vanity makes some brave, he observed, ignorance others, and fear of shame almost everyone; some are carried away by the crowd, either fleeing in panic or joining in hopeless attacks; some fear the sword, others muskets; and no one dares as much as he would if he were certain he would come through alive and unhurt. Friendships were fleeting, lovers transitory, vain and changeable, and national interest was something entirely foreign. Yet Rochefoucauld was widely admired, even more widely appreciated, and must be ranked among the most insightful and unsuccessful French politicians ever.

Rochefoucauld's attitudes were widely shared, quoted by men and women of less wit and no wisdom who believed that common soldiers were expendable, workers and farmers unworthy of notice, and that even friends and family could be sacrificed lightly. After all, one mourned not for the departed friend, but for one's own loss. To lose a father was sad, but to acquire his property and titles was joy. A mistress was a treasure, but she will betray you as easily as you would her; therefore, act quickly, before you become the butt of jokes.

The closest Rochefoucauld came to thinking about the common soldier was a reflection on why men can express contempt for death, something they would never do if they thought about it – great men have a greater love of glory than fear of dying, while common men are insufficiently intelligent to understand what they would lose.

He knew well Marshal Turenne, who was defeating the Habsburg armies in Germany and Italy, making the Catholic forces realise that the Thirty Years War could not be won.[11] When Turenne turned his energies to defeating Spain in the Netherlands, it appeared that fortune was smiling on him – as it often does on generals who are capable, self-confident, and supplied with sufficient resources. However, Rochefoucauld understood that in a world that rewards the appearance of merit more than merit itself, men of true genius are likely to be unhappy. Few soldiers would have understood such elevated cynicism. They had good reasons to be cynical, but none for sneering at their own behaviour.

Rochefoucauld's literary popularity helped make French the dominant language of Europe. There was no competition. Germans in those days identified with their local lord or their city, not with a nation. They understood that they had a common written language (with different dialects), shared many common Christian beliefs (though Lutherans, Catholics and Calvinists often saw their differences more clearly than the points they shared). Latin had passed away,[12] and was too closely identified with Catholicism to be used in the north. German officers and courtiers had little experience in Italy.

French was the logical common tongue, because France was the largest political unit, the most populous single country, and the richest, but also because France had the most attractive music, literature and courtly life. The wine was a bonus.

To the east, however, German was more practical as an international language.

The Fronde

The breakdown of the Western kingdoms began with Spain. As the expenses of the great European war became more than Philip IV could bear, he had sought to persuade his Catalan subjects to make greater contributions to the royal exchequer. The Catalans, however, refused to give up their exemptions from tolls and their right to vote on taxes, even when French troops pressed across the border. Catalan peasants did not blame the French for the robbery and pillaging, but the 'king of Castile', as they saw him. By 1640 they had suffered enough – they rebelled.

As the insurrection spread, becoming a separatist movement, the Portuguese likewise declared their independence. Royal ministers had assisted both insurgencies, reasoning that whatever weakened the Habsburgs in Spain and Austria was good for France. However, examples are contagious. Soon enough similar unrest broke out in France. This even more complicated rebellion, the Fronde, was assisted by Spanish authorities.

Cardinal Richelieu had utterly ignored the pope, supporting Protestants in Germany, and intruding on what was now called the Spanish Netherlands; his armies had fought in Lorraine, Alsace, Italy and Catalonia. This had worked throughout his lifetime, but in 1648 his successor encountered difficulties.

The French civil war began with opponents of Cardinal Mazarin breaking windows in Paris (a *fronde* was a sling, used to hurl the rocks), protesting that the cardinal was collecting ever higher taxes and undermining the feudal rights of nobles, cities and law courts. At first the rebels achieved considerable success, but when the Peace of Westphalia freed Prince Louis of Condé from his campaign in Flanders, he restored order in Paris quickly.[13]

Rochefoucauld was a witness to all these troubles. His role at court was important enough to be noticed, but less than that of courtiers of higher birth; his military resumé was good, but not exceptional – he seemed to have more courage than good sense, and he was recovering from battle injuries at the time that commissions were awarded for the next campaign; his mistresses were numerous, but only one was important – the sister of Condé, by whom he had a son. He was associated with a literary clique that resembled nothing so much as the late nineteenth-century artists and poets of the Decadent movement – light-hearted, empty-headed, openly effete and deliberately offensive to Anne of Austria and Mazarin. They paraded their lack of interest in politics, physical culture or conventional morality. Calling themselves the 'Precious' (*précieux*), they spoke and wrote in coded phrases, a combination of Victorian circumlocution and academic jargon, but cleverer than either Victorian prudes or post-modern scholars.[14] They were hated by coarse and profane warriors such as Condé, but Rochefoucauld – thanks to his dalliance with Condé's sister – was able to flit from party to party easily.

The court was so dissolute and corrupt that Rochefoucauld could joke, 'It is possible to meet with women who have never had an affair of gallantry; but it is rare to find one who has had only one' and 'We have all of us sufficient fortitude to bear the misfortunes of others.' Status and prestige were all-important. Rochefoucauld, for example, was not much enamoured of his wife (he quipped that there are some good marriages, but none with many delights), but he was offended that the queen would not allow her to own a stool, so that while important ladies at court could sit in comfort, she had to stand. Then, when promised a stool, the promise was not kept. It was a reflection upon Rochefoucauld personally, a reflection that he took so seriously that, without fully thinking it over, he entered into the first Fronde, a protest by the *parlement* of Paris against Mazarin's decision not to pay the judges' salaries. Mazarin and the queen slipped out of Paris by night, Condé blockaded the city, and the Spanish proposed an alliance with the rebels. At length, as hunger and fear of the block sank in, the rebels proposed a truce. When Mazarin and the queen agreed to most of the demands, Rochefoucauld obtained the promise of a stool for his wife.

Almost immediately, members of the royal party became dissatisfied. They had seen the rebels rewarded, while Mazarin's resources were insufficient to provide for them, too. Their complaints annulled some of the earlier concessions – Rochefoucauld did not get the stool for his wife. Satisfying the malcontents would have been out of the question anyway, because Condé now insolently demanded more lands and honours and, essentially, to replace Mazarin with himself. Had Condé possessed even minimal manners and a pretence of humility, he might have done better, but pulling the cardinal's goatee (in public, no less) was not a way to make friends. Mazarin bided his time, then struck. In early 1650 he arrested Condé and his friends. Civil war – the second Fronde – followed quickly. Once again, Mazarin was better organised than his rivals. He struck down his principal enemies quickly, then forgave all but a handful.[15]

It helped Mazarin's cause that the example of England – a king executed, noble families destroyed, commerce ruined, the nation slipping into the hands of a military dictator – caused many to stay their hand, to hold back from turning a quarrel among the elites into a war to the death that involved the nation as a whole.

There still remained a rebel army in the east, led by Turenne, the only general equal to Condé, and Condé's friends began to clamour for his release from prison. Mazarin, meanwhile, alienated his erstwhile allies, the party that had prevailed in the first Fronde. In early 1651, when the cardinal fled Paris, the queen released the prisoners and gave Rochefoucauld the coveted stool for his wife. Rochefoucauld brought Condé and his fellow captives back to Paris in his carriage, then watched as the prince failed to take advantage of his opportunities – he could have put the queen into a convent and become regent himself, but he was less skilled in intrigue than war. In short, although on the battlefield Condé knew how to recognise when an enemy was in a weak position, then how to strike him down and finish him off, at court he lacked both manners and common sense. He simply did not have the most essential qualities of a king – poise and manners – whereas Mazarin, who was neither well-born nor rich, understood how to manipulate men and win them to his side. Young Louis XIV was taking in every lesson, carefully and quietly.

By summer Condé realised that he had been outmanoeuvred. Panicking for fear of a second arrest, he fled to his fortified chateau. When he returned to Paris, it was to intimidate his enemies. In September 1651 the third war of the Fronde began.

This time the Spanish intervened more forcefully, aiding the rebels. The royal party, however, now had the allegiance of Turenne. As for Rochefoucauld, Condé's sister had been with Turenne for a year and now took up with a handsome young officer (and perhaps also her own unathletic younger brother) – it was another lesson about love that Rochefoucauld later expressed in several oft-quoted maxims. It was much the same with political allies. If the queen spent too much time in Mazarin's company, how was that different from what other women did? Her son's legitimacy was never in doubt. That was what counted – it sufficed to rally many to the queen's cause.

Meanwhile, Mazarin collected a mercenary army and marched to Paris. The royal party, thus reinforced, kept the loyalty of all those who wanted peace and quiet or who reckoned that the queen would eventually prevail. Condé had three scattered armies, the people of Paris, everyone who hated Mazarin, and Englishmen flushed with victory over King Charles I (1600–49) – giving rise to speculation about a similar beheading of royalist enemies in the future.

Condé collected two of his armies, marched on Paris, then fought a desperate battle against Turenne outside the city walls. The battle was a draw, but Condé was finished – unable to capture Paris, he fled to the Spanish Netherlands. When he subsequently became a Habsburg general, it was a treason that no Frenchman could ever forgive.

Rochefoucauld was wounded in both eyes, and it was not clear whether he would ever recover his sight. Still, he continued to intrigue until it was obvious that the rebellion had failed. Making his peace with Mazarin, he retired to what was left of his estates. After several years he was allowed to return to Paris, where he lived quietly, composing maxims and cultivating the art of boredom. When his eldest son was wounded at a crossing of the Rhine in 1672, and two younger sons were slain, Rochefoucauld accepted his fate stoically; he had little choice, he reflected. He now opined that friendship with women was better than passion, but that was because he was too fat and infirm to exert himself; the same was true of his political ambition. He conversed occasionally with Condé, who had similarly received royal clemency on the condition that he stayed out of sight, and he established a good relationship with his son by Condé's sister. The son accepted the arrangement – Rochefoucauld was a more prominent father than his mother's husband. Rochefoucauld died in 1680, at what contemporaries considered an advanced age – sixty-six.

When Mazarin died in 1661, Louis XIV became his own prime minister. The most important carry-over from the old system was having Turenne as marshal-general and constable – the highest offices in the land. The king never forgot the sight of foreign mercenaries, even Spanish soldiers, in the streets of Paris. Had Louis XIV been satisfied with Turenne's victories and the peace settlement of 1659, rather than trying to extend French control to the Rhine and beyond, he would have better deserved to be considered the greatest man of the era. His later wars, though initially successful, eventually cast a shadow over his reputation as the 'Sun King'.

Louis XIV continued the centralising policies of the past – reducing the nobles to ciphers, expanding the frontiers and crushing the Huguenots (who held military powers as well as a Calvinist belief that their allegiance was to God before the king). In 1682, three years before revoking the Edict of Nantes, stripping the Huguenots of their rights to worship as they pleased, he sent his bully boys into Orange, smashing the Protestant establishment in that southern French province. This was his signal to the Dutch and their foremost protector, William of Orange (1650–1702, later king of England), that their days were numbered.

As states assumed a monopoly over military activities, warfare was changed forever, and then the nature of the state, too.[16] Until the Fronde, French kings had mercenary units, but the practice was still to keep a small core army, then expand it in time of war; in effect, the kings had to raise a new army for every crisis. Louis XIV understood that he had to be better prepared – if a strong standing army stood ready to fight, no noble would dare to rebel. Or even contradict him.

William McNeill, in *The Pursuit of Power*, calls this the moment that the states north of the Alps caught up with those to the south. Earlier Venice and Milan each had maintained small standing armies composed of cavalry, infantry and artillery, supported by tax revenues and led by professionals. Louis did the same, but on a far greater scale and with more emphasis on drill. Drill made soldiers more obedient and more efficient, reduced idleness and boredom and magnified unit solidarity. For the 'human flotsam and jetsam' that composed the armies of the era, it provided a stable, structured and controlled society that contrasted strongly with the crude buying and selling of services that had previously characterised military life.

The greater reliance on infantry may have partly reflected the high cost and low quality of horses. Population growth required more animals to draw ploughs, while simultaneously reducing land available for pasture; artillery required draught horses, and cavalrymen wanted improved breeds based on Ottoman lines. While northern Germany was blessed with a cool climate perfect for livestock and oats, and with many regions being so liable to flooding that ploughing was unwise, raising horses and cattle was easier than growing crops; France, being rich in everything, also produced fine horses.[17] Regions concentrating on the products that they could sell was nothing new, but the increased emphasis of exporting these products was another aspect of modernisation.

The same was true of consumption – and there was no great consumer than a king. Louis XIV may not have said, 'L'État, c'est moi' (I am the state), but this was still the age when the monarch often mattered more than the nation, and though the king's will was limited by traditional practices, the circumstances of the moment, and his personal resources, when he truly wished to have his way – as in revoking the Edict of Nantes in 1685, abolishing the special privileges of Protestants, then driving most of them out of the kingdom – he found ways to achieve it. Moreover, the public often applauded. Order, even tyrannically enforced, was better than anarchy; and if those who suffered most from royal despotism were despised nobles, arrogant clergymen and troublesome Huguenots, well, that was just fine.

Louis could overawe princes and prelates. He quailed only before a handful of women – those with sufficient personality to make themselves his mistresses, or even his wife, but most of all his mother. He became truly a king only after Anne of Austria died in 1666.

France as a Model for its Neighbours

Louis XIV emerged from the Fronde more powerful than any of his ancestors. The provinces, though often markedly diverse in culture, customs and language, and all different from Paris, now tolerated more centralised royal authority; the king, in turn, allowed many ancient practices to survive. It was a relationship that worked until the eve of 1789.

The king dedicated his life to seeing that he dominated France, and that France dominated Europe.[18] But what his efforts achieved in securing autocratic power, professionalising administration, improving the army and navy, encouraging commerce, eliminating religious dissent and curbing the power of the nobles – all clearly marking the way of the future – also made France resented and feared. Even the pope was worried.

Louis XIV did not achieve these results alone. As Martin van Creveld demonstrates in *Supplying War*, two secretaries of war, father and son, created first a system of frontier fortresses that held enemy armies at bay, then a field army of unprecedented size and effectiveness; the key to both was logistics – the care and feeding of troops.[19] Louis XIV achieved much, but part of his success lay in trusting his administrators. Indeed, one sign of genius is the ability to identify men of talent, another is allowing them to use those talents, then holding them accountable. Still, the secretaries of war could not free field marshals from a dependence on local supplies, which partly explains why French armies advanced so often into Germany to collect foodstuffs rather than staying quietly in their fortresses.

Spanish kings did not fare so well with subjects who resented central control – the Dutch and Catalans. Why this was so has been debated by historians and political philosophers for many years. Perhaps it was because Spanish kings and their ministers had so many distractions. Their worldwide empire was not easy to administer, and to the very end of the century the Spanish Habsburgs were poor specimens of that subspecies of humanity known as royalty. Perhaps Catalans and Dutch were simply ungovernable. It was easy for foreign powers to give assistance to rebels there, and flight to safety was always an option. Certainly foreign intervention was important in the Spanish decline, and it may be that Castilian willingness to accept a grandson of the Sun King as the successor to the last Habsburg monarch was a reasonable means to bring an end to French interference in the governance of Catalonia and the Spanish Netherlands.

There were also pirates: swarms of them coming from Holland and England, supporting William of Orange's war effort. Fewer pirates came from France after 1700, thanks to Louis XIV crushing the Huguenots and to the new alliance of France and Spain, but their absence was hardly noticed – Dutch and English privateers took their place.

German and Scandinavian princes, even Polish and Russian ones, hurried to copy French practices – building imitations of Versailles, importing French musicians, artists and philosophers, and speaking French. Those whose lands were not as rich as France (and few were) or as populous (none was) found it difficult to afford those luxuries. Some tried to stimulate their economies; some rented out their armies to friendly powers.

Even the imperial court of Leopold I (1640–1705) succumbed somewhat to the fascination with French practices. The emperor was in no condition to offer cultural leadership – his Catholicism was a spectacular art form, but Vienna was still too much at the edge of Christian civilisation to draw many visitors, and Leopold's court was as dull as the emperor himself. Leopold understood that he needed Protestant assistance against the sultan and the Sun King. Righteous assertions of Catholic superiority would attract no Protestant volunteers to fight the Turk, nor to defend the empire against Louis XIV. Most importantly, only the very richest territorial rulers could aspire to cultural leadership; the emperor barely had enough funds for his peacetime army, his courtiers and the Church.

France Leads the Way towards the Enlightenment

The rule of Louis XIV is associated more with grandeur than toleration, but without tolerating diverse ideas, great ones cannot be born. Certainly the Sun King understood much about art and architecture, poetry and literature, and the nature of the good life. Nonetheless, in his old age he was ruthless and demanding; his treatment of Huguenots, harrying hundreds of thousands of them out of the kingdom, was both cruel and self-defeating. He thought it necessary, of course, both to consolidate royal authority, to eliminate potential rebels and to satisfy his insistent wife, who was advised by her spiritual counsellor to get rid of the heretics.

Even Louis XIV could not oversee everything, however, or see the logical consequences of seemingly inconsequential subjects – like literature, which formed attitudes that were essential to the later success of the Enlightenment. One literary figure of immense importance in this was Rochefoucauld, whose witty aphorisms on the futility and foolishness of love also warned readers against ambition and expecting better of others than of oneself. His thoughts fit well the society of his times, even his sly condemnation of the king's wars, noting that there are some crimes made glorious by their number and their excess, that robbing the public was proof of talent, and seizing whole provinces unjustly was justified by calling them conquests. He believed that fortune (or perhaps the stars) determined events, but that self-deception, jealousy, indolence, incompetence and foolishness were also important – and universal.

His scepticism of his contemporaries' certitude was echoed by Blaise Pascal (1623–62): 'Men never do evil so completely and cheerfully as when they do it from religious conviction', and 'I have discovered that all human evil comes from this, man's being unable to sit still in a room.'

For those who could sit still, fairy tales were popular, particularly in France. *Puss in Boots* became a parable of advancing by one's wits – in this case, the servant's wits making his master, the ignorant third son of a deceased miller, into a noble; the boy in the parable believed that his talking cat could make him rich if he only somehow could provide him boots and a bag, and the clever feline achieved more than he had ever imagined. The importance of boots might remind one of Kleist's *Kleider Machen Menschen* (Clothes make the man), which taught that dressing correctly was essential to social success. But Rochefoucauld reminds us that our origins are betrayed by our ways of thought and feeling, not just our accents and our tailor – ideas elaborated by Fénelon.

François de Salignac de la Monthe Fénelon (1651–1715) was an aristocratic cleric best known as the tutor who broke the spirit of Louis XIV's son and was the spiritual adviser to the king's wives and mistresses. As such, Fénelon did more damage than many a barbarian chieftain. He made up for this in part by writing a sequel to the *Odyssey*, calling it *The Adventures of Telemachus*. Though modern audiences find it unreadable, it was an international sensation, partly because of his representations of impossible virtue, partly because of his effort to describe what good government was, partly from his sentimental condemnation of war and partly because the novel was a precursor of the next century's rage over nature and naturalism. The author's fame survived not only into his declining years, but for many years thereafter.

Fénelon had initially supported Louis XIV's aggressive wars against Protestants, but came to change his mind. Indeed, many of his contemporaries ceased to think that religion was a sufficient justification for killing anyone, and some even questioned that it was logical to murder foreigners to sustain a monarch's claim on someone else's land.[20]

While it was relatively safe to hold such subversive beliefs in France, it was difficult to persuade either kings or government officials to share them – and certainly not Louis XIV. France was a powerful country, and it appeared that France would prevail over any combination of its enemies.

Voltaire and Montesquieu were Fénelon's successors. Both found much to admire in Britain, just as prominent Britons were finding much to admire in France (the quality of the beer being a major exception). The love–hate relationship of these two nations colours the centuries covered in this volume. Robert and Isabella Tombs made this into witty repartee in *That Sweet Enemy*, she defending France, the land of her birth, he defending his natal land.

England and Scotland

The political, military and religious cultures of these two kingdoms are too well known to summarise, and too complex. Both experienced the violent passions of party and faith during the Reformation, both rebuffed kings who wanted to make themselves supreme (or at least secure), and both remained relatively immune from European politics until the second half of the seventeenth century.

The English people, despite having lost the Hundred Years War, remained proud of their martial accomplishments in that conflict, but Europeans did not share those opinions – as far as they were concerned, monarchs such as Henry VIII were better remembered for having promised to capture Paris than for having come close to doing so; Elizabeth was to the Spanish an illegitimate usurper and heretic. For unimaginable reasons God allowed foul weather to save her rather than giving fair winds to the great Armada of a Catholic king. Her successor, James I, dithered during the Thirty Years War and his son, Charles I, managed to lose his head, literally, to bands of commoners. Only Cromwell, the worst of all the Protestants of his era, understood how to win battles, to govern unruly peoples and to make hostile monarchs respect him.

These stereotypes – and they are stereotypes – have just enough truth in them to explain why England concentrated first and foremost on assuring that no hostile monarch held a port along the Channel coast. This meant first, opposition to Spain, then to Holland, and finally to France.

Scotland was too poor to be a great power, and perhaps too proud to care. What mattered was to avoid being taken over by England. It was more acceptable to take over England, in the sense that King James VI of Scotland became James I of England, but tensions remained. If Scots had been united, perhaps they could have established colonies, but the best hope for a young man was to leave Scotland, to become a mercenary in European wars or a settler in Ireland.

It was in constitutional philosophy that England and Scotland made their most enduring contributions – their parliaments established the principle that nobles and commoners alike had the right to be consulted in the making of laws and policies. That was a principle that most 'right-thinking' people on the Continent rejected – the examples of France, Poland and Russia showing that a strong hand was needed to protect the borders, establish law and order, and promote trade. As is too often true, received opinion was wrong – though that was not apparent until the 1700s.

The Polish–Lithuanian Commonwealth

Because England's Parliament had retained its powers long after similar institutions had disappeared or become impotent across much of Europe, there was considerable interest in the practices of the Polish–Lithuanian state, where the aristocracy, the Church, the knights and gentry, and the cities remained strong – too strong, foreign observers began to think. By 1620 demands to be consulted, even to have a veto, had begun to erode royal power. But how could such a large state be ruled, except either by having a single despot make the decision – as in Russia or Turkey – or by sharing power widely?

Eastern Europe was a vast, complex region marked by the domination of the Orthodox Church, great rivers, fertile lands bounded on the south by a great rolling grassland that stretched into Asia. That part which is now Ukraine and southern Russia was largely unsettled; the northern reaches were rich in forests, rivers and people, but its short growing season caused peasants to look longingly towards the rich black soil of the steppe. The climate was hot in the summer and cold in the winter, allowing Russians to brag that they were a tough people who could endure anything. Fortified by vodka, they seem to do so. Vodka was apparently invented by Poles, but this was not a problem – Russians were becoming accustomed to taking whatever they wanted from Poland–Lithuania. That had not been the case until the 1600s. Historically Lithuanians had ruled western Russia, and Poland had expanded southeast towards the Black Sea.

Poles were Roman Catholic Slavs who thought of themselves as culturally superior to the non-Slav Lithuanians; this created tensions in the multinational Polish–Lithuanian state. Germans, Jews and the handful of Tatars insisted on the protection of their rights, but in practice only the voices of nobles (especially those powerful ones called magnates) and churchmen were regularly heard.

Scholars – eager perhaps to emphasise that the rolling plain north of the Carpathian mountains was not part of Russia – have recently adopted the practice of calling it east-central Europe. Central Europe was thus reduced to the mountain-girded lands of Germany, Bohemia and Austria.

To the north the well-ordered lands of Livonia had been divided between Poland and Sweden, but were highly desired by Russian tsars. To the south, in the Crimea and on the steppe, were Tatars. Only the latest of many steppe peoples who have occupied the region, the Tatars collecting people for the slave markets of the east made Russians and Poles occasional allies. So great was the Tatar threat, in fact, that the Orthodox–Catholic religious disputes were often put aside to deal with the common enemy. The practical problems were first how to defeat the Tatar horsemen, then how to prepare for the war that would follow against each other for control of the borderlands and the steppe. These problems could have been more easily resolved if Swedes, Germans and Turks had stayed out of the conflict.

By the 1640s Poland was, in the words of C. R. L. Fletcher, a huge, unwieldy carcass: a conglomeration of conquered provinces unified by a tendency to anarchy and a stubborn adherence to Catholicism. Like most carcasses, Poland attracted its share of vultures, creatures who had no difficulty describing their interests in high-minded terms, most significantly the defence of various religious communities, the rights of ethnic groups and the nobility, and the balance of power. Added to this was an election process that destabilised the Polish–Lithuanian Commonwealth every few years, persuading neighbouring observers that hereditary monarchy, whatever its many faults, was better than a republic, even one with a titular king.

Sigismund III had never recovered from exchanging royal powers for votes in his election, nor from the loss of Sweden; he failed even to persuade the Sejm to pass laws by a majority vote instead of unanimity. The motto *Rex regnat et non gubernat* (the king reigns, but he does not govern) was all too true. Subsequent generations considered Sigismund's reign the era of 'Golden Freedom' (*Złota Wolność*), but they were blinded by later catastrophes – crises that this freedom had helped create – and therefore could not see how unhappy the decades of his reign had been. Sigismund had hoped to compensate for his early concessions and mistakes by intervening in Russia's troubles, hoping to acquire a foreign land where his authority would be less challenged; at the very least, he could prevent his powerful Lithuanian vassals from taking that region for themselves. He occupied Moscow from 1610 to 1612 and seized valuable provinces in what is today Belarus (reclaiming them, he argued, for his Lithuanian grand duchy), but his Polish nobles gave him minimal assistance, fearing that he would grow too powerful; and his Lithuanian subjects were hardly more helpful.

Meanwhile, the Swedish king from 1611 onwards, Gustavus Adolphus, was understandably concerned that Sigismund was plotting to reclaim his northern throne. Sigismund had little time for that, his attention being drawn to challenges by Turks, Tatars and Cossacks, but there were vassals and clerics in Sigismund's entourage who intrigued in the northern kingdom on his behalf, perhaps even without his knowing. Since Sigismund was unable to prevail militarily in the southeastern parts of Poland–Lithuania, he was unwilling to be diverted into far-fetched conspiracies at the other end of his realm, but Swedes worried about what he would do when peace came. Attaining peace depended on what happened on the eastern borders, especially the border with Russia.

Russia

Russian rulers, once Ivan the Terrible managed to re-establish tsarist power in the 1550s, could devise programmes for expansion that were more cold-blooded and single-minded than any Western ruler's. This was because the threat from the south came in the two-fold challenge of Islam and steppe raiders. Organising national defence gave the tsars more moral and political authority than their Roman Catholic rivals possessed; and they had more human and material resources than their Islamic foes. Still, historians disagree why national defence required such great expansion of national borders. Many Russian historians argue that the campaigns to the east and south were the result of careful planning to deal with specific threats; Russia's confrontation with Islam was, therefore, similar to Spain's *Reconquista*. Western historians tend to believe that the tsars were opportunists motivated by expansionist urges.[21] Since tsars explained their strategies in formulaic terms rather than in reflective analyses, we are unlikely to resolve this disagreement soon.

Westerners have long asked why the state centred on Moscow did not adopt foreign practices that seemed self-evidently logical and useful for correcting inefficiency and backwardness. A Western explanation is that traditional cavalry – the shaggy ponies that could survive on grass alone, the nobles armed with bows and swords – were more effective against nomads than either infantry or heavy cavalry, which required oats. Russians, in contrast, often explain that their ancestors saw themselves as God's warriors fighting God's enemies, seeking to save their state from paganism, Islam, heresy (Roman Catholicism and Protestantism) and rationalism. In short, theirs was a sacred task, the preservation of the nation's ancient practices from foreign influence and worldliness; to achieve salvation they had to reject or ignore Western advice and Western examples. The boyars and clergy were to serve the grand duke of Moscow, God's representative on earth. Ivan the Great had changed the grand duke's title to tsar (Caesar), a reference to Byzantine emperors who were his wife's ancestors and a challenge to the Holy Roman emperor. The tsar's duty was to maintain and defend the state, not to change it. Change was dangerous; change would challenge the authority of the Orthodox Church, the ancient noble houses and the holy men inside and outside the monasteries.

Mysticism and miracle were central to this view of the world. God had his own plans for humanity and for individual humans, and perhaps great sinning was part of it. Certainly, great men felt themselves called to a divine service – whatever they did was not altogether of their own making or even their own choice, but part of a great design that one could only discern from a distance, that is, after the fact. This generalisation, like many useful ones, can be misleading. The point is that those who attempt to understand traditional Russia in terms of modern Western concepts are likely to be badly mistaken.

Russia was a relatively exotic world, much influenced by Byzantium, the Tatars and its own relative isolation; so it must have seemed, too, to visitors from the East, though the strange influences would have come from the West. Tatar delegations entered the great Kremlin in Moscow, perhaps to marvel at the strange concoctions of Italian architects, perhaps to compare those marvels unfavourably to the great buildings of the Ottoman and Persian empires; certainly, they were not impressed by the crudeness of Russian manners and dress. The isolation of women they would have understood, but not the drunken revelry.

The 'Time of Troubles' seemingly confirmed long-standing Western stereotypes about Russia. That great land, though not as vast yet as the modern state, was considered the antipode of the West – that is, it was the far side of the world, where strange beasts ruled, not men. It was part-European, part-Asiatic, totally backward and uncivilised, and beyond understanding. That reputation, despite vigorous protests by Russian historians, has lingered on to the very present.

A parallel reputation, that of a land rich in people and resources, became ever more true in the years to follow. The Romanov dynasty did not instantly make Russia a great power, but it restored stability and confidence. This led to a doubling of the population within a century and to an increase in international trade that allowed the tsars to keep taxation within limits that the peasantry could bear. The dynasty released most of its foreign mercenaries, but retained the foreign officers needed to turn illiterate recruits from the lowest ranks of society into passable soldiers.

The difficulty of fighting on the steppe, a combination of logistical problems and the nature of the Tatars' light cavalry, is easily ignored by those who have no experience on such a broad expanse of grasslands. The story of Russia's rise to prominence in European politics is intertwined with overcoming the physical and human barriers to taking this southern plain from its Tatar possessors and Polish competitors.

However, the story is not one of a continual advance into Tatar lands. The decades to come would see the Tatars striking north, almost bringing down

the Polish–Lithuanian Commonwealth and threatening the existence of
the Russian settlements along the frontier.

In the early 1600s Russia was only one of several states suffering from
disunity. The kings of France were still trying to cope with powerful nobles
and zealous religious factions; and there were fierce struggles before they
could even tax commoners easily, but in the end they would succeed. In
Poland–Lithuania the nobles prevailed and, to keep the elected kings weak,
they often chose one of the weaker candidates.

The process by which kings managed to acquire the authority necessary
to make their states powerful was not always pretty, and it certainly did
not instantly create more just and civil societies. Nevertheless, many
subjects would have agreed with the later philosopher Hobbes that the
new Leviathan represented by authoritarian rulers was an improvement
over the rough methods of local strongmen and much superior to chaos.
Prelates, too, resisted the tendency towards centralised power, but with
mixed enthusiasm and usually without success.

The most important figure in developing the theory and practice of war
in these years was the son of William the Silent, Maurice of Nassau. He
reorganised the Dutch army into smaller and more flexible units with greater
firepower and increased mobility, but rather than face larger Spanish forces
in the field, he demonstrated how to frustrate and weaken besieging armies.

As stadtholder of the Dutch Republic, Maurice was merely the foremost
citizen and, therefore, ignored by royal houses as a suitable husband for any
available princess; but his personality, perseverance and reputation drew
Protestants from far and wide to learn the art of war from him.

Less well known as a contributing factor to his success was Maurice's
insistence of paying troops directly rather than giving money to the colonels.
This was made possible by the profits of Dutch businessmen, who not only
had hard cash available for taxes and loans, but also understood the principle
that all workmen should be paid. Troops who were paid regularly were more
willing to train hard and to labour on fortifications. This reform was not
instantly copied elsewhere, but it was an important step in a long process that
by 1700 replaced the private owners of regiments with state appointees.[22]

CHAPTER SIX

Years of Intense Conflict

During the 1600s changes in state structure occurred slowly but steadily, part of a paradigm shift in European society. It was insufficient just to buy weapons. (The contrasting experiences of Europeans were like those of China and Japan in the nineteenth century – the Japanese adapted their entire society and flourished, the Chinese did neither.) As weapons became better, new skills were needed to employ them effectively. Artillerymen, for example, had to have specialised knowledge: not just in how to fire the weapons, but also in getting them to the battlefield, making certain that the powder worked properly, and understanding how to fire under adverse weather conditions. Infantrymen had to be able to load quickly and fire in volleys. Furthermore, unless the troops were in the right place, facing the enemy at the right angle and at the right distance, such firepower was wasted. This meant constant drill in marching and firing. To a significant degree, only professionals had these skills; at the beginning of the century there were relatively few professionals, but this would change soon. Since formal instruction in the military arts was uncommon until the end of the century, most future officers learned their craft by observation – accompanying commanders as aides and pages.[1]

Light cavalry, whose lack of discipline was offset by their ferocious habits and love of war, became more important. Flocks of such irregular troops surrounded the professional core of every army, acting as scouts, rounding up food and fodder, and would even be pursuing defeated armies right until they reached their enemies' camp, where they often stopped to loot the tents and supply dumps.

Traditional feudal forces still appeared when summoned. Heavy cavalry and semi-trained militia were welcome, but no commander could count on their serving through until the campaign was concluded, or that they would stay long after fighting became intense. Unlike the mercenaries, they had families to return to; while they were facing death in wars that they hardly understood or that seemed pointless, faces of loved ones would still be fresh in their minds.

This may have been most true in east-central Europe, where the average peasant must have wondered why Christian rulers were fighting one another rather than joining to oppose Tatar raids that were carrying so many people off to Muslim servitude.

The Swedish–Polish War of 1621

The short-lived union of Sweden and Poland (1594–98) under Sigismund III had not brought regional peace. Not only had the nobles, clerics and parliaments of both states been unwilling to concede the points in dispute, but the possession of Livonia remained unresolved. Poland wanted Reval, Sweden wanted Riga, and Catholics wanted to extend the Counter-Reformation as much as Protestants wanted to defend their reforms; everyone wanted in on the trade with Russia that ran through Livonia, and to control the revenues and patronage appointments.[2]

The origin of this conflict lay in the fear of Ivan IV that had made the two states allies in the Livonian War, then a marriage of the two dynasties. Sigismund, the heir to both kingdoms, however, thought that religious uniformity could be restored by wile and force. He failed. What was left was a Swedish claim on the Polish crown, and a Polish claim on Sweden's. Russia's Time of Troubles acerbated the mutual mistrust so that right as the Thirty Years War began, a new generation of Vikings – very well organised but just as fierce – were ready to fall on the Polish–Lithuanian Commonwealth.

Although Sigismund had abandoned his effort to conquer Moscow in 1618, he had retained possession of valuable borderlands that could eventually strengthen his hand. To prevent this, the Swedish king, Gustavus Adolphus, chose to attack before the dispersed Polish–Lithuanian army could be reconstituted. In 1621 Gustavus Adolphus ordered his governor of Estonia, Jacob de la Gardie, to send word to Sigismund that the truce would end in three months, then to gather fourteen thousand troops for a summer campaign against Polish Livonia and Courland. Considering that the fortifications of Riga were outdated and the garrison consisted of only three hundred

(*Above, left*) 1. Maximilian I (Holy Roman emperor 1490–1519), painted by Peter Paul Rubens.

(*Above, right*) 2. Maximilian's grandson, Charles V (Holy Roman emperor 1519–56), who possessed an unusual jaw deformity which became characteristic of many members of the Habsburg dynasty. Note the medallion of the Order of the Golden Fleece, the most exclusive chivalric order in Europe.

3. Francis I (king of France 1515–47)
Though spoiled and pampered, Francis
made an excellent impression on everyone—
but most importantly on beautiful women.

(*Above, left*) 4. Charles III of Bourbon (1490–1527) The motto reads: 'Rome, under which the earth and the seas trembled in the olden days,/Of this French hero was the prey and honour;/And without his harsh death, which cut short his happiness/The world belonged to him, since he had the head of the world.'

5. Muhammad II (1432–81), painted by Giovanni Bellini a year before his death.

6. Prince Władysław Vasa (1595–1640), painted by Rubens in September 1624.

7. Constantinople in about 1900, a good approximation of the Ottoman capital at its greatest

8. The Battle of Nordlingen, 1634, which gave the emperor ascendancy over the Protestants in the Thirty Years War. The infante (pictured with the blond hair, and feather) commissioned several pictures by Rubens to commemorate the battle. Rubens painted from a combination of imagination and sketches of the two Habsburgs; apparently spears made for a more dramatic effect than muskets – the picture tells us nothing about the battle itself

9. Rembrandt, *Allegory of the 1648 Peace of Westphalia*. Here we see the chained lion, the army standing in wait, muskets still at the ready, a knight with an upraised spear.

10. Cardinal Richelieu's funeral monument in the Church of the Sorbonne, Paris

11. A famous tapestry showing Louis XIV visiting the Gobelin works

12. Every self-respecting ruler had to have an extensive palace and gardens This sketch, loosely modelled on Versailles, was drawn by Paul Decker for his book, *Der Fürstliche Baumeister*.

13. Rembrandt, 'Portrait d'un cavalier polonaise' (*c.*1665). This painting may be the grand chancellor of Lithuania; scholars have long disagreed about whether this was Rembrandt's work or merely his 'school'.

14. In 1658 Marshal Turenne joined his French force to an English detatchment sent by Cromwell to besiege Dunkirk and prevent a Spanish-Royalist invasion of Commonwealth England. Dunkirk fell a few days later and came into English hands.

15. Jacques Callot (1592–1635), 'The Robbery' from *Misères de la guerre* (Sufferings of War), *c*.1633.

16. Andreas Schlüter, 'Memorial to the Great Elector' on the Langen Brücke in Berlin.

mercenaries and 3,700 militiamen, the city should have fallen quickly, but it did not. Gustavus Adolphus, though angered at the losses in battle and to disease, controlled his emotions sufficiently to offer generous terms of surrender – essentially that Riga would belong to whichever power won the war.

The Swedish army then crossed the Daugava River into Courland, capturing the duchy's capital at Mitau. By winter, however, the Swedes were on the defensive – Mitau was under siege, and the Swedish monarch could not find mercenaries to replace those who were fallen, crippled or ill. Despite great efforts, his recruiters could provide no more than 350 hussars for the badly depleted cavalry, and most new infantrymen were untrained peasants without proper weapons. The king's commissioners 'scoured the mercenary market', with only limited success.[3]

Sigismund's commander had it no better. His unpaid soldiers began to form 'confederations' in the hope of extorting wages from him. Troops freed from the Turkish war failed to appear, and plots to replace the king abounded. Luckily for him, his foe had similar problems. Armies had wills of their own, wills that few employers could consistently bend to the requirements of the moment – leadership required a strong personality, stamina and charisma. These characteristics were all possessed by the Swedish king, but even he could not always find ways to win victories.

When Gustavus Adolphus failed to relieve Mitau, the stronghold surrendered. But the Polish inability to capture Riga made it clear that neither side could expect to achieve victory soon. Meanwhile, the king of Denmark seemed ready to retake lands in southern Sweden that had long been an important part of his kingdom.

The two sides signed a truce in July of 1622, then made a 'sixty-year truce' in 1623. Sigismund resisted this to his utmost, refusing to ratify his general's terms, but at length, as Geoffrey Parker put it, 'common sense, or common weariness, prevailed'.

The Swedish–Polish War of 1624

When Christian IV (1577–1648) of Denmark entered the Thirty Years War in 1625, taking on the emperor's powerful armies, Gustavus Adolphus no longer had to worry about him attacking Sweden. Quickly raising a mercenary army, he sailed for Livonia. He left his Swedish troops at home, confident that his mercenaries could sweep aside the three thousand troops that Sigismund had managed to scrape together as garrisons. He pushed up the Daugava River, then captured Dorpat. In the late summer he crossed into Courland, taking all the fortresses there.

Negotiations were opened, but Sigismund was more interested in reversing his generals' failures than in abandoning his claims to the region. Not that Livonia helped the situation for either side, with epidemics raging across the war-torn regions, and the armies melting away from disease and desertion, although Gustavus Adolphus inspired his men into making a forced march through freezing January weather to surprise and defeat the commonwealth army.

When Gustavus Adolphus looked east, to check the other power interested in Livonia, he could see that Michael Romanov was fully occupied with problems to his south: there was a civil war among the Nogay Tatars, and the arrival of the Kalmyks in 1622 had upset the balance of power along the Volga; the tsar's only means of stopping Tatar raids was to use the Cossack brotherhoods – but they were complicating the process of making peace with the Turks by making independent naval raids across the Black Sea. The difference between defence and offense was always blurred on the steppe; now it really seemed to be all the same thing.

If the Swedish king moved on Prussia (and the valuable mercantile centre of Danzig) no German prince was likely to interfere – they were all fully engaged in the Thirty Years War. The way seemed open for Gustavus Adolphus to expand his empire, if only he could push over the rickety edifice of the Polish–Lithuanian state, which claimed the allegiance of the Hohenzollern duke of Brandenburg–Prussia. With more mercenaries he just might accomplish this – but where to get them? Most mercenaries were already collecting good wages in Germany and Russia.

He sent recruiters to Scotland and England, the only two important lands currently at peace. These kingdoms had provided many mercenaries for past wars, men who brought their wealth and exotic clothes and customs home with them to make strong impressions on family and friends; these were natural recruiters now, able to tell how many others had grown comfortable in Poland and Russia, where opportunities were good for men willing to grasp at them. Such men, hardened in the European wars, also helped make the later Civil War in England and Scotland so shockingly brutal.

The Thirty Years War

This great conflict came to involve directly or indirectly all western and central Europe: Germany, France, Spain, Holland, Denmark, Sweden and later Poland all directly, and then indirectly England, Scotland and Ireland. It was a complex war, on one hand being a struggle between Catholics and Protestants, on another it was a war between dynasties (Bourbon versus Habsburg). A further perspective was that it was a conflict of states (France versus Spain and the Holy Roman Empire), as well as an opportunity for newly important states (Sweden, Russia, the Tatar khanates) to exploit the chaos. Minor political leaders, both secular and clerical, sought to acquire lands and reputation (or simply retain what they had). There were zealots, opportunists and cowards – with occasionally all these characteristics being combined into one person. Most mercenary soldiers and officers, whatever the allegiance of the army, were Germans – because all armies replaced losses by recruiting locally, and most of the fighting was in Germany.

The conflict had begun in 1618 when the Bohemians refused to acknowledge Ferdinand of Habsburg (1578–1637), the heir of the dying emperor, as their future king. All too aware of Ferdinand's record of bigotry, they believed that he would end their tradition of religious tolerance that predated the Reformation by a century, and that he would curtail their political rights. To demonstrate the depth of their feelings, protesting nobles in Prague threw two of Ferdinand's representatives and their secretary from the windows of the royal palace into the moat – surprisingly, the victims hobbled hurriedly away and escaped, which was a foretaste of the many unexpected events of the coming decades.

This Defenestration of Prague might have been forgiven, but when the Bohemian nobles and clergy met to elect their monarch, they voted for Frederick (1596–1632), elector of the neighbouring Palatinate. After that, war was inevitable. The issue was more than religious, though Frederick was a Calvinist who had been ruthlessly confiscating Catholic Church lands – without Bohemia's vote, Ferdinand II would not be elected Holy Roman emperor, and without Bohemia's resources, he would be an impoverished ruler indeed. The Palatinate, part of which lay along the Rhine, also threatened the Habsburg supply route from Italy to the Netherlands.[4]

Peter Wilson has argued in *The Thirty Years War, Europe's Tragedy* that it is inaccurate to emphasise religious differences and forget how the checks and balances of the Holy Roman Empire made everybody reluctant to make basic changes. Certainly each prince had personal ambitions that went beyond religious beliefs and many, even Catholics, feared the growth of this Habsburg emperor's power. However, distance and lack of communication made it difficult for conspirators to co-ordinate their activities – the peasants of Upper Austria rose in rebellion, hoping that the Bohemian revolt would spare them the necessity of fighting, but that miscalculation left them facing a victorious Habsburg army that dealt with them ruthlessly; second-rank German and Italian rulers were unwilling to similarly hazard their fate on long odds. The most significant aid to the Protestant cause came from the duke of Savoy, Charles Emmanuel (1562–1630); knowing that in any case Ferdinand would seize his Alpine lands, he sent two thousand men to support Frederick, together with a German soldier of fortune, Ernst von Mansfeld (1580–1626), the illegitimate son of the governor of Habsburg Luxembourg. Then he allied himself with Cardinal Richelieu, who was fighting Protestant Huguenots in France.

Mansfeld had fought in the imperial army against the Turks until a minor Habsburg, the Archduke Leopold (1586–1632), had somehow offended him – an entirely plausible scenario. Leopold was a bishop though not a priest, he was married to a de'Medici, he was regent of the Austrian lands and he was a skilled leader of mercenary troops, but tact was never listed among his virtues. Mansfeld's army was typical for the era, hurriedly raised, indifferently equipped, and more interested in the pay than reasons for fighting. It was the money that was his undoing – he collected a fortune in his camp, but did not distribute it to his soldiers. Some of his Protestant troops, too long without pay, actually went over to the larger Catholic army commanded by Johan Tserclaes, the count of Tilly (1559–1632), on the eve of the climactic battle outside Prague in 1620. More importantly, Mansfeld found himself also facing the army of Protestant Saxony, while the princes of the Protestant union who had originally voiced support now declared neutrality and kept their armies at home to ward off attack from the Spanish Netherlands.

Tilly was a highly regarded veteran of wars against the Dutch and the Turks; commander of the army of the Catholic League, he trained his men in *tercio* formations – a deep phalanx of pikemen and musketeers. Such was the strength of his personality that historians often forget that there was a second army in his coalition, raised directly by Ferdinand. The battle of White Mountain (Bílá Hora, roughly where Prague airport is located nowadays) was such an overwhelming Catholic triumph that Ferdinand II came to believe that he could crush Protestantism everywhere. As a warning to others, he executed the Protestant leaders he could catch and confiscated the properties of those who fled. Frederick became an exile – the 'Winter King' – but lacked the military talent necessary to recover even the Palatinate, and his zealous Calvinism irritated his Lutheran hosts. Honour, mistrust and a belief in his destiny sustained him even after he became an irrelevant exile in Holland.[5]

The emperor had won the initial point of dispute – possession of Bohemia – and peace might have come about quickly if he had not attempted to re-establish the authority of empire and Church as Charles V had envisioned them. Ferdinand had been taught the theory and practice of imperial power even though his predecessors had found that day-to-day politics frustrated even their least ambitious efforts. Ferdinand must have made his tutors proud in his insistence on exercising an authority that no living person, nor any person's grandfather's grandfather could remember. He hoped to roll back the Reformation, maybe even stamp out the Protestant heresy forever.[6] The pope could be tamed, maybe even the French, whose internal conflicts suggested that young King Louis XIII would present no difficulties.

This was mostly a collection of pipe-dreams, the euphoria enhanced by the tobacco being newly imported from the Americas, propaganda and paranoia. In reality, each imperial success was a close-run thing, and several times it appeared that the emperor might lose even his core domains to foreign invaders or native rebels. That explains his bloody reprisals, his expulsion of Protestants, and his inability to think beyond the mental constraints of his time.

Ferdinand's main problem was that his army, like Frederick's, was not under his direct control. Tilly was more or less an independent entrepreneur, hired for the moment by the duke of Bavaria, a rival for German leadership. Ferdinand soon corrected this by building up a new army under Albrecht von Wallenstein (1583–1634), a Bohemian officer experienced in war. This gave the Catholic forces a great numerical advantage – if they could keep the loyalty of their mercenaries.

Soldiers professed whatever religion their paymasters represented, willingly changing sides, happily looting whatever communities their commanders directed them to, or whenever hunger and lack of pay drove them to ignore orders to show restraint. Deficit financing was soon out of control. Protestant and Catholic leaders alike found that they could not dismiss their armies, partly out of fear of their enemies, but also because they could not pay off their troops.

Mansfeld continued to fight, as did Frederick and other Protestants, and he won his share of battles – more than one would expect, given his lack of money. However, Germany was large and the imperial armies were too small to occupy all of it; moreover, the desire for peace and stability was so strong – almost overcoming distrust of imperial ambitions – that ongoing negotiations seemed likely to bring the war to an end soon. Alas (so says the Protestant narrative), the emperor was pushed by zealous and ambitious advisers not to miss his historic opportunity to restore imperial authority and religious uniformity.

Mansfeld ended up penniless in Holland, where he reconstituted his army and re-entered the war in 1625 as an ally of the king of Denmark. Three times he went to England to ask for money, and once to Paris. What he obtained was insufficient, since each monarch was reluctant to raise taxes. Mansfeld then went to Hungary to lead the rebel army there, but had to flee after his employers made peace with Ferdinand; discouraged and becoming ill on the Adriatic coast, he subsequently died, just before Sweden entered the war. His courage and daring made the Mansfeld Thaler, with its image of Saint George, the indispensible lucky charm for cavalrymen.

Combat 1618–1648

From the very beginning of the war it was apparent that there was a great difference between old-fashioned units hurriedly raised and haphazardly trained and those which were handled more professionally. Recruits needed to develop self-confidence before being exposed to the sound and smell of gunpowder, and to learn not to panic when the enemy ranks became obscured by smoke. Experienced soldiers looked more favourably on employers with well-filled treasuries – even the usually dependable Scots in the Danish and Swedish armies, who were considered deeply committed to the Protestant cause, were unwilling to fight for free. Although Ferdinand II had the deepest pockets of any German, his lands were far less rich than France. Still, he had access to the wealth of the Spanish Netherlands, the heart of contemporary industry and commerce; and he could obtain loans from German bankers and from his Spanish relatives. Nevertheless, he too found it hard to maintain his armies in the field.

After a decade of fighting, many observers began to think that a compromise settlement was preferable to peace imposed by the sword. The emperor alternated proposals for peace and threats, but his concessions and promises could not win over the Protestants, and even Catholic princes mistrusted his intentions – too often it seemed that he was determined to reorder the Holy Roman Empire completely. His greatest captain, Wallenstein, was a gifted organiser, whose armies soon operated on widely scattered fronts, and while it was impossible to provide enough food and fodder to bring them together on one battlefield, he demonstrated how co-ordinated operations could be managed. Logistical realities, together with the need to exercise effective command and control, limited the armies of this era to about thirty thousand men.[7]

Generals such as Wallenstein were needed because the time had not yet come when armies were firmly under state control. Regiments continued to be partly private and often dissolved when the commander was slain, removed or retired.[8] Colonels and generals who were poor businessmen did not last long. Redlich estimated that the imperial army contained over six hundred such officers, while the Swedish army contained a third to a half that number, other armies far fewer. Command was dominated by nobles who often operated their regiments and armies as family enterprises. Their concern for higher salaries and better pension benefits reflected the greater risks of war in this era. Commanders' ties to the aristocracy involved allegiances that limited what rulers could order them to do, and although armies and commanders did not change sides, everyone was aware that this was possible. Individual units did; and Wallenstein was murdered out of fear that he would do exactly that. Rulers had to reward success lavishly – often with confiscated lands – and pay ransoms in case of defeat, and then re-equip the entire army.

As minor states were priced out of contention, the Thirty Years War was fought to an ever greater extent by Austria, France, Spain, Holland and (thanks to French money) Denmark and Sweden. The monarchs were only occasionally commanders of the armies, though; they were more valuable at the court, supervising the bureaucracy through their councils and assuring the populace that there was little chance of a stray bullet throwing politics into disarray. Military professionals were more competent in the field, in any case, and often more competent at diplomacy. All the colonels, generals and field marshals could not do was to serve as objects of feudal reverence, and as flesh for the marriage market, which was an important aspect of diplomacy at the highest level.

Field commanders were not long-lived. Few survived the war, and few became rich. They became professional soldiers because of family tradition, and they were proud of their heritage; they enjoyed flaunting their clothing and jewels, their horses and carriages, their silverware and servants before their peers. More importantly, it being impossible to escape the destruction of towns and estates, they preferred to be the hammer rather than the anvil. Younger sons who rose in status far beyond their expectations found the power and prestige addictive; they were eager for knighthoods, titles, estates and noble wives. Though few made fortunes, many were drawn by the love of adventure. Some were motivated by religious beliefs, patriotism and hatred of their opponents. And lastly, what else could they do? There was a practical limit to the number of courtiers, abbots and bishops.[9]

Many soldiers were probably, in the beginning at least, decent men driven into military service by desperation. The recruit gave his bonus to his family, rented his land or trade to a neighbour for a pittance, then shouldered a musket and marched off to lifetime employment – however long that was. As one French contemporary quoted by Redlich wrote, a mercenary was one *'qui doit mourir pour avoir de vivre'* (who must die to have something to live on). The Germany described by the novelist Grimmelshausen allowed no refuge for the pious pacifist, the aged or the weak;[10] on the other hand, army life was attractive to criminals, runaways, orphans and half-wits. A few soldiers of fortune could rise in status, especially those lucky enough to have accumulated enough loot to bribe a commander into giving them a promotion; otherwise, only experienced soldiers too aged to serve effectively in the ranks became officers. In the meantime, there would be episodes of gluttony and drunkenness, gambling and fornication. Most importantly, the army became the recruit's new family; otherwise, the heat and cold, the flies and fleas, the lack of food and overabundance of illnesses could not have been endured. Fear of punishment had its role, too, and discipline kept the troops in line as long as the commander could pay them – without money to buy food, they would collect it from peasants and townsfolk, and once that began, officers lost all control.

It was at such moments that soldiers deserted. Then, or when they realised that the officers would flog and hang enough of their number to cow the rest. The cleverest took off, the dumbest ended on a gallows. Defeats were similarly followed by swarms of soldiers seeking safety, food and money. Many men ended up in new regiments – new families, as it were, perhaps to change employers again when falling out during a march because of illness or looking for food. Capture provided another such opportunity – serving among former enemies was better than being hanged or starving in prison, and it lightened the task of the recruiting sergeant.[11]

The longer the war lasted, the less money there was for wages, so soldiers ended up fighting for a combination of food and promises, with hope of loot and booty offsetting the irregular pay. They were undoubtedly aware that whatever coins came their way had less silver content than those minted earlier – then, as now, inflation was the way that governments paid off their debts. Understanding that if they died, their wages would never be paid, some must have refrained from fleeing the chaos of battle because while victory promised loot, defeat meant losing everything; if scattered in flight, they could count on nothing from the peasantry except vengeance for other soldiers' misdeeds.

The life of a soldier may have been short, but it had its attractions – vice was more exciting than virtue. Most observers were appalled at the behaviour of soldiers whose drunkenness, violence and undisciplined habits turned Christian morality on its head, but some observers – male and female alike – were attracted by the hope of escaping humdrum existences. To make matters worse, the only way to stop the excesses of hostile troops was to have an army of one's own, an army that soon acquired the vices of those it opposed.

As for the women, once kidnapped by soldiers, there was no going home; the best they could hope for, perhaps even better than marrying a soldier, was to become a sutler, supplying men with the necessities of life and even a few luxuries. After a few years, the same was true for the men – their only skill was war, and perhaps theft and brawling, and once injured or laid low by illness or depression, they could not even practise the veteran's traditional retirement trade as a barkeeper. To return home meant a quick march to the poorhouse or jail. All these minor, personal tragedies were dwarfed by the immensity of the conflicts playing out across the rolling landscape of Germany and the plains of Flanders.

Sweden's Decision: Germany or Poland

Gustavus Adolphus faced a significant choice in 1630 – to continue his successful war against Poland–Lithuania or enter the conflict in Germany. His inclination had been to concentrate on making the Baltic Sea into a Swedish lake, but now it appeared that imperial armies would undo that programme. With Wallenstein building a fleet, the king had to choose between abandoning his Baltic empire and fighting for it. As a firm Protestant and a Swedish patriot determined to protect his nation's commercial interests, not to mention thwarting Danish and Polish designs to 'recover' lost territories, he felt that he had to strike down the Habsburg forces before they became entrenched. Only he had an army capable of challenging the victorious imperial hosts; and only by taking the offensive could he defend the conquests he had already made. His chancellor, Oxenstierna, who was well aware that the king had almost no money to pay his men, thought the policy unwise, but neither he nor the other counsellors could deter him.

Swedish observers had long seen control of the Baltic as essential for the prosperity and safety of the kingdom. The traditional foe was Denmark – as it remained – but Russia and Poland–Lithuania were old enemies, too. In addition, Sigismund had a better claim on the Swedish throne than did Gustavus Adolphus. The moment seemed right – the emperor had dismissed Wallenstein for being too ambitious and had sent Tilly into Italy; there was no commander of similar talent present in the north of Germany.

It was for these reasons that the Swedish king entered the Thirty Years War in 1630.[12] The issue between Sweden and Poland had always been control of Pomerania, Prussia, Livonia and Courland. For both monarchs it had been a matter of economic necessity, historical precedents and pride. But if Gustavus Adolphus had to worry about an imperial navy operating on the Baltic, Ladislas IV, who became Polish king in 1632, had to contend with Russian designs on his Lithuanian provinces – the outbreak of war that year over possession of Smolensk made it impossible for him to take advantage of the Swedish involvement in Germany, and, simultaneously, the sultan had declared war on Poland. Awkwardly, the Habsburg emperor was not eager for his Polish brother-in-law to become too strong, lest he challenge him for possession of Silesia, and he wanted to use his resources in Germany; on the other hand, it was highly desirable to have Poland strong enough to help him expand Catholicism.

Gustavus Adolphus, lacking the money and men for a long war and not being able to count on Poland remaining weak long, had to seek out a decisive battle in Germany as quickly as he could.[13] Adding to his haste was awareness that even Catholic rulers were unhappy with the emperor's recent efforts to gather more lands and authority into his hands, but there were limits as to how long they dared delay before providing more assistance to the imperial armies; Protestant rulers were almost as cautious. National, religious and personal reasons required Gustavus Adolphus to be aggressive.

This was not easily accomplished – a barrier of political alliances, strong fortifications and armies stood between him and central Germany. Gustavus Adolphus first occupied Pomerania and then, after 'rough wooing' of the elector of Brandenburg,[14] moved his army to the Elbe River – arriving too late to prevent Tilly's massacre of the citizens of Magdeburg, one of the greatest atrocities of the war.

The Swedish king took revenge for this in two battles, one in Saxony, the other in Bavaria – with Tilly being fatally struck by a cannonball. The emperor, desperate to reconstitute the Catholic armies, reluctantly recalled Wallenstein.

The confrontation of two gifted generals – Wallenstein, the imperial commander, and Gustavus Adolphus, the Protestant champion – still makes for exciting, if sometimes confusing reading. The story can be understood as a bitter combination of heroism, professionalism and tragedy. Both men, either of whom might have changed history forever, died at the height of their power and potential. Their successors were capable men, but were limited by the stalemate on the battlefield, the instructions of distant courts and their armies becoming impossible to control. Once commanders could not pay their men, the soldiers turned to looting; as commanders felt it necessary to have larger and larger armies, their ability to pay the soldiers diminished proportionately.

The military arts evolved more swiftly now. The *tercio*, the almost universal battle formation at the time, relied on musketeers weakening the enemy formation until the deep ranks of pikemen could push forward, then the cavalry would charge through to capture the enemy camp and artillery. Gustavus Adolphus, who lacked the manpower for this tactic, trained his musketeers to stand in lines, their ranks only a few men deep, then advance slowly on the enemy, the first rank firing, then standing still to reload as the next rank moved past them to fire, then the next rank. He reduced the danger from opposing pikemen by using his cavalry to force them into a static formation, then once they had melted away from the devastating hail of musket balls, he sent his horsemen in pursuit. This was not as easy as it sounds.

The contrasting temperaments of the king and his chancellor, Oxenstierna, made for a fruitful combination – the more widely educated but less gifted chancellor and the swift-thinking, swiftly acting king. The king lived lustily, the chancellor lived long.[15] The king's death in battle in 1632 did not end Swedish domination of the battlefield – his army had routed Wallenstein's at the end of a day of bloody combat – but no general could take the risks a monarch would dare.

Oxenstierna did not see that the war involved any basic Swedish interest, but he was willing to continue the military stalemate that set in after the Catholic revival in the mid-1630s. He understood that it was not as easy to get out of a war as it was to get in. One Swedish war aim – to obtain a decree of toleration for Protestants in Catholic lands – had to be abandoned. It was not a demand that even his ally, Catholic France, could support. After all, Cardinal Richelieu, the director of French policy, had crushed the Huguenots at La Rochelle, and he was unwilling to give them hope that they might recover the autonomy they had previously enjoyed.

Richelieu kept France out of the war as long as he could, but when the Habsburg armies gained the upper hand, he knew that Ferdinand would soon make war on France. Afterwards, with the French and Spanish armies engaged in the Low Countries, the war in Germany became stalemated – armies could march through the countryside, destroying farmsteads and villages, but they could not take heavily fortified cities. With nobody willing to give up on the fundamentals of religion and power, mercenaries envisioned their employment lasting forever.

We remember this part of the war, to a certain extent, as a series of anecdotes preserved in local folklore. One from 1631 recorded the desperate situation faced by the citizens of Rothenburg ob der Tauber. The citizens, allied with the Protestants, knew that the Swedish army was not far distant; however, with Tilly's Catholic army at the gates, the councilmen decided to surrender; only afterwards were they told that the councilmen would be killed and the city burned. As the councilmen fell silent, only the mayor's daughter kept her head – she suggested that the guests might like a drink. Surprised, Tilly agreed. When he tasted the local wine in the huge tankard (a bit over three litres), he said that he would spare the city if one of the citizens could drink it all down in one long gulp. The mayor agreed to try. To universal amazement, he succeeded.[16]

The Thirty Years War in the Spanish Netherlands

The era of brilliant achievements in what eventually became Belgium dimmed after the outbreak of the Thirty Years War (1618–48). As noted earlier, the conflict began when the Bohemians came to believe that Ferdinand II, the heir to the dying Habsburg emperor, would be another duke of Alba – that he would revoke promises of religious liberty that predated Luther by decades and impose his narrow version of Catholicism on them. When Tilly's army routed the Bohemian forces in 1620, the emperor confiscated the property of Protestant rebels and began warning both Protestant and Catholic rulers in Germany that this was a new era – the emperor was no longer the figurehead of the past.

Subsequent successes of Habsburg arms against first Denmark, then (less decisively) Sweden, were accomplished more by Wallenstein than Tilly, because he had created a mass army that could operate on several fronts at once and serve as an occupation force for captured cities. He raised huge sums ('contributions') from communities in lieu of being sacked to pay his men, but what he gathered was usually still insufficient to avoid allowing his troops to supply themselves.[17]

After Wallenstein's assassination in 1634 – which he had provoked by ignoring imperial commands and secretly opening peace talks with the Protestants – armies roamed across Germany and Poland, extorting huge sums of money and burning towns and villages that could not pay. When commanders could not control their angry and often starving troops, it mattered little whether the army was Protestant or Catholic; when supplies were short each preyed upon the local population regardless of religious beliefs. The uneasy stalemate drew France and Spain into the war because victory there might well determine who would win the struggle for control of the Low Countries.

Both Spanish and French monarchs had been discreetly involved in the Thirty Years War from the beginning. Louis XIII had been advised that if Ferdinand conquered all of Germany, the imperial forces would join with the Spanish army in the Low Countries and fall on his realm; because that would, inter alia, disturb Louis's hobby of hunting, something had to be done about it; eventually, the French monarch intervened directly, ordering armies to invade neighbouring Habsburg lands – Catalonia, Italy, Germany and, most importantly, the Spanish Netherlands. In theory, his adversary, Philip III (1578–1621), could send reinforcements to the Low Countries – with money and supplies – by sea, but a new generation of English, Dutch and French pirates made this even more uncertain than before. Intrepid Protestant sailors were attacking the Spanish Main everywhere, forcing Philip to divert resources to protecting his possessions in the Caribbean, the Mediterranean and even in Asia. Then there was the weather. The uncertainty of sea communications made the Spanish Road from Italy to the Low Countries more attractive.

One of the French goals in the war was to interrupt this supply route. Thus expansion towards the Rhine was not simply a Bourbon desire for more land, but to achieve a geo-political advantage. In short, the religion the French shared with Spaniards was important, but national interests were vital.

The Spanish equivalents of Richelieu and Mazarin were Francisco Gómez de Sandoval y Rojas (1522–1625), the duke of Lerma, and Gaspar de Guzmán y Pimentel (1587–1645), the count of Olivares. The monarchs they served, Philip III and Philip IV (1605–65), were as incompetent as Louis XIII and as inconsequential as Louis XIV during his childhood, but their state was not as wealthy and populous as France. Their ambitious schemes, when continued by less competent successors, led to bankruptcy and decline. The weakness of their plans was not immediately obvious because the Spanish army had a momentum based on traditions of victory and Roman Catholicism, as well as gold and silver from the New World.

The Spanish army that fought in the Low Countries was originally composed of Spaniards and Italians, but attrition from disease, desertion and combat led to local recruitment for replacements; this added regional rivalries to the already fierce religious divisions. The same process affected the French armies opposing them, except that it was easier for the French commanders to recruit new men at home.

As the Low Countries were filled with powerful fortresses surrounded by low-lying fields that could be easily flooded, there had been few battles in the open field.[18] This began to change after 1640, when Germany was too ravaged to support armies in the field and it became clear that the outcome of the contest in Flanders might be decisive. Armies there were accustomed to sieges, not battles, which might account for the alternate bursts of enthusiasm and panic when the Habsburg and Bourbon armies met in 1643 at Rocroi.

Francisco de Melo (1597–1651) was the Portuguese-born governor of the Spanish Netherlands, a cool and competent professional. The French commander was twenty-two-year-old Louis of Condé, the king's cousin and, therefore, likely to govern France once the fatally ill Louis XIII passed away. The armies were closely matched in number, each about twenty thousand strong, but Condé had the advantage of fighting on the defensive, and of possessing a line of fortresses behind which he could manoeuvre.

De Melo had penetrated into northern France in the hope of forcing Cardinal Mazarin to recall troops from Spain and Italy to save Paris. He was besieging the fortress at Rocroi when news arrived that reinforcements led by Johann von Beck (Jean de Beck, 1588–1648), a veteran of Wallenstein's army, former governor of Prague and now governor of Luxembourg, were not far away. This seems to have made him confident that he could take Rocroi quickly, then move into France.

Condé, understanding that the campaign would be lost if he could not prevent the union of the two armies, ordered his troops to move around the Spanish flank through irregular, woody ground. From the top of a ridge, he could see the Spanish moving out of their fortifications and rearranging their lines to meet him, forming the traditional squares – men with pikes protecting the musketeers – with the cavalry on the flanks. He sent his men forward.

Condé's attack was a failure. The Spanish *tercios* remained intact and their cavalry drove away the French horsemen and captured several cannon. De Melo, however, failed to send his infantry forward to complete the victory. This allowed Condé to reorganise his cavalry, then send it back into the contest under a dashing officer, Jean de Gassion (1609–47), who had learned his skills in the Swedish army. This charge hit the Spanish hard, after which there were charges and counter-charges, until at last de Melo's cavalry fled the field, followed by those infantrymen who had been raised locally, then the Germans and Italians. De Gassion pursued the fugitives, making certain that they could not regroup, while Condé rallied his foot soldiers and brought them in on the flank of the Spanish infantry. The Spaniards faced about – one of the strengths of the *tercio* formation – and continued to fight. Though surrounded, the Castilians refused to yield. At last Condé brought up cannon and proceeded to blow huge gaps in their formations. Still, he could not obtain their surrender, though 7,500 men now lay dead and dying. Admiring their courage, Condé offered to allow them to march away with all their flags and weapons; in contrast, he made prisoner the thousands of soldiers who had scattered across the countryside. French losses were about four thousand. De Gassion became a French marshal at age thirty-four. This was to become the traditional award for valour and victory.

Rocroi was the turning point in the war, ending a century of Spanish domination of the battlefields of Europe. This was not immediately apparent, however, because France itself was on the verge of dissolution – the first Fronde was in the making.

The Impact of the Thirty Years War on Germany

The war removed the fiction that Germany was a unified nation. Several German states were now closely associated with neighbouring non-German lands, the emperor was not trusted, the Church was divided, tariff barriers hindered trade, petty lords ground down their peasants, and proposals for imperial reform barely got a hearing. Germany was a geographical expression, a place where princes could scheme at inheriting new lands, bargain for their loyalty, and dream of a return to days when they could hunt safely in their many woods, listen to good musicians and even burn a few witches. It would take Louis XIV's aggression late in the century to revive national feelings, but when those wars ended, so too did the patriotic feelings.

Even so, memory of the destructiveness of the Thirty Years War lingered in Germany for generations.[19] The physical damage was made good sooner, though estimates of human losses run as high as a third of the population in some regions, and property damage can hardly be calculated. In *Swords for Hire* James Miller writes eloquently about the cycle of hungry, cold and poorly clothed soldiers taking what they needed from the peasants, the peasants murdering soldiers whenever they felt safe to do so, and the soldiers taking brutal revenge later (perhaps on completely different communities). Soldiers storming towns massacred those who had not surrendered promptly, causing their enemies, when the roles were reversed, to slaughter them even as they tried to yield.

What did the many female camp followers think about the robbery and rapes? Did female solidarity come into play? Probably not. The camp followers, whether prostitutes, whores (cohabiting for the duration of a campaign) or wives, seem to have been more voracious plunderers than the men; as for rape, they seem to have looked upon that as one of the fortunes of war, perhaps even witnessed it with some satisfaction – providing them a sense of revenge for similar humiliations inflicted by the enemy.[20]

It was a situation where everyone was to some extent a victim and nobody saw how to end it, short of capitulation, which was unthinkable – the enemy was obviously weaker, too, so enduring a little longer might well bring victory. There was no lack of intelligent commanders or even competent diplomats, only a lack of manoeuvring room and a narrow range of options. There was little difference between them. The story was not altogether black, at least not everywhere – some peasants gave information and acted as guides, some communities hosted dances, and some local girls married soldiers. Some peasants came to sympathise with the soldiers' plight – by 1648 both Protestant and Catholic armies were in such poor shape that no one had sufficient food and clothing, no one could replace equipment and animals, or even buy ammunition; there was barely enough to keep the armies together and to hope for better days.

After 1648 most of the soldiers took their back wages and went home. Recruiters managed to lure individuals into Venetian, Polish, French and Spanish service, but none was able to persuade an entire regiment to volunteer for a new war.

Protestants had managed to keep their armies in the field during the Thirty Years War largely thanks to subsidies from Cardinal Richelieu, the de facto ruler of France.[21] Cardinal Mazarin continued this policy, which required gathering more authority into his own hands and collecting ever more taxes. This provoked the Fronde. While a popular slogan of the rebels was '*Vive le roi sans gabelle*' (Long live the king who does not collect taxes), the civil war involved constitutional issues and prominent personalities as well.

Once Louis XIV took personal control of the government, and peace had restored prosperity and population growth, he revived his late ministers' plans for expansion. After that, nothing could be done by Germans or Italians regarding the Turks without a look backwards to see if Louis had taken his knife and fork out, ready to carve a few provinces off the Holy Roman Empire for himself.[22]

The Turks had observed the European wars with alternate alarm and amusement, but they did not take advantage of the Christians' willingness to slaughter one another. Except for coming to the aid of the Tatars, they did not repeat the great offensives of the previous century. The siege of Malta in 1565, the capture of Cyprus in 1571 and the subsequent battle of Lepanto were all gigantic events involving huge number of men and dreadful slaughter. It had been widely expected that the Turks would repeat those efforts while the Christians were at one another's throats. Why this did not happen requires some explanation.

Turkish Wars

In *The Rise of the West* William McNeill states that by every standard except comparison to Europe (the only one, in hindsight, that really mattered) this was a great period for Islamic civilisation. Still, even though Islamic law and culture flourished, those achievements were essentially backward looking – traditions were praised, new ideas were discouraged. Sunni Orthodoxy, personified in the Ottoman state, emerged triumphant from its long war with the Shiites, but the Persian war had been such a fundamental challenge and the outcome had been so long in doubt that religious conservatives viewed every proposed experiment with suspicion. This was especially true of military reforms.

There had been a Turkish 'military crisis' between 1571 and 1580. The army, having grown in size and been deployed on ever more distant frontiers, could no longer support itself from the countryside. Buying supplies and storing them was expensive, and the new emphasis on firearms meant large financial outlays for purchases and, occasionally, desperate expedients such as collecting weapons from the battlefield – which first required a victory, then some means of dealing with the wide variety of calibres acquired. Raising more musketeer units required other new bodies of troops to keep the janissaries from overthrowing the sultan; heavy taxes to pay these troops provoked rebellions. Reform was needed, but reform seemed impossible.[23]

The very size of the empire worked against making fundamental changes. In *Europe's Steppe Frontier* William McNeill described the rhythm of military campaigns: since no army could march before grass had grown high enough to feed the horses and it had to be home before winter, the time required to march from Adrianople (Edirne) to the Austrian border, dragging siege cannon, left too few campaigning days to mount a successful siege. If the Ottomans had possessed a forward base where supplies and cannon could be stored, these problems would have been less significant, but the borderlands lacked the population to support a closer base, and the sultan's council of state worried about the governor of such a fortress becoming a rival to the sultan or his grand vizier. The problems of transportation were the same that Christians faced later, the only differences being that spring came somewhat later in the north and winter slightly earlier, and the Austrians could sail down the Danube relatively swiftly.

As the Ottoman military lost influence, civilian corruption had less to fear. The sale of offices allowed for the promotion of incompetent administrators, and sultans reared in seclusion were unlikely to be intelligent rulers. In spite of every effort to curb the authority of regional governors, the need to make timely decisions required the sultan to give them more authority and even independent military commands; decentralisation made it difficult for sultans to give directions to officials in distant provinces, or to put down rebellions.

As a result of these accumulated problems, the Ottoman Empire failed to achieve victory in its long war with Austria (1593–1606). Instead, Austrian armies penetrated briefly into Hungary and the Balkans, and Transylvania obtained what amounted to self-government. Previous sultans had not seen any necessity for fortifying strong points (they had never imagined being on the defensive) and would have been hard pressed to regain the pre-war frontiers if there had been any Christian unity.[24] These years were, in the words of William McNeill in *Europe's Steppe Frontier*, the 'Ottoman Time of Troubles'. The borderlands became so desolated that raids were no longer profitable, and with the 'locus of predation' shifting to the taxpayers – or, through debasement of the currency, to all subjects – there was a financial crisis. Every effort to cut the budget produced riots.

Worse came after the Persians defeated the Ottoman army in 1624. This had an impact on Christian Europe in that Protestants who had counted on Turkish pressure to limit the emperor's ability to strike at them now found themselves facing all of Ferdinand's mercenary armies. The emperor demanded total capitulation before he would even guarantee Protestant lives and property. Honour did not come into the question – his enemies were expected to forfeit that.

The imperial programme was, as Geoffrey Parker said in *The Thirty Years War*, 'pure folly', but belief in religious uniformity was central to the mentality of the times. It was, as Ferdinand's contemporary, James I, said, 'No bishop, no king'.

India

After Shah Ismail had been defeated by Selim I in 1512, he was unable to dominate the nearby regions of Central Asia as the Persian empire had done in the past.[25] The vacuum was filled by Babur (1483–1530), a descendant of

Timur (Tamburlane), who subsequently recognised opportunity in Indian civil wars. In 1526 he led an army of Turks and other Central Asian peoples there across the mountains from Afghanistan, then, using a combination of wagons, firearms and archers on horseback, he crushed the Hindu army near Delhi and made himself master of northern India. This was the beginning of the Mughal Empire, a magnificent amalgam of Islamic and Hindu thought and art best known for the achievements under Akbar the Great (1542–1605), a tolerant ruler who brought his varied subjects to appreciate the greatness of Islamic (that is, largely Persian) culture. Akbar's military power, however, rested on Hindu vassal princes who governed their territories with minimal oversight from the centre.[26]

Simultaneous with Babur's conquest of Delhi, a new religion arose in the Punjab – the Sikhs, whose monotheism reflected aspects of both Islam and Hinduism. The Sikhs might have remained another marginal Indian cult except that in the seventeenth century they reacted to Muslim fanaticism by creating their own large and admirably tolerant state. Another force, that of Hindu rulers in the hilly plateau of the south, the Deccan, copied Mughal light-cavalry tactics, a strategy that became more effective after the Muslims turned to reliance on heavy cavalry.[27] The sultans of the south preferred light cavalry because of the hilly nature of their country, but also because they could import horses by sea more easily than the Mughals could acquire them from hostile rulers to their north and west; lastly, they did not encumber their armies with hordes of servants, wives and courtiers as did the regal sultans who pretended to rule all India. Wealth from trade enabled these Hindu rulers to attract Turkish mercenaries into their service. Not surprisingly, they saw the Portuguese as welcome allies in their struggle against Islamic foes who had dominated what the newcomers came to call the 'Indian Ocean'.

The Rise of the West

The gunpowder revolution was an important step upwards in the rise of the West to world leadership. It was closely connected with the increasing mastery of production that culminated in the Industrial Revolution.[28] Making a musket was not an easy task, but a rifle was essentially beyond the existing technology, and cannon production was possible only for a handful of foundries. Nor was it easy to adopt even small practical innovations. As William McNeill reminds us in *The Pursuit of Power*, once any weapon had been widely adopted, economies of scale worked against changing it; such was the cost of re-equipping an entire army that rulers hesitated to adopt even obvious improvements. In contrast, discipline and drill could be modified relatively cheaply. Therefore, improvements came less in the weapons themselves than in the ways they were employed. As for non-Western states, some increasingly lacked the ability to make firearms themselves, most despised infantry, and their leaders reacted sharply against any suggestion that they had fallen behind their once-despised Western rivals.

Geoffrey Parker's thesis in *The Military Revolution* is, first of all, that the change did not come about all at once. There was first the new artillery, then a new concept in fortification (the *trace italienne* described in Chapter Three), followed by a vast increase in the size of armies; these required states to develop systems of supply. For some it meant creating a proper navy that could outflank fortifications and attack the enemies' commercial lifelines. More important than technology, one might argue, were leadership skills that traditional societies were reluctant to share even with foreign peers, much less with talented members of the lower classes. When commanders could not be sure that orders would be obeyed, when there were too few intermediate ranks between the ruler and the troops, the best that armies could do was line up opposite one another and fight – or, all too often, figure out which one would run away first.

It is wrong to think that Western superiority rested on technology alone, but that mistake had been made by rulers and generals again and again. Superiority came from the ways people were trained and the responsibilities they were given.[29] Western societies were far from free of class prejudice, but though everyone was supposed to know their place, many were coming to realise that they would have chances of rising above it.

Perhaps nothing shows this better than the Western ability to employ sea power. The Chinese, Indians and Arabs all had long maritime traditions: they all built ships as large as those of Western states, all had long experience with gunpowder weapons and none lacked courage. Yet they failed to drive away relatively small fleets of Portuguese, Dutch, French and English ships. They were able to sustain the fight for a long time because the oceans were large and the Westerners few, but after their main ports were taken, they lacked the warehouses and repair yards needed for commercial exchange; without experienced seamen and captains, they could not raise a great navy. There remained only the niche occupation of pirate – as a result, both native and Western pirates flourished in succeeding centuries.

No one state could establish a monopoly, or long maintain superiority, in weaponry or tactics. Nor were all generals men of ability and imagination. Men who seemed capable at court, or at drills, or in lower commands, or when younger and slimmer, could always falter at a critical moment. Health, weather, oddities of terrain, the quality of lower-ranking officers, the support of political leaders, the willingness of the public to support a war and to pay for it – all these were important, too, at least in the short term.

Above all, it was important to believe that one's fate lay in one's own hands. To abdicate responsibility to God was to court defeat. This was especially important for the Muslim world, where adopting Western practices was often equated with accepting Christianity – or, worse, adopting a secular outlook that threatened to undermine Islam's claims to be a social system that was inseparable from its religious message.

The European world of 1500 would be changed fundamentally by 1700. Should aliens have visited the leading civilisations of the earth in 1500, it is unlikely that they would have been able to pick the European one that was most likely to dominate the world; even by 1700 it would have been a long shot, but Western guns and discipline were changing the odds.

Spain and France had struggled for supremacy since 1500, but by 1700 it appeared that the French king, Louis XIV, was likely to prevail.

France prevailed in the centuries-long struggle, not by military might alone, but through marriage contracts and intimidation. When Louis XIV's grandson became king of Spain in 1700, threatening thereby to upset the balance of power, the War of the Spanish Succession quickly followed. That led to the total eclipse of Spanish pretensions to great power status, then to the surprising rise of England (soon to be joined with Scotland as the United Kingdom) as France's principal rival.

In 1700 it was not yet clear that France could be frustrated in its drive for hegemony in western and central Europe. When it was subsequently realised, it must have come as a surprise to those who had learned French and adopted French culture, assuming that France represented the future of European civilisation.

At the other end of Europe was another surprise. Poland–Lithuania, which by the late 1600s was the cultural and intellectual leader of Eastern Europe, had been in as much trouble, half a century before, as contemporary France.

Poland Moving Towards the Deluge

The Polish–Lithuanian Commonwealth had exhibited signs of decreasing vitality even before the death of Sigismund III in 1632. The combination of Russian and Tatar attacks had made it possible for the Swedish king, Gustavus Adolphus, to march into Germany without worrying about an attack on his Livonian conquests. The drift towards paralysis ended by 1650, although not as patriots would have wished – the great state was subsequently battered by every force coming across the Baltic Sea, from the steppe and from the west. The failure to rebound came as a surprise: earlier times when the great Polish–Lithuanian Commonwealth had appeared to be ill, it had revived. Supine again, it was now more alert to dangers, but was unable to rise to meet them. Many Poles chose to think that their national troubles were passing annoyances that God would soon decide to remove. Complaints by their Orthodox subjects about over-zealous Catholic policies were dismissed by their Jesuit advisers as what anyone would expect of backward and ignorant peoples. God would take care of them, too.

In this world of Sarmatism – a belief that Polish knights and aristocrats were descended from noble Iranian horsemen, not Slavic ploughmen – influential men argued that national salvation lay in returning to the simpler manners of an era they remembered inaccurately as the age of 'Golden Freedom'. Their thinking was reinforced by looking at their impressive architecture, literature, chivalry and good manners; their superiority was confirmed in sartorial excess, their exotic costume being widely copied by the nobility of neighbouring states. However, there were ominous political implications to a class system based on a belief that nobles were a separate race and that the Polish constitution was based on Greek and Roman models. The nobles not only claimed a right to oversee royal administration and determine national policy, but they believed they had a right to rebel whenever they felt a king exceeded the very limited authority they conceded to him. In a normal parliamentary system, where a majority can decide matters, such recalcitrance would be only an annoyance. But in this state, where a small minority or even a single individual had the ability to challenge royal authority, it was very nearly fatal.

Poland was suffocating from 'an excess of liberty', a malaise that can be traced to the *Nihil novi* (nothing new) legislation of 1505. While foreign rulers had been surprised that the patient kept recovering just as he seemed to be gasping his last breath, they may have considered it necessary to keep the invalid alive in order to keep themselves geographically separated and, therefore, less likely to go to war; if the patient occasionally rose from his sickbed to accomplish great deeds, that merely disguised the depth of his illnesses. At such moments the neighbours would begin to quarrel again as to how to divide up the inheritance.

The fundamental problem was that the complicated system for electing kings and approving laws made it easy for foreigners to interfere in the Polish–Lithuanian Commonwealth's affairs. It was not the case that all nobles were in the pay of outsiders, but there were always some whose interests coincided with foreign powers or who thought that an outside alliance was preferable to giving in to royal autocracy or to rivals for offices and authority. As a result, there were reasons to mistrust every foreign offer of aid. In 1626, for example, when Wallenstein gave Sigismund assistance to keep Gustavus Adolphus busy, that should have led to a Polish–Austrian alliance. However, many Poles were suspicious that this would benefit the Germans more than themselves. Even later, when the war against Sweden and Russia was being lost, Poles still refused to call on the Habsburgs for help, no matter how useful this might have been. The only respite came when Gustavus Adolphus turned to face Wallenstein in Germany, removing Swedish troops from the commonwealth's territory. Since Russia had not sufficiently recovered from its own Time of Troubles to interfere with Sigismund's efforts to pacify the eastern frontier, the future looked promising.

Ladislas IV became king in 1632, the very year in which Gustavus Adolphus fell in battle in Germany; with that the Swedish threat had receded even farther. On the eastern frontiers Ladislas concluded the war with Russia victoriously, abandoning the empty claim to be tsar for the rich lands around Smolensk. The remaining years of his reign were remembered fondly by later generations.

This 'Golden Freedom' applied mainly to nobles and clergy, but also perhaps to free peasants who were moving east on the promise of fewer taxes and more land. This migration came at the cost of increased dangers. The Ukrainian steppe was the most promising in every sense; not only were the rewards greater for those who survived Tatar and Cossack raids, but the lords promised even more. Immensely wealthy and powerful Polish and Lithuanian nobles, known as magnates, tried to adjust to this migration, both to attract more farmers to their estates and to keep their present labour force from leaving. Both efforts were difficult to accomplish in a time of war.

To the north, in Livonia, serfdom had expanded in the fifteenth century, as free men and women carried away by Russian and Lithuanian raiders were replaced by prisoners taken from Russia and Lithuania. Then came the terrible Livonian War of 1557–82, which created hundreds of thousands of refugees, followed by war between Sweden and Poland; in those years farmers accepted work under whatever conditions they could get it, which often meant abandoning their free status. Because of this we can say that the development of serfdom was a 'natural process', not a conspiracy of German nobles (at least no more than a well-organised programme to benefit Polish and Lithuanian magnates), but the Livonian nobles took advantage of it – for them it was not merely a matter of increasing their wealth, at least at first, but of survival: no workers, no estates, no income.

This was similar to the problem faced by Lithuanian magnates, the great lords who provided armies to defend the frontiers and the republic's liberty. For them life was a constant struggle – against external enemies, against other families and against jealous relatives. They resisted royal proposals that would take them away for long periods. Who, they asked, would protect their lands and people against small bands of raiders and gangs of common criminals? War always provided opportunities for such people, and if the military elite rode off to foreign conflicts, could those remaining at home ward off foreign attackers, or even constrain robbers and cattle thieves? Their properties became islands of population, with little connection to the rest of the commonwealth. To prevent their farmers from leaving, they bound them to the land.

Polish and Lithuanian nobles (and Russian boyars, too) saw little point to having infantry, which would have been effective only if recruited from free farmers, but foot soldiers also moved too slowly to deal with raiders from the steppe; and no noble was willing to descend from his warhorse to lead such miserable troops as could be raised from serfs – not even the many knights who could not afford a good horse.[30] The magnates tended to vote against taxes for raising troops, knowing that much of the money would go to foreign officers and infantry, not to cavalrymen such as themselves and their followers. Moreover, a centrally directed army might well march off to some distant strategic point, taking them along and therefore leaving their estates undefended.

The king could not rely on the very large class of knights and gentry, which formed as much as 10 per cent of Poland's population. Those men were often too poor to be effective warriors, but they nevertheless clung to their pretensions to be better than peasants and burghers, and they saw that changes in military organisation would make them totally obsolete. They disliked mercenaries because such professionals threatened their tenuous hold on social status, and because the foreigners might well support royal tyranny, eliminating their voice in the government as well. Minor nobles and knights could be counted on to vote against taxes that would strengthen the king, and foreign rulers knew that they could find support among those classes, which would make their political intrigues effective. With the magnates demanding control of the local military forces and the knights unable to pay their own costs during campaigns, the king found it very difficult to raise large armies for his own purposes.

It would have helped if Ladislas IV had been more competent. Alas, he was merely corpulent; his gout was so painful that his screams could be heard throughout the castle. No wonder he preferred to conduct state business from bed and entrusted great lords with the military commands. None of this was unusual for the times – almost everyone ate excessively and drank too much. Hygiene was often minimal and medical care was miserable. To escape the smells, diseases and dangers of the towns, nobles lived in the countryside as much as possible. Public assemblies were large, so only the most important persons – and those with loud voices – could speak. Decisions were often impulsive, reflecting the crowd's enthusiasm; those who lost thus felt justified in taking up arms against the majority.

There were moments when the Polish constitutional crises could have been resolved, but fate intervened. *God's Playground*, the name of Norman Davies's popular book, was not a happy place for the people who lived there. The death of Ladislas IV in 1648 brought an end to the happy days. His brother and successor, Jan Casimir (1609–72), was both mediocre and contradictory. A Jesuit and a cardinal, he married his brother's widow and preferred drunken parties to discussing politics. Some say he was addicted to sex, others that he merely loved his wife so extravagantly that he neglected public duties.[31]

Yet the failure was not due to one man's shortcomings, but to institutional flaws – when the Cossacks demanded social equality with Poles and Lithuanians, and the equality of Orthodoxy with Roman Catholicism, they were rebuffed. Then the Polish–Lithuanian army sent to crush the Cossack uprising fled in disorder without having fired a shot.

The Deluge

The Polish–Lithuanian Commonwealth had ignored the problem presented by a growing national feeling in the eastern borderlands that was intertwined with hostility towards Catholicism. Also, the Cossacks were becoming too numerous either to employ as mercenaries or to control. Peasants and runaway serfs had made their way from Russia to the Cossack communities, then taken an oath renouncing all former allegiances and proclaiming their loyalty to the Orthodox Church; not all became Cossacks, but their labour increased the importance and self-image of Cossack leaders, who began to consider themselves equal to Polish nobles. This was a controversial point, because Polish nobles usually owned some land and possessed proud lineages, and they almost always fought as cavalry – while in theory Cossacks owned nothing individually except their small houses, were of common origin (with manners to match) and as often served as mounted infantry or sailors as they did on horseback. The religious issue, the class issue and the demands for pay were matters that infuriated Poles. The first was offensive to the Catholic Church, the second to the nobility and the last to the treasury officials.

Nation-building usually requires a number of widely shared elements – whether it is language or religion, loyalty to a dynasty or common political interests – but imposed unity inevitably antagonises those who do not share those concerns. The Catholic Church, which thought of itself as a unifying factor, was actually contributing to the dissolution of mutual trust. Counter-Reformation zeal frightened Lutherans and Calvinists, and even moderate Catholics; Orthodox and Uniate subjects and allies called on the tsar to save them from this newly aggressive Western heresy.

The result was the 'Deluge', a Polish nation overwhelmed by foreigners, drowning in misfortunes. To give a preview of the events to follow, not only were the nobles contentious, but Jan Casimir mismanaged every challenge, internal as well as external, turning crises that could have been resolved peacefully into wars that could not be won, or not won at a reasonable cost. The king's close ties to the Jesuits and Austria were seen as signs of personal weakness, unhealthy foreign influence and a conspiracy against the toleration that kept the multinational state together. He was not solely to blame, nor could contemporaries have been faulted for electing him king – his half-brother's reign had been a happy one and the only other candidate had no military experience. Moreover, Ladislas's last great political action – to deal with the Tatar challenge once and for all – had gone badly after a good start. Passing over the Cossack leader, Bogdan Chmielnicki (Khmelnystky, 1595–1657), to command the army in 1648, and not even including Cossacks in the largely Lithuanian army, he had set off a rebellion that no one understood how to end, then he had died, leaving his country leaderless until an election could be held.

Chmielnicki was an exile from Poland–Lithuania whose education and experience had assisted him in rising to leadership – he could speak with Polish representatives as an equal. Although his initial programme seemed to have little point except revenge for slights to his honour (a problem made worse by excessive consumption of alcohol and the superstitions common to the age), he was a brilliant general. However, when the Sejm rejected his appeals for constitutional reform, he understood that his Cossacks lacked the strength to take on Poland–Lithuania alone; consequently, Chmielnicki made an alliance with the Tatars that allowed him to spread destruction far and wide through the commonwealth. After obtaining concessions from Jan Casimir, some of them secret, which amounted to Cossack autonomy, he began to drive Jesuits, Uniates and Polish officials out of the Ukraine, and loosed on the Jews the greatest pogrom until Hitler.

When the magnates ignored royal commands and counterattacked, the Ukraine was soon at the mercy of roving peasant bands and rampaging Polish and Lithuanian forces; the epidemic that began there soon spread into Poland, prostrating even the king. Civil conflicts broke out, and when the 1652 debate on the crisis lasted too long, the Sejm was dissolved by the first 'liberum veto' in Polish history – the first of many that would paralyse future governments.[32]

When Chmielnicki turned to the tsar for help, he earned the admiration of later Russian historians as a nationalist, an Orthodox hero and a champion of the lower classes, although Polish historians, whose kingdom had been shaken to its core, held very different views. When Chmielnicki died, his short-lived state was in total disarray. Some Cossacks submitted reluctantly to the tsar, others maintained their traditional ties with Poland–Lithuania and some sought an alliance with the Tatars.

When the tsar accepted the submission of Chmielnicki's Cossacks in 1654, he knew that it was a clear violation of the existing peace treaty and would lead to war. However, with armies marching all across Poland–Lithuania's eastern frontier, peasants suffering terribly and Jews being massacred by everyone, he could not ignore the crisis. Sweden stayed out of the war until the erratic Queen Christina (1626–89) abandoned the throne in 1654 to Charles X (1622–60); the following year Charles invaded Poland and occupied much of the country almost without resistance; then Transylvanians under Georg Rákóczi I (György, 1591–1648) entered the country, too, followed by Moldavians.

Jan Casimir proposed creating an autonomous Cossack state, or even one having a status something like Lithuania's, but his subjects, after briefly and belatedly agreeing to his proposal, decided that it would be better to crush the rebels by force. The decisive factor may have been warnings by Roman Catholic and Uniate Christians that they would be eradicated by Orthodox fanatics. In any case, this was not the moment for a quiet discussion of constitutional reform. Everything was going wrong – Cossacks terrorised Vilnius, Swedes and Transylvanians plundered Cracow, and Russians were on the advance, capturing Smolensk in 1654. Two years later the bottom was reached – while Jan Casimir was in exile in Habsburg Silesia, the crown could have been seized by Sweden, Russia or Austria, or even Transylvania – but the tsar and king of Sweden, instead of dividing up the occupied lands, began to fight over Livonia. The Tatar khan hurried to punish the Cossacks for having betrayed him, and Poles such as Jan Sobieski (1629–96), who had briefly recognised Charles X as the rightful king of Poland, began to wonder if the Swedish monarch had the resources to absorb all of Poland, or if a Protestant king could be accepted by Catholic Poles – or even if Protestant Swedes could accept Catholic equality. When Denmark attacked Sweden in 1657, the English and Dutch sent fleets into the Baltic to reopen trade; Austrian and Russian armies entered the war, allowing Jan Casimir to raise a new force and join in the assault. Sweden could not cope with so many enemies at once.

The decisive blow was struck by Austrians under the command of Raimondo Montecuccoli (1609–80) and by Frederick William, the elector of Brandenburg and duke of Prussia, who promised to assist the Polish king in return for a declaration that he was henceforth freed of obligations to the crown. Though the splendid professional army of Sweden was driven out of the commonwealth, Jan Casimir's efforts to raise taxes for a permanent army provoked revolts, and the Sejm quarrelled with him over constitutional rights. Not surprisingly, he lost important battles to Charles X.

Nevertheless, within two years, Jan Casimir brought some order out of this chaos, winning two victories over the Russians in 1659–60.[33] Charles X subsequently died; when the peace treaty ended the war with Sweden later that year, Poles looked for someone to blame for the difficulties – and then took out their anger on foreigners, Protestants and Jews. Austrians may have been Catholics, but they were Germans. The Holy Roman emperor, Leopold I, was easy to blame, though he had been a staunch ally of the commonwealth; certainly Leopold did not look like a forceful man – his Habsburg lip was perhaps the most pronounced of anyone in the family and he was careful to avoid putting himself in danger.

This was the moment that Jan Casimir might have turned everything around, but his magnates refused to grant him money for military operations when the tsar was weak; when they later agreed to co-operate, it was too late. Nor could he persuade them to make an accommodation with the Cossacks. In 1668, he gave up the many-sided struggle, resigning his office and retiring in France. He took his art collection with him, a sign that he had no intention of returning to a nation in chaos.

Contemporaries wondered how all this could have happened. Jan Casimir had been a competent general in the war against Russia in 1633 and in Habsburg service in 1635. Of course, there was the episode in 1638, on his way to become viceroy of Portugal, when Cardinal Richelieu detained him as an honoured prisoner in Paris, and the earlier frustration of having the Sejm refuse him permission to become duke of Courland. Then there was his brief experiment with clerical life in 1641, and the woman he may have loved from his stay in Paris marrying his half-brother before becoming a widow and his own wife. Wracked by depression all his life, his mental health deteriorated even further after her death in 1667. Doctors called in to consult about her condition were stunned to find that she had never learned Polish. Their children had died earlier – it was the end of the Vasa dynasty, but few wept.

The most prominent candidates in the election of the next king included Charles of Lorraine, a minor German prince who was related to almost everyone, including Louis XIV (who supported a German candidate from the Palatinate) and the Grand Condé (who saw himself as an excellent choice); all candidates were backed by large sums of money. The foreign candidates, however, could not overcome Polish national pride and the memory of a previous French-born king (Henry III, 1573–4) who had fled the country upon hearing that he had inherited the kingdom of France. The foremost of the Polish candidates was Jan Sobieski, whose French wife assisted him in winning Louis XIV's support; she had been lady-in-waiting to the French-born queen of the last two monarchs, and he had been on the French payroll for some time. However, while the combination of Sobieski's larger-than-life personality and his military victories impressed many of the great lords and clergy, it was the second candidate, Michael Korybut Wiśniowiecki (1640–73), who was elected. He was the richest man in Poland and the last of the old Jagiellonian line.

The election was conducted by the gentry without consulting the magnates – a highly irregular procedure – and marred by Habsburg interference, which was quickly followed by Michael marrying Leopold of Austria's sister. This was disadvantage enough, since thereafter the magnates trusted neither him nor his Habsburg wife, but they also thought him stupid. A recycled traditional witticism went around that the king could speak eight languages, but had nothing interesting to say in any of them. Although the magnates had feared that Michael would be like his father, a forceful and even tyrannical ruler, he proved to be quite the opposite – lethargic and weak, short, overweight and covering his baldness with a wig. Moreover, he had never wanted to be king and therefore never learned how to be one, and he may have been impotent, too. These were major disadvantages in a nation proud of its courtly manners and sexual energy. Furthermore, the French ambassador continued to funnel money to the king's opponents.

Though Turkish inroads continued amid the civil conflicts, the state somehow slowly righted itself. Still, only the Habsburgs mourned Michael's passing away after only four years. His death was sometimes attributed to poison, sometimes to overeating – it did not matter much.

Those who lived through this terrible period had widely divergent views of what had happened and why, and what should have been done. Modern historians reflect these ancient disagreements – Russian, Polish, Ukrainian and Lithuanian nations each having their own historical narratives and mythologies. Since most historians see their own peoples as having been victims of foreign intrigue and invasion, they tend to ignore the role played by mercenaries, but the many largely faceless and nameless mercenaries complicated what was already a very difficult collection of problems. Had the rulers been able to do without them, or to pay them, events might have played out differently.

The impact on national confidence, especially in Poland, was perhaps more important even than the physical damage.[34] Poland–Lithuania survived the Deluge, but emerged weaker. The old constitution had failed to meet the new challenges. The Protestant and Jewish communities had been hard hit; Orthodox gangs had massacred Catholics, Catholics had retaliated, and the currency became seriously devalued. Since mercenaries would not accept coins worth only a third of their face value, many believed that it would be impossible for the next Polish king to defend his nation from invasion and anarchy.[35] However, events once again proved that expert opinion can be wrong.

CHAPTER SEVEN

The Process of Change Accelerates

Searching for a Philosophy of Government

Norman Davies tells of eight sermons of Piotr Skarga (1536–1612), rector of the Jesuit College in Vilnius and Sigismund III's chaplain, which offended many listeners in the Sejm of 1597. His defence of royal authority and the supremacy of the Roman Catholic Church included criticisms of the concept of noble anarchy. Skarga observed that while there are three kinds of 'good' freedom – from sin, from invasion and from a tyrant – the fourth kind, to live without law, was evil.

This was a comment appropriate to any land at any time, but it was easier to repeat it as a Polish proverb than to discuss it in the Sejm. When does liberty become licence, how does one balance freedom with responsibilities? Is absolutism the only answer to anarchy? Is honour more important than patriotism? Religion more valuable than the nation?

In the centuries to come Western philosophers came to very different, though compelling, conclusions to these questions. Hobbes saw no alternative to strong royal government (the 'Leviathan'), Locke emphasised a constitutional balance between crown and parliament (the 'Social Contract'), Rousseau advocated consultation with the people (the 'General Will'), Robespierre called for the overthrow of ancient traditions (the 'Terror') and Burke advocated slow change based on consensus ('Conservatism').

Meanwhile, change was being forced by men and women who paid little heed to philosophers and scholars: rulers who realised, as Mao would in the twentieth century, that power comes from the barrel of a gun. Those who were wise used this power responsibly, winning the support of those nobles, clergymen, burghers and peasants who valued law and order over abstract principles that they could not enjoy in any case. The Time of Troubles in

Russia, the Thirty Years War in Germany, the Fronde in France, the Civil War in England and the Deluge in Poland demonstrated that tyranny comes in various forms, but the worst despotism is not that exercised by a distant autocrat, but by small bands of armed men unrestrained by law or conscience. These bands might be invading foreigners, but they were more often merely outlaws. Either way, communities called out for protection against them. Unfortunately, restoring law and order was possible only for rulers who possessed an effective army that was not identified with local factions – in short, either a truly national army or foreign mercenaries. Until the nation existed, with an army composed of patriots, it was necessary to make mercenaries ever more the core of the royal army, not merely support troops.

Mercenaries in Russia

In 1649 a new law extended serfdom across Russia. Landlords had been forcing increasing numbers of peasants into servitude since the fifteenth century, but it was only recently that they had become truly desperate to prevent their labourers from leaving. Free peasants still existed, but their numbers had shrunk, and continued to shrink under the demands of the tax collectors and military officers desperate to enlist the number of draftees assigned to them. With serfdom becoming more universal, slavery declined rapidly.[1] Serfs made adequate workers, since there was little competition or incentive, but because war is the most competitive of all human activities, they made poor soldiers. It had long been obvious that the tsars had to supplement the boyar cavalry with infantry, but since their nobles refused to command foot soldiers, they had to recruit foreign officers.

'New select infantry regiments' were created in 1642, one of which was commanded by a William Drummond.[2] Unfortunately, the expectation that these elite soldiers would feed themselves meant more agricultural work and trade than drill, so that when they went into combat, some hardly knew how to fire their weapons, much less march well or change formations quickly; fire discipline – discharging their weapons only when ordered – was almost unknown. Consequently, although these units were supposed to be shock troops, it was safer to shelter them behind the wagons of the supply column, relatively safe from cavalry attack. Tsarist armies continued to rely on cavalry, both because so much of Russia was open prairie and because the nobles insisted on it. Responding to this, a number of new regiments created between 1654 and 1667, units that ultimately totalled sixty thousand men, were modelled on Western cavalry – dragoons armed with sabres and hussars using lances. This would be the nucleus of the army that later fought against Poles and Turks – bringing an end to invasions that carried off people, cattle and horses, and creating the conditions for a more orderly life. With peace came a growth in population that permitted the tsars to raise larger armies and to supply them with the food and weapons needed to be effective.

These changes were not immediately apparent outside Russia. Tsarist successes were attributed to Poland being in the process of disintegration – the western and northern regions invaded by Swedes, the eastern lands devastated by Cossacks and Tatars.[3]

The Later Thirty Years War in Germany and Poland

Peter Wilson's recent book was intended to correct the defects of earlier historians' work caused by their seeming to lose interest in the conflict after 1635. He may have succeeded better with historians than lay readers, because these years contained many dreary repetitions of slaughter and cruelty without any central personality sufficiently memorable to drive the narrative forward. There were great captains present in these years, of course, men whose careers deserve more study, but none as interesting as the great captains who preceded them.

Johan Banér (1596–1641) was the first of Gustavus Adolphus's successors. In 1636 he reversed the downturn of Protestant fortunes by a victory at the battle of Wittstock, then eliminated the Brandenburg army and almost crushed Saxony. After retreating from Saxony to Torgau and thence to Pomerania, he returned in 1640 to overrun Bohemia and almost capture the Reichstag delegates in Regensburg (Ratisbon). As it became clear that the war was stalemated, talks preliminary to the general Peace of Westphalia (1648) began; individual rulers signed truces and peace agreements, but Banér died before he could see the process through to the end.

His successor, Lennart Torstensson (1603–51), crushed Saxony again and moved through Bohemia into Moravia.[4] After capturing Olomouc in 1642, he turned south to threaten Vienna. So crippled from gout that he could not mount a horse, he was carried about in a litter, but that did not hinder him from moving his army at a lightning pace and striking with incredible suddenness and power.

Torstensson knocked Denmark out of the war, then struck at the imperial armies that had come up behind him. Pursuing them south, he made an alliance with the Calvinist Hungarian rebel, Georg Rákóczi. This became important in 1649, when Chmielnicki, Rákóczi and the prince of Wallachia and Moldavia joined the war, overwhelming Jan Casimir's outnumbered and underpaid forces. Rákóczi entered Cracow in triumph in 1655, but could not hold the city after the Swedish troops withdrew.

Oxenstierna, the hard-pressed chancellor, sought ways to get out of the war, but he understood that peace could only be obtained on harsh terms. In any case, Swedish taxpayers could support an army only as long as it was out of the kingdom, taking food, money and recruits from occupied lands. Moreover, he had to deal with Queen Christina, one of the most difficult monarchs any royal adviser ever had to work with.

Queen Christina, for all her quirks – becoming a secret Catholic and refusing to conform to society's conception of femininity – was no pacifist. She was aware of her father's contribution to Sweden's military reputation, and of his glorious death in battle, but as the situation changed – especially the problem of dealing with unemployed officers and soldiers – she began advocating first peace (1648), then war (1652).[5]

One of her problems was that copper was a declining export, and while iron production was soon to happen, incomes from its sale were still in the future; consequently, royal incomes were insufficient to cover her expenses. Returning the nation to Roman Catholicism was an option for her, but peace with Poland on those terms would leave Sweden as the junior partner; and it was unlikely that either Protestants or patriots would accept that. In 1654 she separated her personal faith and her political duties by abdicating the throne; she travelled to France, and then to Rome, where she made herself both a nuisance and a symbol of reviving Catholicism.

The turning point of the Polish war, as far as public opinion was later concerned, was a year later at Jasna Góra monastery at Częstochowa. When a small body of Swedish cavalry demanded that the well-fortified monastery surrender, the abbot and his monks – fearing that the Protestants would destroy their miracle-working Black Madonna – first hid the icon and replaced it with a copy, then hired 160 mercenaries and persuaded about eighty men, some nobles with military experience, to volunteer their services. Should the deception be detected, torture might reveal the icon's location, so it was thought best to prevent the monastery from being captured. The Swedes brought in reinforcements and more artillery, but abandoned the operation after a month. Little was thought about the Polish victory at first, but the impossible odds, fighting an unbeatable enemy, eventually made the monastery a centre of pilgrimage both for Catholics and nationalists.

Christina's cousin and successor, Charles X, resolved his military/ political problems by reclaiming royal lands that she had given to her friends and supporters, then borrowing money – eventually acquiring a debt of ten million silver daler, four times the state income. Once the Northern War of 1655–60 began, however, his army could live off Polish peasants, and because he filled the ranks with foreign recruits, there was no manpower shortage in Sweden.[6]

Charles X won several easy victories, then occupied Poland and coerced the elector of Brandenburg, Frederick William, into an alliance.[7] Soon enough, however, Charles faced a national uprising, partly because he insisted on religious toleration for Lutherans, but mainly because Poles wanted to govern themselves, no matter how badly they did it. Even a monarch as hopeless as Jan Casimir seemed better than a foreigner.

When Jan Casimir's new army began moving north in 1656, it drove the Swedish garrisons out of one place after another. In response, Charles called on Frederick William to honour his commitments, then moved up the Vistula River with an army towards Jan Casimir's capital at Warsaw. This was a fateful moment for Frederick William, who had already discovered the means to make his lightly populated state into a major German power – his army was a larger and more disciplined mercenary force, better drilled than any earlier Brandenburg army. Moreover, he was willing to cut a few corners of conventional political morality: this made him reviled, hated, feared and ultimately respected.[8]

At the end of July, Charles encountered the Polish army dug in at a narrow passage between the Vistula River and a marsh-filled forest. Having only eighteen thousand men, half Brandenburgers, against perhaps double that number or more, he was unwilling to make a suicidal head-on attack;

instead of retreating, however, he led the Swedish troops on a flanking march through the forest while the elector captured a small hill – which could have provided the Poles a view of the line of march, had they chosen to station more troops there. When the Polish commanders sent troops to retake the hill, the fight distracted them from the movement of the Swedish army until it came in on their flank.

The Poles valiantly tried to reorder their lines, then launched a desperate cavalry attack that almost broke the opposing formations. When night fell, the battle yet undecided, the two armies slept on their arms and resumed fighting at daybreak. Charles's order for the elector to seize a grove at a critical point in the improvised Polish position was compatible with the conventional Swedish strategy of allowing its allies and foreign mercenaries to suffer the most severe casualties, reserving the elite Swedish troops for a decisive strike. As the elector's German infantry stormed the grove, Frederick William led his cavalry over some sandy rises to come in behind the Polish lines. The Swedes then moved forward on the other flank, routing the shaken Poles.[9]

The next year Frederick William changed sides, to support Jan Casimir, in return for the king releasing him from his vow to be a Polish vassal. He did not succeed immediately in achieving complete independence, but neighbouring rulers no longer despised Brandenburg as an inconsequential power.

More distant rulers paid little attention, of course. Brandenburg–Prussia could be dismissed as a state based literally on sand, a region that nobody particularly wanted. They had a very different opinion of Austria, which was being threatened once again by a Turkish advance out of Hungary.

The Revival of Turkish Power

When Köprülü Mehmed became grand vizier in 1656, western Christendom had not yet recovered from the Thirty Years War, the French–Spanish conflict in the Low Countries and the Deluge. With a vigour belying his eighty-plus years, Köprülü proceeded to execute four thousand troublesome administrators and enemies.[10] Köprülü was the perfect administrator for a sultan such as Mehmed IV, who had become supreme ruler at age seven. The sultan revered Köprülü Mehmed, but he did not heed the grand vizier's 1661 death-bed warning to ignore advice from the harem, to fill the treasury and keep the army busy. If Mehmed IV had been any better educated than his wives and concubines, or had more backbone than his mother, he would have done so. Instead, he spent his time hunting.

Mehmed IV constantly ridiculed and belittled his next grand vizier, Ahmed Köprülü (1635–76); encouraged in this by ambitious rivals and shallow-minded courtiers, while immersing himself in sex and alcohol, he made orderly administration difficult. In response Ahmed Köprülü made intrigue into a fine art and revenue enhancement into a cynical and brutal business, while ignoring the insults; though he was addicted to wine and Polish brandy, this did not interfere with his judgement. He saw Vienna, small though the city was, as a doorway to Austria, Moravia and Poland. He began planning to seize it.

Transylvanian Complications

When the final peace treaty of the Thirty Years War was signed in 1648 the difficult problem of demobilising the armies remained. The mercenaries were not happy being unemployed, and many had claims for months of unpaid wages. There were stages of demobilisation, the most important being in 1650, the last in 1653. It had not been practical to move these armies to new theatres of war, in the Balkans or on the steppe, partly because there was too little agricultural production to support them, partly because the troops preferred either staying where they were or taking their money and going home. Most of what remained of the imperial army, perhaps twenty-five thousand men, were stationed in those western portions of Hungary that were under Habsburg control; Transylvania remained autonomous but under Turkish control, and central Hungary was an Ottoman province.

For Hungary 1648 was also a pivotal year – with the death of Georg Rákóczi I, governor of Transylvania and a zealous Calvinist. Four years earlier, at the instigation of France and Sweden, he had briefly seized control of Royal Hungary (much of which is modern Slovakia), demanding recognition of Protestant religious liberty and the rights of Hungarian and Croatian nobles. His mountainous Transylvanian lair, long known as the Seven Cities (Siebenbürgen), was a tangle of nationalities and religions. Magyars tended to be Calvinists, Germans Lutherans, Romanians Orthodox, but all accepted the leadership of this elected Magyar governor who was an Ottoman vassal. Given that scholars consider Hungarians of this era among the most difficult people in Europe to govern, Rákóczi must have been a man of great talent. His successors were not.

Georg Rákóczi II (1621–60) involved his multinational state in affairs well beyond its resources. He began by defending Protestants in neighbouring Wallachia and Moldavia, then intervened in the war between Sweden and Poland. He infuriated the sultan, brought death and destruction on his people and died in battle. The Turks bore in celebration through the streets of Constantinople the heads of thousands of his warriors.

The sufferings of Transylvanians were nothing, however, compared to the population of Hungary proper. In contrast to traditional Ottoman policies for dealing with Orthodox Christians, whose leadership was left some responsibility and honour – which often led to conversions – the sultan's governors dispossessed the Roman Catholic Magyar lords, taking some lands for the sultan, giving more to warriors. Areas that had once prospered under Ottoman rule went into economic decline. Wherever rebellions alternated with brutal repressions, river valleys became swamps and plains turned into moors; mosquitoes swarmed, while people fled.

Magyars, being inferior in numbers and equipment to Turkish armies, had to meet strength with speed and cunning. Hungarian light cavalry became highly respected, but they could not be counted on to fight in a hopeless situation; nor did they want to be ruled by Austrians – they were as distrustful of the emperor as they were of the sultan.

Croatia, traditionally a part of the Hungarian kingdom, became a Habsburg military frontier, a zone inhabited by warlike clans of Croats and Serbs. They were visited almost annually by Ottoman raiders, some of whom passed farther north into Slovenia and Austria. If not for the frontier fortresses in Croatia and Slovakia, Austria could hardly have been defended – its valleys and fields would have resembled Hungary's.

The Battle of St Gotthard

Turkish preparations for an offensive became obvious in 1662, then the offensive became a reality in 1663: Grand Vizier Ahmed Köprülü advanced on the principal fortress on the Slovakian frontier, Nové Zamky (new castle), undermined its cannon-proof walls by a combination of mining and sapping, and captured it. In response, the Reichstag, that ancient assembly of electors, princes, clerics and representatives of the cities, met in Regensburg and ordered church bells tolled throughout the Holy Roman Empire. In addition to arranging for troops to be sent to Austria, the delegates agreed to remain in session until the emergency passed. As it happened, they dissolved only in 1806. A winter counterattack led by Croatian governor, Nicholas Zriny, destroyed many of the roads and bridges that the grand vizier would need for the next summer's campaign. As a result, when Ahmed Köprülü opened his campaign in May of 1664 with one hundred thousand men, he left behind the siege guns that would be needed to take another great fortress. Nevertheless, the immense size of his army caused garrison after garrison either to flee or to surrender quickly. By 1 August the Ottoman army was within a few miles of the Cistercian monastery at St Gotthard (Szentgotthárd), well on the way to Vienna.

The Christian army of forty thousand took up its position at a ford on the Raab (Rába) River, hoping to prevent the Turks from crossing to more open country, which the Timar cavalry and their Tatar auxiliaries would be able to plunder at will. Small units had come from Brandenburg, Saxony and Bavaria; and 5,400 French and German mercenaries under Comte Jean de Coligny and Archbishop Johann Philipp of Mainz, who insisted on a separate command from the imperial forces led by the hereditary imperial marshal, Leopold William (1626–71) of Baden-Baden.[11] After quarrelling over the overall command, the responsibility was finally given to the Habsburg general, Montecuccoli, who believed that he could defend the ford until the lack of supplies caused the grand vizier to retreat.

For the grand vizier the choice was instantly clear – either break through quickly or retreat. However, that wasn't much of a choice – he did not want to face the sultan, even the pasty Mehmed IV, and confess to having been too cautious. In any case the water was too low to be an effective barrier. After Köprülü's janissaries waded across the river and seized the far bank, his engineers began constructing makeshift bridges. Montecuccoli wanted to attack, but he could not persuade the French units to join him. Then it began to rain – when the bridges were swept away overnight, Montecuccoli saw that Köprülü could neither send the rest of his army across the river nor withdraw the exposed troops. Though Montecuccoli only had his imperial troops, he could not pass up this opportunity. A spirited Turkish response almost drove his men back, but now Montecuccoli was able to persuade the French to join the fight. When exhausted Turkish troops fled in panic from this new attack, they pressed into the river, many being swept away and drowned. Some were saved by Tatars; the rest were slaughtered. The worst aspect of the disaster for Ahmed Köprülü was that the heaviest losses were among his finest troops, the janissaries.[12]

Montecuccoli made no attempt to follow up the victory – there were still powerful Ottoman formations on the other bank, and a river too strong for Turks to cross would be no safer for Christians. Though Montecuccoli had won the campaign, the peace treaty left all contested territory in Turkish hands; the weakling emperor, Leopold I, even paid a bribe of one hundred thousand thalers to the sultan to approve the treaty. It was Köprülü's salvation. Christians far from the battlefield could not believe it, but those on the spot understood. The army was mired down by heavy rains, the Hungarians remained in rebellion, the Germans wanted to go home, and the French were believed to have nefarious plans of their own – encouraging the Hungarians to revolt being only part of a long-term strategy of weakening the emperor.

The Croatian–Magyar Conspiracy

The lords involved in this widespread plot against Leopold were many and diverse. A number held prominent positions, some even in the Church, and a few were Germans. Of course, once these lords consented to participate, their promises did not remain secret long. Not even the French instigators of the treason could hold their tongues.

There was, moreover, little popular support for the conspiracy, a result of failing to explain what they hoped to achieve – a stronger monarch, Zriny, they hoped, to defend the country. Perhaps they suspected that their peers in Austria and prominent churchmen would not have approved. Leopold was able to arrest the leaders, put them on trial and then behead them. Had the Ottoman threat not been so great, the brutal treatment of the magnates might have sparked a real revolt. However, as it was, not even the execution of the heroic Zriny, the representative of the greatest family in

Croatia, did little more than provide a figure for later folklore and national pride.

Repression of Protestants in Royal Hungary followed. Although Magyar priests put nationality above Counter-Reformation zeal, the newly converted nobles were eager to demonstrate the purity of their beliefs by forcing their peasants to become Catholics again. The emperor was determined to press the policy through and for a moment even contemplated making the grandmaster of the Teutonic Knights, Johann Kaspar von Ampringen (1619–84), the governor of Royal Hungary.[13] Rebellion followed; the cruel regional specialty, impalement, was employed by both sides and memories of the horrors persisted for generations. For decades to come Leopold had to keep a large portion of his army in Royal Hungary, chasing rebels, rather than pursuing the war to the south or along the Rhine.

Soon a new rebel leader appeared in Hungary – Imre Thököly (1657–1705). Vengeance was his original motivation, but it was soon overshadowed by his ambition to become ruler of an independent state, or at a minimum the governor of Royal Hungary. Playing the sultan against the emperor, proposing to make the imperial borderlands into a second Transylvania, he was so successful at defying Leopold's authority that the grand vizier, Ahmed Köprülü, believed that the moment had come to strike at the Habsburg heart – Vienna. Victory there would guarantee the independence of Hungary under Ottoman sovereignty and would open the way to attacks into the German and Czech lands and through the Carpathian passes into Poland; he already foresaw more successes to the east of the Carpathians, moving past the Polish and Lithuanian borderlands into their heartlands as well. However, he did not live to implement these plans.

Köprülü's successor, Kara Mustafa Pasha, wanted to continue his policies, especially to take revenge for Austrian assistance to Hungarian rebels, but also to restore imperial prestige, which had shone less brightly in recent years.[14] That could be done most forcefully by taking Vienna. However, before he could lead an army up the Danube River, he had to settle matters on the steppe, north of the Tatar homeland. He had been in command of the Ottoman forces there, and knew his Polish and Lithuanian foes very well. Much had happened in their nation in recent years.

After the Deluge

The collapse of authority in Poland–Lithuania had been corrected slowly. It had not been easy to curb the massive incursions of Tatars and Cossacks, because, in their element, on the steppe, those swift horsemen would either overwhelm the commonwealth's forces or just ride away. Given the ability of neighbouring rulers, or even powerful magnates, to build up their own parties among the Cossacks or just cause trouble by arming them, controlling the brotherhoods was impossible for both Poles and Russians.[15]

Polish nobles had to perform military service before qualifying for any office; and since the Polish knightly class was large, there should have been more cavalrymen in the army than there were. Such horsemen were, moreover, difficult to command: to many, being noble meant being exempt from taking orders. There was also a levy of infantrymen from among the peasantry, but peasants who have been deprived of arms for generations do not easily develop the habits of warriors. Foreign mercenaries – sometimes incredibly exotic and often barbaric – were of erratic discipline and unpredictable usefulness (some being very good on one battlefield, but mediocre or useless elsewhere) and, if not paid, would change sides instantly.

The Polish aristocrat who eventually mastered the situation was Jan Sobieski. Born in a castle near Lwów, reputedly with the sounds of a thunderstorm and a Tatar attack ringing in his ears, Sobieski inherited both high status and private wealth; after study at the university in Cracow, he made a two-year grand tour of western Europe (learning French, German and Italian) before joining the royal army. As a hostage in Constantinople, he observed Turkish customs (some of which appeared later in his exotic dress) and he acquired a working knowledge of the language; later he commanded Tatar cavalry. He was engaged in numerous combats, emerging from each with a greater reputation and promotions, though after his commander surrendered to Charles X in 1654, he thought it wise also to acknowledge the Swedish monarch as king of Poland. To no one's surprise, after Jan Casimir made a surprising recovery, Sobieski changed sides again and was given the responsibility of defeating the Tatars and Cossacks, a task that was complicated by Russian offensives into eastern Lithuania.

Poland was not alone in its troubles. Russia was even worse off, protected from defeat and potential dismemberment only by its immense size and, ironically, its backwardness – which made it difficult for 'modern' armies to support themselves off the land. The Russian army almost dissolved through desertions, leaving the tsar's fortresses short of men and supplies. Had Jan Casimir's war effort not collapsed at that same time, the tsar could not have maintained his hold on the recent conquests.[16]

Jan Casimir had enjoyed a few successes in 1666, thanks to hiring Tatar auxiliaries. However, once the steppe warriors had gathered enough captives to supply their slave markets, they had gone home; when, soon afterwards, the king had to dismiss many of his foreign mercenaries, he was essentially powerless. The Sejm and the provincial diets had given him a tax only for the immediate emergency – seeing how popular he was among the foreign officers, the magnates and nobles began to fear royal absolutism more than Tatar and Cossack raids. When Jan Casimir removed the grand hetman (supreme commander) of Lithuania for refusing to continue the war against the tsar, many Lithuanians renounced their allegiance to the king; unpaid troops returned home, plundering along the way. When Jan Casimir sought to force through procedural changes, civil war resulted – and the king lost.

This crisis allowed the Cossack hetman, Peter Doroshenko (1627–98), to become a major, if momentary, political figure. Doroshenko was of noble Cossack ancestry, the grandson of a hetman and a follower of Chmielnicki. After he rose to leadership of the right-bank Cossacks in 1665, he crushed his pro-Moscow competitors on the left bank of the Dnieper River, and began to imagine a Cossack state arising on the steppe. Building on the lessons of Chmielnicki's rebellion, he understood that he needed an alliance with one of the major states other than Russia, and then he had to unify all the Cossack brotherhoods. He first approached Jan Casimir, then the Tatars. There was but a small Polish presence left in Ukraine in 1666 – German mercenaries, a few Polish volunteers and some royal Cossacks – which he believed he could easily rout with his army of twenty-five thousand Cossacks, thirty thousand Tatars and a unit of Turkish janissaries.

At hearing the news of Doroshenko's invasion of Lithuania, the long-deadlocked Muscovite and Polish peace delegations decided against prolonging negotiations. The Russians came off better in the treaty, retaining Smolensk and obtaining a claim on the Ukraine east of the Dnieper; but that mattered little, since this was more a truce than a peace agreement – each expected to resume fighting once the crisis had passed. Nonetheless, it could have been the foundation stone for a wider Christian alliance; in the next year the tsar's emissaries went west as far as the Atlantic states and as far east as Persia to see if such a grand coalition was possible. The plan was premature, but it may have cleared the way for less ambitious alliances in the future. This was the moment that Moscow emerged onto the wider European political stage.[17]

As grand hetman, Jan Sobieski pursued negotiations with Doroshenko, the Tatars and the Turks through 1667, but was unable to persuade anyone to make peace – Poland–Lithuania appeared just too weak, too vulnerable. The Tatars wanted to collect slaves and cattle for sale; the Turks wanted Cossack raids to end – a promise that the Poles could not make the Cossacks honour; and important Cossack leaders disagreed with Doroshenko, who was not only becoming autocratic, but arguing counter-intuitively that the best chance for Ukrainian independence was an alliance with the Turks and Tatars. Ultra-Orthodox Cossacks found this distasteful, conceding only that it might be temporarily expedient.

Knowing that war was unavoidable, Sobieski used a combination of earthen barriers and wagon forts to limit the horsemen's range. By defending river crossings and attacking small units immediately, he was able to force Doroshenko into accepting a two-year truce. This did not bring peace – for every troublemaker removed from the scene, another appeared to take his place.

Stenka Razin

Stenka Razin (1630–71) was not associated with the important Zaporozhe brotherhood that lived along the Dnieper River, but with poorer Cossacks living in the Don Basin – that is, farther away from Poland–Lithuania. The tsar had been paying an annual subsidy to the Cossack brotherhoods for protecting the borders, but when one trouble piled on top of another in the 1660s, he could not pay the subsidies. Working on the ensuing discontent, Stenka Razin became the spokesman of those who wanted to return to the freebooting ways of the past. A violent man, often drunk, but also courageous and charismatic, in 1668 he began leading his followers on raids into Persian and Russian territories. His successes brought him ever more followers, including some Zaporozhe Cossacks, who were traditionally associated with Poland–Lithuania. When Tsar Alexis (1629–76) was threatened by dissident boyars, Razin invaded Astrakhan, slaughtering thousands, murdering government officials and boyars, and calling for the end of serfdom. In September of 1670 he besieged Simbirsk (Ulianovsk), but was wounded badly. The well-trained garrison shot down hundreds of his followers, then followed after the retreating horsemen, torturing prisoners to death. As the Russian army advanced into Cossack lands, the number of atrocities soared, costing Razin his last supporters; in April of 1671 he was taken prisoner by Cossacks associated with the tsar and turned over to the Russian army. Taken to Moscow, he was executed by quartering.

The Russian advance into the steppe was based on simple principles – fortified bases along a line of rivers, long ditches and walls that blocked routes north, then using a *Wagenburg* to protect the army during marches. This moveable fortress was easily constructed of supply wagons and could be effectively defended by musketry and light cannon. Infantry was necessary to defend the wagons, but the heart of the army was cavalry.[18]

Meanwhile Sobieski had learned to counter this strategy by surrounding the wagon forts, cutting them off from supplies and water, building artillery emplacements and waiting for the garrison to sally out. Since horses suffered more from a lack of fodder than men from insufficient food, the surrounded forces usually chose to fight before their mounts became weak. Then it was a matter of Russians using sabres against Polish hussars' long lances.

On the steppe lances were less effective, because Tatar horse-archers would retreat when charged. Unless the hussars could close with the enemy quickly, they would find themselves at a distance from help, their horses blown and the enemy firing endless volleys of arrows at their backs as they tried to retreat.

Ottoman Intervention

The nature of the war changed completely when eighty thousand Ottoman troops arrived in the disputed territories. Assisted by Doroshenko and observed by Sultan Mehmed IV (1642–93) himself, the Turkish army besieged the poorly garrisoned Polish fortress at Kamieniec Podolski. The fortress had almost as many cannon as men, meaning that there were too few crews to service the guns. When it fell, a discouraged King Michael signed a humiliating peace treaty that ceded the frontier lands to the sultan and provoked Sobieski and other magnates to declare themselves in legitimate rebellion, then to persuade the Sejm to reject the treaty.

As the war resumed, this time more energetically pursued by the Poles, Doroshenko lost the loyalty of his Cossack followers, the support of the sultan and the alliance with the Tatars. When he asked for help from the tsar, swearing loyalty to him in 1674, it was a fatal blow to hopes for creating an independent Cossack state. Doroshenko retired to an estate in Russia, never to roil Ukrainian politics again. The vacuum was filled by the Ottomans.

Sobieski routed several Ottoman armies during these years. In November of 1673, at the climactic battle of Chocim (Khotyn), on the frontier with Moldavia at the site of an ancient castle then in Ottoman hands, his troops surrounded the fortified Turkish camp. They bombarded it with rockets, then they stormed the walls; they slaughtered twenty thousand fleeing enemy at the cost of fewer than two thousand men.[19] It helped immeasurably that the Turks were almost paralysed by freezing rain and wind, while Poles found the weather merely stimulating. Sobieski was frustrated by the Lithuanians wanting to go home rather than follow up the victory, but such was the prestige he earned in these campaigns that he was elected king of Poland the following year. It did not hurt that he had been on the payroll of Louis XIV for years, and was supported financially now in the hope that he would neutralise the regional influence of the Habsburgs; also that Sobieski's vivacious and ambitious wife, Marysienka, was French by birth and inclination.[20]

During the next few years Sobieski reformed the army completely, both in equipment and organisation. He placed his confidence in the cavalry, especially the heavily armoured winged hussars; artillery was useful, he felt, only if it was mobile. Since pikemen were not particularly useful on the steppe, he replaced many of them with musketeers; still, he used them sparingly, and he gave little attention to engineers and specialists in siege tactics because he did not expect to use their services often. With his finances limited by the Sejm, he relied heavily on the private armies of the great magnates to increase the size of the royal host from twelve thousand to thirty-six thousand, and the Lithuanian army from six thousand to eighteen thousand – even so, his armies were still vastly outnumbered by the Tatar and Turkish forces.[21] A French subsidy – part of Louis XIV's scheme to isolate and surround Austria – provided temporary relief, but Sobieski soon tired of the French diplomats stirring up trouble in his kingdom, emphasising the need to fight not Russians and Turks, but Austrians. Sobieski did not see how this would stop Tatar attacks.

It became apparent in the years to follow that Sobieski's conflict with the Turks precluded him from achieving success in White Russia – traditionally closely associated with Lithuania. He had to fight in the Ukraine, where he had little support from Lithuanian magnates, and along the eastern shore of the Black Sea, where Hungarians and Romanians were reluctant to turn away from their Ottoman masters.[22]

So brilliant were Sobieski's later achievements that it is often overlooked how difficult the early years of his reign had been. The Cossacks had not been a Polish problem alone, but one shared by the tsar. Both Christian monarchs were on the defensive, and pacifying the steppe and even the coastlands of the Black Sea seemed ever less likely – the Turkish sultan and the Tatar khan were extending their control over the Cossacks and besieging major Christian fortresses. Unless the Christians began to co-operate, they would all be defeated.

The Ottoman Offensive 1676–81

The Ottoman grand vizier, Kara Mustafa Pasha, was a dangerous foe for both the weakened Poland–Lithuania Commonwealth and the Russian tsar. Although his personal defects were well-known (including the possibility that he was mentally ill as well as corrupt and greedy), when Ahmed Köprülü died in 1676, the sultan saw in Kara Mustafa the man most qualified by talent and temperament to continue the empire's expansion.[23]

Two years later, when the Zaporozhe Cossacks rebelled, and the local Ottoman commander did not crush the rising quickly, Russian troops came to the Cossacks' aid. This prompted Kara Mustafa to send an Ottoman army against the Cossacks' main settlement, which was defended by a general with the German name of Tauernicht.[24] The siege progressed slowly because it was so difficult to transport the siege guns and equipment overland, and then because the Turkish commander sent so many men to face the Russian–Cossack relief army that he had too few to push the mining operations swiftly. (This was a lesson that Kara Mustafa seemed to remember in 1683, when a Christian relief force came to break up his siege of Vienna.) In a matter of days the Turks changed from besiegers to besieged, then to fugitives. Only the covering squadrons of Tatars prevented the total destruction of the army.

When Kara Mustafa studied the reports, he concluded that the failure was not due to an overly ambitious plan, but to the Ottoman commander. In 1679 he took personal control of the army that marched north, only to encounter a much-improved Russian field army. Russian infantry moved outside the *Wagenburg* to attack, supported by mobile artillery and cavalry; this may have been the result of increased self-confidence from the campaign of the previous year, but it may also have reflected the presence of more foreign officers.[25] The grand vizier, unable to prevail against this army, made peace in 1681, sacrificing all the territorial gains made earlier. Not surprisingly, he looked around for an easy victim, hoping to erase the humiliation of this defeat.

His eye fell on Vienna.

Brandenburg–Prussia

In the meantime there had been large changes in the north. The great winner in recent wars had been the elector of Brandenburg. This was not expected: Frederick William's village-like capital of Berlin was surrounded by lakes and rivers; his lightly populated lands in East Prussia, with only Königsberg as a significant city, was more suitable as a great hunting preserve than the basis for a great state. More important were his lands along the Rhine – Cleves and Mark – which would eventually become centres of German industry. That his ancestors had been electors meant little most of the time – while their role in imperial pageantry must have been emotionally satisfying, there was only one contest for the imperial crown between 1637 and 1705 – the Habsburgs were a long-lived dynasty. His only opportunity to haggle a price for his vote was in 1658, and the outcome then had not been in doubt.

The Thirty Years War had rolled over an unresisting Brandenburg – its citizens plundered, its young men forced into foreign armies. When Frederick William succeeded his unlucky father in 1640, no one expected much of him. Authority was held by his chief councillor, Adam von Schwarzenberg, an ardent Catholic who believed that bowing to the emperor was preferable to placating the Swedes. Schwarzenberg pampered his spoiled mercenaries and the local *Junkers* (the petty nobility of the region). To make it impossible for the elector to build a party against him, Schwarzenberg first sent the young elector to Holland on the pretext that he should learn the arts of war, then to Königsberg, where he would be 'safer'. He himself thought Berlin was not particularly dangerous. He was, in effect, sending the young man into a form of internal exile, to reside in a distant backwater where he could not woo supporters or even learn what policy options existed.

Good fortune smiled on Frederick William sooner than he had dared hope. Schwarzenberg fell dead in early 1641, perhaps from over-indulgence at a feast – restraint not being a characteristic of the times. The young elector then called in his officials, first demanding an accounting of expenditures, then using loyal troops to put down their rebellion. His making peace with Sweden angered Catholics, but his marriage to the eldest daughter of the stadtholder of Holland pleased Protestants.[26] He made his little army more effective, then raised its numbers from 2,500 to 8,000. This was sufficient for him brazenly to confront the parties negotiating the Peace of Westphalia, winning more lands for himself than anyone expected. If the diplomats did not give him Pomerania, that was because Sweden had to be given some territorial compensation for losses elsewhere.

The elector was a fanatical follower of the religion of hard work and responsibility. An arch-Calvinist, he saw work as the proper lot of a Christian man, duty as part of work, and living on little as a duty. Such virtues made for good officers, judges, tax-collectors and councilmen. In this spirit he gave his *Junkers* greater authority over their peasants and serfs, but he required them to serve as officers or in the state bureaucracy. No longer could a petty noble retire to his estate and hunt pheasants – Frederick William would conscript him into the army, even in peacetime.

Understanding the importance of a strong economy for increasing state revenues, he invited immigrants from Austria, Holland and the Palatinate – Protestants driven from their farms and towns by French armies – and, after 1685, Huguenots expelled from France by Louis XIV. Fleeing France with nothing but memories of robbery, murder and rape, the industry and commercial acumen of the Huguenots allowed him to hire more mercenaries, until he had forty thousand men in his army. He was also able to avoid the necessity of selling commissions; instead, he could award them on the basis of merit. Since he could afford to recruit mercenaries from other German states, he could spare his own subjects for work and paying taxes.

The elector sought out competent foreign officers. The most important of these was Georg von Derfflinger (1606–95), one of the numerous Austrian Protestants who went into exile in protest of Habsburg Counter-Reformation policies.[27] He fought in the Swedish army in the Thirty Years War, then married into Brandenburg nobility. At age forty he purchased property in Brandenburg from his wife's impoverished relatives, an action that brought him to Frederick William's attention – the elector was then replacing Catholic officers with Protestants.

Derfflinger was a far from model citizen: having come up from poverty, he personified all the vices and virtues of a mercenary soldier. Woe to the town where his soldiers were stationed and woe to the barkeeper who expected him to pay for his drinks. He was vain, pompous and proud, but able to get an instant overview of any battlefield and courageous in taking advantage of geographic features and opponents' mistakes. He was unusual in one characteristic – he believed in giving lower-ranking officers the authority to act. This *Auftragstaktik* allowed the Prussian army (as the Brandenburg forces became known) to strike faster than any opponent.[28]

Derfflinger made his mark in the 1674 campaign against the French in Alsace, where the German coalition faced Marshal Turenne. At one point, seeing an unoccupied height overlooking the French lines, he suggested to the council that they place their artillery there, then strike. He was overruled on the grounds that the troops were too exhausted to move. Derfflinger took the rebuff as a personal insult, and the next day missed no opportunity to point out that Turenne had realised how dangerous his position was and prudently retreated. Since caution remained the primary characteristic of the coalition, the bolder Turenne was later able to manoeuvre the German army back across the Rhine.

After Frederick William had put his army into winter quarters at Schweinfurt, a major crossing of the Main River, he learned that the Swedish king, Charles XI (1655–97), had accepted a French subsidy in return for invading Brandenburg. Soon afterwards, a Swedish army of twenty thousand men occupied the entire country – Brandenburg and Prussia alike – then settled into winter quarters, expecting to supply themselves from the stored grain of the peasantry and the savings of townsfolk until the elector agreed to pull out of the French war. It was universally agreed that even if the elector decided to fight, he could not get his army home before mid-summer – encumbered by hundreds of supply wagons and thousands of camp followers, such a march could not be made in winter, when fodder was lacking, nor even in the spring, when rains made marching difficult. By summer Brandenburg would be bankrupt, unable to provide the money, supplies and men to keep the army going – he would have to leave the imperial coalition.

Little did they know. Frederick William put the sixty-nine-year-old Derfflinger in charge of the march. He broke camp at the end of May without warning, as soon as grass was up, sending small units along different roads and moving through the difficult Thuringian forests to avoid major cities. Although Derfflinger had provided money to buy supplies from local farmers, in Thuringia there was little to sell. That made it a difficult march. Nevertheless, he covered 250 kilometres (150 miles) in two weeks, moving so stealthily that the Swedes were not aware that they were being approached by the entire army until it was too late. Derfflinger struck at Rathenow, a crossing of the Havel approximately half-way between the two main Swedish garrisons. Derfflinger took the first fortress by guile, providing money to a councilman for a banquet at which most of the Swedish officers became drunk, then impersonating a Swedish officer fleeing Brandenburg troops – his experience in the Swedish army decades earlier allowed him to pull off the farce. He then seized the gates and brought the army inside.

Frederick William did not wait for the infantry to come up, but went into pursuit with the cavalry. He caught up with the retreating Swedes at Fehrbellin, where they were hurriedly trying to repair a bridge across a small river. Seeing that the Swedes had not fortified a small height overlooking their position, the elector put his artillery there, then charged. The losses in the combat were about equal, but it was the first time a Brandenburg army had ever defeated a Swedish one. The Great Elector, as Frederick William was subsequently known, drove the Swedes out of Brandenburg–Prussia.[29] He next invaded Pomerania, taking strong Swedish fortresses one after the other until at last he reached the strongly fortified ports. If he could take them, the Swedish king would be unable to land troops or supply them, and the rest of the country would fall. Charles XI had only one means of saving these strongholds – distracting Frederick William. To this end, he sent the governor of Estonia, Henrik Henriksson, Baron Horn (1618–93), south with twelve thousand men. Horn left from Riga, crossed Courland into East Prussia, then bypassed the fortress city of Königsberg and drove into the heart of the province.

Frederick William did not panic. First he concluded his siege operations, then in January, when the northern winter was at its worst, he moved against the Swedes in their scattered garrisons. He had at that time forty-five thousand troops available, by far the largest army he had ever possessed, but he only took about nine thousand of the best. Marching east swiftly, he took advantage of frozen ground and ice-covered rivers and lakes to come upon the Swedes by surprise.

Horn's men were short of supplies, and of the nine thousand that had survived combat, the weather and disease, at least a quarter were too ill to fall into ranks. Retreat seemed the most prudent course – Horn could have outrun ordinary pursers easily, but he had not anticipated Frederick William's ingenuity. The Great Elector had already sent word to Königsberg to collect 1,200 sleighs and horses to pull them, then, dashing ahead with his cavalry across the frozen bay south of the fortress, he put his men (and his now much overweight frame) into sleighs and hurried after Horn.

It was a merry chase – for the Germans. For the Swedes it was a disaster. Although Horn escaped, only a quarter of the army that had marched so gaily out of Riga managed to slink back inside, and he lost all his artillery.

Frederick William's army was now widely admired for its discipline and efficiency. The Great Elector was reluctant to lead it into combat, but he was also hard-pressed to afford to keep it at full strength during peacetime. His compromise solution was to provide more units than required to the emperor for his wars against the Turks and the French. The advantages were mutual and obvious: a small state could afford to maintain a large army, while the larger state could rent units ready to fight.[30] As the practice spread, Brandenburg became a prized source – its soldiers were simply the best. The legal fiction was that this was a subsidy contract to an 'ally'. It was nothing particularly new, of course – the French having supplied money to allies during the Thirty Years War; it had merely become more respectable, more open. It had also became a bidding war. Louis XIV provided 'subsidies' to some, Leopold of Austria others, but it was awkward that the two great Catholic powers were bidding for the services of Protestants. The gulf between Catholic and Protestant narrowed significantly when Venice and Austria hired Lutheran troops to fight the Turks, and it turned anti-French when Louis XIV seemed to be in league with the sultan.

Austrian Recovery

Emperor Leopold I, whose long reign began in 1658, had reluctantly accepted the fact that Germans would accept his leadership only when his actions would benefit the entire nation, not the Habsburg dynasty alone, and while no action was more necessary than military reform, he could implement it only in those lands he held directly – Austria, Bohemia, Moravia, Silesia, parts of Italy and Royal Hungary. Foreign experts contributed significantly to the rebuilding of the imperial army, but none more than Raimondo, count of Montecuccoli, duke of Melfi. Montecuccoli had been wounded and captured at Breitenfeld, wounded again at Lützen and captured again in 1639. While imprisoned he began a book on military theory, *Memorie della Guerra*, that served as a manual of arms for many years. He fought in Italy in 1643, and two years later against the Hungarians, the French and the Swedes; in 1661–4 he commanded the army fighting the Turks, then was on the council of war, became field marshal, and in 1673 led the imperial armies on the successful defence of the Rhine against the French army.

Montecuccoli was a cautious commander, which was nothing unusual. He understood that battle was occasionally necessary, but he calculated the likely benefits and losses carefully. The principal loss, even in a victory, was in trained men and officers, then in equipment. Forcing an enemy to abandon lands and fortress without serious fighting was by far the better strategy.[31]

Montecuccoli's army was composed of mercenaries, men recruited from a wide variety of lands, most German-speaking, but some Italians like himself, some semi-professional warriors from border regions and many local boys from regions where his armies were engaged. In 1682 he began recruiting seriously, urging the 'circles' of the Holy Roman Empire to contribute money and men.[32] Ominous reports were coming from Turkey that an army was being raised for a campaign into Austria. Many thought this was a scare tactic, but Montecuccoli knew better.

Innocent XI, who was pope from 1676 to 1691, was also aware of the Turkish plans. His calls for crusade were long dismissed as an overused ruse to exalt the role of the papacy in both religious and foreign affairs, but his ability to contribute enormous sums of money to Christian armies was taken seriously. The pope's actions were timely, because, as Rhoads Murphey reminds us, the Turkish army was now well paid, well fed and well led. The recent turmoil at the top of the system, in fact, testified to the essential strength of the empire – whatever happened in the harem and Sublime Porte had little adverse effect on prosperity and administrative efficiency. Moreover, Turkish weapons were much the same as Western Europeans possessed – partly because the same skilled workmen were producing them. Turkey was open to outside talents and rewarded handsomely anyone who would apply them to the empire's benefit. Ottoman resources were not unlimited, but contemporary observers tended to think they were. Certainly no one outdid the Ottomans in ceremony and pageantry, an aspect of military life that everyone valued highly. Their bands were so inspirational that, should the musicians stop playing, the troops knew that the battle was lost; on the other hand, as long as the famous attack march could be heard, there was hope for victory. The loud music was rarely interrupted.

The Great Habsburg–Ottoman Confrontation Approaches

Kara Mustafa Pasha's first step towards Vienna was to end the war with Russia. Then in the spring of 1682 he persuaded Thököly to declare his truce with the emperor ended. After that he began to work on distracting the emperor. Although his military preparations in the Balkans were no secret and were not intended to be – intimidation was a tactic known to work – he wanted the emperor to worry about the French king.

Louis XIV did not want to be seen as an open ally of 'the Turk', but his ambassador, Guilleragues, responded to Turkish questions about French intentions, saying that at the present time the king was at peace with the emperor, but that it was not Louis's practice to leave three hundred thousand troops unoccupied for long.[33] The ambassador's position was temporarily undermined when a French admiral pursued Barbary pirates to Chios, where he bombarded the city as punishment for protecting the fugitives, but the relationship improved when Mehmed IV – never very well versed in the details of international politics – understood that he and the king had a common enemy in the Habsburg emperor.

As diplomats scurried across Europe, desperate to obtain promises of support from wavering princes, the emperor's attention was focused on Thököly, who was demanding to be recognised as king of Transylvania, to receive five hundred thousand florins annually as a subsidy, and permission to marry Helena Zriny, whose estates were to be restored.[34] The emperor, however, believed that Thököly's price could be negotiated down – way down.

This was a mistake. In July Thököly took advantage of unrest in Royal Hungary to capture Košice, and the following month a Turkish garrison arrived to hold it. Thököly was momentarily frustrated in taking more territory because the commander of a small fortress refused to surrender, even mooning him in defiance. Though his assaults failed three times, costing him four thousand men, Thököly was so close to success that the mutinous garrison surrendered.[35] Thököly's reward was the sultan naming him prince of Hungary in return for a nominal tribute. With all of Hungary east of the Vah River now subject to Turkey, the way was open for the Ottoman armies to reach Austria. The sultan and grand vizier concluded that, with only scattered German units coming to reinforce the Habsburg army, Vienna was now vulnerable. However, their intelligence service missed the Polish king's intent to come to the rescue; and they failed to perceive that Thököly's optimistic reports were more self-serving than accurate.

The Christian Coalition in 1683

The imperial army was now more disciplined and better armed than it had been in 1648 or even 1664. Freelance commanders of regiments were rare and competent officers more common. There were, however, too many titled amateurs who counted on the subsidies for their units to supplement their personal revenues. They paid poorly when they paid, and had many phantom soldiers on the rolls.

When the princes of the Holy Roman Empire were informed that the Ottoman army was on the march, they ordered their officers to fill the ranks of their armies, to buy equipment and to teach the newest drills. There was considerable competition for soldiers, with recruiting officers spreading across Germany with tempting offers – imperial agents, Bavarians, Brandenburgers and Saxons. The rulers of minor states sought to limit the activities of these agents, because they knew that the reputation of the military powers would draw men away from the forces they hoped to rent out for the coming conflict. Recruiters were encouraged to concentrate on country boys, but they were willing to sign up the unemployable and even criminals from the cities; they knew that such men were often more trouble than useful, but a quota was a quota.

Reflecting this hurried enlargement of the armies, it was impossible to provide proper uniforms for all the troops. All wore long overcoats and floppy wide-brimmed hats, with a cartridge pouch slung over the left shoulder. Special insignia on the hats and lapels distinguished units, but the general impression was drab. Only the generals were dressed in expensive, bright colours; they also wore wigs and hats with impressive feathers. They were more experienced in small-scale battles than in confrontations such as the one that awaited them.

The soldiers were no better off. Armed with matchlock muskets, half-pikes and a few old-fashioned pikes, most were accustomed to wars of position, with each commander seeking small advantages – high ground, better access to food and water, cutting the enemy's communications – not to pitched battle against the seemingly endless hordes of Ottoman soldiery. German and Polish cavalry, the best of the Christian forces, were more lightly armed than before – except for the Polish hussars with their magnificent wings that spread out during a charge; the hussars wore a bullet-proof breastplate, wielded a sturdy sword with a basket hand protector, and carried two pistols.

Only in artillery did the Christians have a distinct advantage. The cannon could not yet be manoeuvred swiftly, nor fired rapidly. However, there were more state munitions works and more arsenals, and most master-gunners were state employees. The wagon train necessary to transport ammunition and shells was not easy to find, but like everything else, the supply services now began to shape up.

The traditional calling up of militia applied only to threatened districts and then only to defend local refuges. There was no place for untrained troops except as scouts, teamsters and sappers. Commanders wanted steadiness, a characteristic acquired only slowly and never attained without a tradition of victory; they sought to raise morale through impressive ceremonies, parades, and by music (drums, fifes and bagpipes, with trumpets for the cavalry) so loud that marching troops were kept at a distance lest their hearing be affected.

Enthusiasm was high. Typical was the archbishop of Trier, Johann Hugo von Orsbeck, who volunteered troops to the emperor, then served personally as a chaplain and eventually took part in the combat himself. To do this required him to ignore the threats of Louis XIV, whose army invaded his diocese that summer, but remained in occupation a much shorter time than after the invasions before he took office in 1676 and the future one of 1688.

Although news that 150,000 Turks had reached Vienna in mid-July galvanised the Germans into a more hurried response, volunteers were less numerous than the pious folk who filled the churches to petition the deity for aid. Leopold became so frustrated at Sobieski's letters reporting that his troops had not yet gathered that he asked him to come alone, if necessary, because his name was worth more than an army – when the Polish king arrived, only to discover that the German troops were not assembled yet either, he was furious. Fortunately, his first army was not far behind, and a second was forming up in Lithuania.

Leopold himself lacked troops even to prevent Tatar marauders from spreading terror across Austria. When the raiders got as far as Linz, Leopold fled with his pregnant wife farther up the Danube, leaving orders for isolated communities to defend themselves. His army was slowly collecting north of the Danube under the leadership of Charles of Lorraine;[36] Pope Innocent XI sent money, promising even to pay the expenses of Protestant forces (a promise easily forgotten later). Although there had been no decision as to how this army was to cross the mountains to Vienna, when Sobieski arrived he took charge. There was no time to spare – Vienna was at the point of falling, its walls collapsing from the explosion of mines and constant cannon fire, and its garrison reduced to a fraction of its original, insufficient numbers.

Fortunately for the Christian host – about eighty thousand infantry and cavalry – the grand vizier had made no effort to destroy the bridges over the Danube or to attack the first units to cross. He had staked everything, it seems, on his enemies being too divided and too weak to accomplish anything, and he had counted on a screening force of thirty thousand Tatars – which vanished when it was most needed. Sobieski, who had faced Kara Mustafa before, knew that the grand vizier would take no risks, and therefore he could be daring himself – on 11 September he ordered a night march over the intervening mountains where Turkish forces could easily have slowed or stopped the Christian advance, trapping exhausted and hungry troops on narrow and steep roads. When Sobieski reached the summit the next morning, he could see that the grand vizier had not prepared extensive earthworks or more than a handful of strong points for artillery.

At the last moment the grand vizier turned to face the oncoming crusaders, but it was too late – moreover, he had committed some of his best units to an assault on the city walls, expecting that he could fight successfully on two fronts. The armies tore at each other all day, but when the Polish winged hussars finally broke the Turkish lines, the battle became a massacre. The garrison and citizens of Vienna, at the limit of their ability to withstand any further artillery bombardments, mine explosions or mass assaults, rejoiced – and Jan Sobieski became an international hero.

The Christians followed up their victory by marching towards Buda; the Poles suffered one defeat on the way to Parkany, then, when reinforced by the Germans, achieved an outstanding victory the next day. It now being October, the Christians decided to return to Austria and go into winter quarters. Imre Thököly now sought in vain to make peace with Leopold, and he might have done so if the combination of his own vanity and imperial anger had not made compromise impossible. Jan Sobieski saw how valuable Thököly's help would be in the wars against the Turks, but he could not move the emperor to forgive him. Since the Transylvania ruler shared the blame for the defeat at Vienna (and was perhaps more to blame than the grand vizier), he was eventually delivered in chains to the sultan for execution. The sultan, however, saw the same potential in Thököly that the Polish king had. He gave him absolute command of small armies and of the cavalry in larger ones; in both Thököly served with distinction until late in life, when he retired to the countryside with his wife. It was a missed opportunity for the emperor: just as Leopold's enthusiastic Catholicism alienated Protestants in Germany, it also cost him the opportunity to recover more of the Balkans.

The Christian position was complicated – some Protestants had gone home angry at the way they had been treated, especially at not being paid; Louis XIV was threatening to cross the Rhine; and Poles were demanding that Sobieski come home. The Polish king had been able to rally the nation earlier because there was so much anger at the Ottoman attacks on the frontier, but now nobles and clerics were ready to believe that was no longer a danger. With so many nobles believing that even a weak king was a greater danger than a strong enemy, it was difficult for a strong king such as Sobieski to continue the war.

Entering the political calculations was a young and still untried ruler, Peter of Russia (1672–1725). His state was huge beyond imagination, with an uncountable population and tremendous potential for economic production, but it was still weak. In short, Russia was backward, impoverished and chaotic, but it had the potential to become a powerful nation. Nothing that would amount to anything, experts thought, in their lifetimes. But life and politics are full of surprises. Perhaps even the Austrian–Polish combination would stay together long enough to capture Buda.

CHAPTER EIGHT

The Turkish Wars

Islam in Retreat, or Maybe Not

After the battle outside Vienna in 1683, the geographic barriers that had separated Christendom from the Ottoman Empire began to break down. From Russia to Poland to Austria, Christian armies were overcoming logistical difficulties that had earlier prevented them from moving south against an enemy they respected for its numbers, firepower, competence and religious fervour. Perhaps equally as important in Christian successes was a willingness to overlook religious disputes that in the past had led them to hope (if not to pray) for Islamic victories over their rivals.

Christians also began to suspect that the Ottomans had lost the vigour that had made them so potent and resilient. The Habsburgs, in particular, who had been on the defensive since the sixteenth century, sensed an opportunity to recover even Christian territories that had fallen to the Turks in the fourteenth and fifteenth centuries. Still, it was hard to believe that there would be a major shift in the balance of power. Traditional enemies – Sweden for Poland, and France for Austria – did not want the victors of the battle at Vienna to exploit this opportunity.

Russia was another problem, but the sultan left that to the Tatars. It would be difficult for the tsar to bring his army across the steppe, which had few inhabitants and fewer resources, and the Tatar fortresses on the Black Sea were strong. Any Russian army moving in the direction of Istanbul would come into conflict with the Poles; should they be successful there, they would compete with the Austrians for the right to liberate the Slavic peoples in the Balkans.

Meanwhile, the Ottoman Empire was broad, rich and filled with skilled warriors. The setback in Austria, a region distant from Istanbul, was not fatal; the failure of 1529 had not been followed by serious consequences. While it must have been disconcerting that the 1683 coalition had not dispersed and gone home – as Christian armies had done in the past – but had followed Jan Sobieski in the direction of Buda, it must have been a relief for the Ottomans to hear that the grand vizier had ambushed the van and routed the proud Polish knights.

Christendom on the Offensive

The Polish army, followed somewhat reluctantly by German forces, had pursued the retreating Turkish army into Hungary. Jan Sobieski – no stranger to Turkish determination and valour – was not discouraged by the first skirmish, but pushed on to Parkany, where his army won a violent confrontation before retiring to winter quarters inside the Holy Roman Empire.

The grand vizier, Kara Mustafa Pasha, who had gathered his forces to defend Buda, must have been astounded at the Polish persistence – the dynamics of Polish–Lithuanian politics surely demanded that the king return home. Once that happened, the situation would return to the *status quo ante bellum*. The grand vizier would not have used the Latin phrase, but he understood what it meant. However, he failed to persuade the Ottoman sultan, Mehmet IV, that all was well, and – as was customary for failed commanders – was ritually strangled in late 1683.

Turkish administration fell into disarray following the ritual strangling of Kara Mustafa Pasha – a silken cord was the only reward that defeated Ottoman commanders could expect, and it was only awarded moments before it was pulled tight around the neck. His three successors were nobodies who left few accomplishments to boast of, each lasting only two years.

The new governor in Hungary used local labour to reinforce the fortifications at Buda, and they had collected all the foodstuffs that a besieging army would require. Surely he could hold the great fortress until the Christian coalition fell apart, then resume the drive north at some convenient moment.[1]

The sultan, undoubtedly kept informed by French connections, followed the emperor's efforts to pull together an even larger European coalition for the next summer's campaign – a new crusade (though not officially called that, to avoid offending Protestant sensibilities) that would bring Catholics,

Protestants and even Orthodox peoples together against him. He knew that Louis XIV was working against this by sending his armies into Germany, knowing that this would draw Austrian troops out of the Balkans. Louis not only wanted territories that he believed were French (he was familiar with Caesar's *Gallic Wars*), but he was determined to prevent Leopold from acquiring Hungary – that would immediately remove the Turks to such as distance from Vienna that they would cease to be a nuisance, and that land, once it began to produce food and revenues, would make the emperor much stronger. Although Louis XIV failed to prevent Jan Sobieski from renewing the offensive in 1684, he complicated the plans of both pope and emperor.

Louis XIV knew that Kara Mustafa Pasha had been very close to capturing Vienna. Had the grand vizier arrived a week earlier, or had the Christian generals been less daring, or had papal money not been available to the emperor, or if the grand vizier had concentrated on the Christian field army instead of taking the city, or if the Tatars had not felt that the grand vizier had insulted them, Vienna would most likely have fallen. The loss of Vienna would have so undermined imperial prestige that Germans might have turned to the French king to save them.

As it was, though the Ottoman army had been bloodied twice, it was still a magnificent war machine. For good reason those princes who had shared in the dangers proudly displayed captured tents and muskets, and the backward-curling headdress of the janissaries still struck fear into Christian hearts. Even so, the Ottoman tradition of victory – when they saw no reason to fortify camps or plan routes of retreat – now worked against them as they faced more self-confident and dangerous foes.

As the Austrian–Polish army pressed into Hungary in 1684, Venetian-led naval forces sailed southeast to Greece and Russians advanced towards the Black Sea, Mehmet IV was unable to find a grand vizier with the talent to master any of these crises, much less all of them at once. In the past he could have relied on raids into Christian lands to pay his soldiery, but now he was on the defensive everywhere. Nevertheless, the Ottoman state had resources and assets that Europeans were hardly able to estimate, much less easily overcome. One was a proud military tradition, another was religious fervour, and lastly, the fact that many of its various non-Turkish subjects believed that Ottoman law and order was better than the chaos that came in the train of invading Christian armies.

The Hungarian War 1684–1687

The immediate challenge for the Christian coalition was to capture Buda, the impressive fortress overlooking the Danube that had long served as the Turkish administrative centre. Unless Charles of Lorraine, who commanded Leopold's army, and Jan Sobieski, the commander of the Polish forces, could work together effectively, the Turks would soon be back at Vienna. So, between them they made arrangements to send guns and supplies by boat down the Danube and marched their troops along the bank, taking several strong points on the way. It was not an easy task, not just because the fortress was so formidable, but also because the Turks had collected all the nearby food and fodder, leaving little for a besieging army. The Christians might have better cannon and better-trained soldiers, but they could not control the weather, and the well-constructed defences of Buda, sited atop high hills, could be held by determined men. The Ottomans were, if nothing else, determined – there was no such thing as a cowardly Turk, and there were ten thousand of them in the garrison.

Jan Sobieski – despite his age, heavy weight and a strong desire to return to his wife – was eager for the fight. Although his subjects had little enthusiasm for the Hungarian enterprise, they agreed to apply pressure on the Black Sea front: acquiring lands there was a traditional Polish goal and required the new grand vizier to divert troops that might have gone to Hungary. Venice, aided by the Knights of Malta, was attacking by sea, requiring the sultan to protect the coastlines. More distantly, Peter, tsar of Russia, was talking about besieging Azov, the main Ottoman base on the Black Sea. He planned to use river transport in much the same way as the Habsburg army was supplying its men, and he could be much more ruthless in dealing with desertion and incompetence, although there was so much less forage and food available en route that his logistical problems were more severe. Far to the west, Spanish Habsburg forces were tying down Ottoman resources in North Africa.

The most important shortcoming in the Christian coalition was the failure to win over the Hungarian Protestants in Transylvania. If Thököly had come over, the Ottoman position would have been completely unhinged. But Thököly's supporters feared the emperor's fervent Catholicism more than they disliked Islam; the sultan had not only left them alone, but even encouraged their preachers to speak out against other Christian bodies. Then there was Louis XIV, who was a Catholic bigot like the emperor, but had not yet displayed that hatred of Protestants that became apparent later – in 1684 his desire to acquire more German lands seemed to reflect simple greed.

Leopold played on the contradictions of the French king's position, calling attention to his failure to support the religious war, while promising to cede territories to France peacefully. The 1684 Treaty of Ratisbon recognised as French all the territories that Louis had taken earlier; however, this secured peace only temporarily, and it was far from clear that the Christian coalition could defeat the sultan's forces before the French king made new demands.

Leopold giving Charles of Lorraine command of the imperial army was not a universally popular decision.[2] Decades earlier, when Charles's lands in Lorraine had been occupied by Louis XIV, he had escaped from France to live on Habsburg sufferance. It was widely assumed that his appointment as general was rather a consolation prize than a recognition of talent. Tall, somewhat overweight, yet an excellent horseman, he had simple tastes and modest habits. These served him well in a situation where so many looked for leadership not to him, but to the Polish king.

Jan Sobieski kept his Polish forces independent, just as Maximilian Emanuel (1662–1726) did with his Bavarian units. Venetians, as usual, followed their own interests, unwilling to make any sacrifice that would strengthen a Habsburg ruler who might eventually have designs on them.[3] Thus, the Christian coalition advanced on Buda in 1684 with a divided command. Normally, such arrangements lead straight to disaster.

No one underestimated the challenges. The besieging army gave up after more than a hundred days of intensive siege operations – two-thirds of the troops were dead, wounded or ill, and an Ottoman relief army had arrived. Even if Buda had been taken, occupying the rest of Hungary would not have been easy – and nothing less than advancing south to liberate the Serbs and Bulgarians would be a decisive blow against the Ottomans. The great plain was crossed by several great rivers that flowed south into the Danube, each river bounded more by swamps than banks. There were few places to load grain for export; years earlier, when Constantinople had ceased to be a reliable market, many farmers had abandoned agriculture in favour of herding. Now that villages were being devastated by both Christian raiders and Ottoman scorched-earth tactics, everyone living in the line of advance was fleeing to safety, taking their herds with them. This left little forage and almost no food for Christian and Islamic forces alike. Coalition commanders who had kept their armies in Austria over the winter incurred expenses that limited their ability to pay their troops in the spring. In addition, Sobieski, who had entered the war with a depleted treasury, was being urged by his advisers to abandon the Danube campaign in favour of recovering eastern lands he had ceded to Russia. Still, since the sultan showed no signs of wanting peace, Sobieski chose to persist in the campaign – the capture of Buda was in Poland's long-term interests. To his great disappointment, the siege failed.

The German armies again withdrew to winter quarters and the Polish army went home. Surely now, the Turkish commanders must have thought, the danger was past. That was not the case, however – the Christian commanders had persuaded themselves that Buda could be taken the following year. They were mistaken; the strong fortress held out.

This was an important development for the young man who later became the greatest general Austria ever produced. Eugene of Savoy (1663–1736) was so hard-pressed to support his men through the winter of 1684–5 that he had sent them to Bohemia, then travelled to the Low Countries to ask for money. He accompanied his influential mother (Olympia, Mazarin's niece) to Spain, then to Turin to ask the duke of Savoy for aid, but did not obtain much more than promises. Sitting out the summer's campaign turned out to be no disadvantage, because it associated his reputation with the successes of 1686, not the failures of 1685. Desperate for money, he became the titular abbot of two monasteries in Savoy; this was not a large income, but his action showed his troops the sacrifices he would make to provide for them, and it blunted criticisms by rivals for command – should he somehow survive sharpshooters wielding heavy Turkish muskets, he would not be founding a dynasty.

Eugene's enthusiasm for combat led to one of the less glorious moments of the 1686 siege, when a much larger Christian army – perhaps seventy thousand men – attacked the fortress. His cavalry had been stationed beyond the siege lines to fend off the Ottoman efforts to relieve the city, but when he saw janissaries attempting to escape, he ordered his horsemen to charge. The ensuing slaughter was considered unnecessary, but it was typical of this war. One horror led to another, each feeding stories to the fascinated and sometimes frightened subjects of both Christendom and Islam. Enhanced by selective propaganda, this brought recruits into each army and heightened the determination to prevail. This was a contest of rival religious and social systems: neither would yield anything to the other.

When Buda fell to an overwhelming force of besiegers, Pope Innocent XI did all he could to encourage the Christian armies to continue the advance south. To keep Catholic rulers from quarrelling, he organised an alliance called the Holy League. More important was the money he sent to hire units from Protestant princes who had previously sent troops more or less voluntarily, but were still wary of Counter-Reformation fanaticism.[4] In 1686 the elector of Brandenburg alone received 150,000 thalers for seven thousand men, the elector of Saxony rented out five thousand soldiers and the king of Sweden one thousand. This was good business practice. Soldiers had become too valuable a commodity to allow foreigners to recruit them, but unless princes sopped up subjects likely to enrol as mercenaries, they would slip out of the country. Also, war against 'the Turk' was popular.

As well-trained units marched south from Catholic and Protestant Europe alike, English and French volunteers crossed the Rhine to join the Christian army. Only Polish contingents were absent, the diets in Poland and Lithuania having given the taxes and draftees to the eastern magnates for defence and defied the king to claim them. The best that Sobieski could do in 1687 was to lead an expedition into Moldavia. Though this advance paralleled that of the Habsburg army, many influential Poles saw less grand strategy involved than the king's desire to carve out lands for his eldest son, who stood little chance of being elected his successor – Poles did not want a strong ruler.[5]

Germans had shared the glories of victory at Vienna with the Poles – indeed, ceded most of the credit to Sobieski – but when Buda fell, it was their victory alone.

With the prospects of more Habsburg victories in the future, Peter of Russia hurried to seize his share of the booty. There were no significant geographical barriers between him and Constantinople, but he had to defeat the Tatar khan in the Crimea before he could march down the Black Sea coast; he could not take his army south with an unprotected flank.

Charles of Lorraine had not been able to move south that autumn, the siege having left too little good weather for a campaign. In any case, the next obvious target, Belgrade, was far away. In the spring of 1687, Max Emanuel took an independent command down the great river to that fortress, with Eugene of Savoy as his cavalry commander. By midsummer the campaign seemed a failure – supplies were so short that the Bavarian duke swallowed his pride and rejoined the main Habsburg army. This was fortunate, because a large Ottoman army appeared soon thereafter and began following the retreating Christians. On 12 August Charles of Lorraine turned to confront his pursuers near the historic battlefield of Mohács. It was fifty thousand against sixty thousand – much better odds than the Hungarians had faced in 1526, when King Louis II and most of his knights had died in battle.

Eugene distinguished himself in the battle by his courageous cavalry charges, but it was the duke of Lorraine's strategy that resulted in the destruction of the new grand vizier's forces. As the victors pushed south into Serbia, the sturdy mountain men of Montenegro ('black mountain') rebelled against the Ottomans. This was no surprise, since the Ottomans had never occupied that region – either their armies were too small to take every fort or they were so large that supplies quickly failed. The mountains were formidable, and the gorgeously moustached tribesmen gloried in the piles of enemy skulls that marked their borders.

The grand vizier was now desperate to reverse his fortunes – before the sultan gave the order for his strangulation. He rallied his retreating army and ordered it north for a surprise attack on the Christian army, only to have his bridge across the Danube collapse in a storm; since the bridge was loaded with men, many of them were lost, as well as most of the supplies. After the grand vizier was executed, the sultan was deposed (to spend the rest of his life as a prisoner in the Topkapi Palace), and the next summer Belgrade fell to the Bavarian duke.

Max Emanuel emerged from the war with a great reputation – as the 'Blue King'[6] he had won the admiration of even his Turkish opponents. His wife being Leopold's daughter (with a strong claim on the Spanish inheritance as well), and his Bavarian lands being rich, he saw himself as qualified to be Leopold's successor.[7] He may have been vain, a spendthrift and ambitious, but he was almost as good a general as he imagined himself. However, he was unwilling to wait for Leopold to die – that might take years (as, indeed, it did) – and there were Leopold's two sons ahead of him in the line of succession. Moreover, it was well known that he and his wife had not liked each other, and after her death two months after childbirth, he married a daughter of Jan Sobieski – which gave him an interest in Polish affairs, although that led nowhere. Slowly losing his interest in the Balkans, where he might have done more for his future hopes than he could see at the time, the Bavarian elector missed his chance to make himself the foremost champion of German arms.

The Ottoman hold on the Balkans had been loosened; even the Hungarian Protestants came over, temporarily, and while the advance into Transylvania was stymied by poor roads, bad weather and a lack of supplies, the presence of fine Bavarian units might have made possible an advance down the Danube from Belgrade.

Everything seemed to be going wrong for the new sultan, Suleiman II (1641–91). The Venetians captured much of the Dalmatian coastline, even taking Athens in September of 1687 – a short but memorable siege marked by a Venetian shell hitting the gunpowder magazine in the Parthenon, blowing the roof off and leaving the ancient structure in ruins. In 1688 the Bulgarians revolted; in 1689 the Ottoman governor of Rumelia (a 'Roman' province that included most of modern Macedonia and Thrace, including Istanbul) led his army against the capital.

The sultan hardly knew what to do. He did not lack intelligence, but the bureaucrats took such care to prevent him from knowing how to interfere in their business that he had neither the education nor experience to judge their effectiveness; like his predecessors, he was being assured that the duty of producing sons was more important than politics. The system allowed talented commoners to rise to power through the bureaucracy, even to become grand vizier, but there was no chance for another Suleiman the Great to appear. The name of the new sultan seemed more a mockery than a talisman of success.

There was intense infighting in the bureaucracy among those who saw themselves better qualified than their rivals, infighting that extended to the harem, where each mother intrigued to advance her eldest son – none had forgotten that in the past each new sultan had murdered all his half-brothers. The silken cord was employed regularly as grand viziers transferred nobles and warriors from one region to another, giving orders that could not be carried out, then fell out of favour themselves. There was no safe and predictable future for those in Ottoman employ – only opportunities, rewards and punishments.

The situation was turned around in 1689 when Grand Vizier Mustafa Köprülü (1637–91) persuaded Suleiman to follow his plans without question. This third member of the Köprülü dynasty made immediate improvements in the army and the hard-pressed financial situation, then drove the Habsburgs from Bulgaria and Transylvania. His counter-offensive found the Austrian forces so weakened by having sent troops to fight on the Rhine that he was able to recapture Belgrade in 1690. Although he was unwilling to make changes that modern historians see as necessary for revitalising the empire, his improvements in the performance of existing institutions and practices were obvious.

The dispute over power was not resolved. The sultan, unqualified to lead an army himself, relied on his grand vizier and the regional governors to act as they saw best to meet the challenges from Austria, Poland and Russia.[8] Since Suleiman II's resources were still great, and his subjects were far from bankrupt, Köprülü was able to lead a vigorous counterattack on the Christian forces. However, he faced immense challenges.[9]

The Christian Dilemma

The Christians were not much better off than the Ottomans. Unity was an illusion. Hopes that there would be a widespread uprising by the sultan's Orthodox subjects faded as hard experience taught local peoples how undependable their rescuers could be. There had been some early successes in winning over native Christians, such as Count Piccolomini impressing the citizens of Priština in 1689 by parading before them captured camels bearing monkeys and parrots – playing on a local legend about a future liberator. However, Piccolomini died of the plague, and his successor, Duke Georg Christian of Holstein, lacked his imagination and energy.

The greater danger was the French king, who was encroaching upon Germany, the Spanish Netherlands and Italy. In 1689 French armies ravaged Baden and the Palatinate and singled out the many Protestants there for rough treatment, driving many into exile. In *The Sun King* Nancy Mitford quotes a letter written to Louis a few years later from one of his most prominent courtiers, Fénelon, which said that an unjust war ruins a nation, that the king was rewarding those who should have been punished, that he loved glory more than justice, and that he neither loved nor knew God.

This tells us much about the Sun King, but absolves him of not allowing freedom of expression. That is, Louis XIV did not throw Fénelon into the Bastille, but appointed him bishop of Cambrai, effectively removing him from court. In France, exile was considered a worse fate than imprisonment – it usually lasted longer.

The king's tolerance had been similarly abused by the Conti brothers, descendants of the brother of the Great Condé and Mazarin's niece. While serving with the Austrian army in Vienna, they had written homosexual love letters to friends in France containing disparaging remarks about the king, unaware or uncaring that censors of the royal post would pass them on. An infuriated Louis XIV did not mourn when one died of smallpox after returning from the Turkish wars, and he banished the other from court for a short while.

The Sun King

Louis XIV was the most famous of the 'absolute rulers' of this era. He was less than impressive physically, but after he had put on high-heeled shoes and gathered more power into his hands than any earlier king had possessed, he radiated authority. His nobles and clergy hung on every word, hoping for some promise that would benefit them. Still, he was not absolute in the sense of having unlimited power. Hemmed in by tradition, ancient laws, requests by wives, relatives, friends and clerics, he needed to buy support, and by the very nature of the bureaucracies he had created, he could not lift the weight of institutions as easily as one of his mistresses' skirts – and even in that department affairs went less easily than he often wished. Still, he built palaces, encouraged the arts, promoted commerce and industry, and appointed capable subordinates to high office. Internal peace produced taxes and products that made it possible for him to support a fine army and buy allies, and the failure of his neighbours to do the same encouraged his sense of invincibility and entitlement. It was mainly when he aged – and his ministers aged, too – that he made mistakes, such as expelling the Huguenots from France and making crude demands that united his opponents. At all times he was impatient, unwilling to wait for the right moment – or thinking too soon that the right moment had come.

The Sun King, as he liked to be called, had a magnificent army. Remembering the Fronde, he trusted foreign officers more than his own nobles, but for the highest commands he groomed grandsons and relatives. When these proved either not ready or incompetent, he tried to co-ordinate operations on widely scattered fronts personally. Given the distances and his lack of accurate, up-to-date information, this was a bad administrative model, but it did give unity to campaigns stretching the length of the Rhine and along the Mediterranean. His successes and failures illustrate the strength and weakness of his position. The conflation of the monarch and the state meant that personal loyalty was still more important than patriotism: it was still 'Vive le roi', not 'Vive la France'.

France was still the most populous country in Europe, and the richest. Louis had many capable officers to choose from, and while some of his judgements were mistaken, on the whole he did no worse than most modern rulers. It was simply impossible to know which generals would be 'lucky' and which not, which could adapt to the skills (or lack thereof) of opposing commanders, and which would inspire troops to undergo hardship or forgo prompt payment of wages. The list of Louis's marshals could easily be used as the starting point for a military hall of fame – which is what the Invalides (the military hospital and retirement home) in Paris eventually became.

All Germans agreed that something had to be done to stop Louis – German lands were being lost, and Holland, an important territory in the Holy Roman Empire, was in danger. However, it was not until the Turkish war was ended that Leopold could take the lead in organising a grand alliance. Immediately after the capture of Belgrade in 1688 he had sent Eugene of Savoy to command imperial units on the Rhine. Similarly, he sent the duke of Lorraine west to reclaim his ancestral lands (which nevertheless remained firmly in French hands).

Only in 1691 could he send another great army into the Balkans, this time under the command of Louis of Baden (1655–1707), already known as 'Türkenlouis'.

Türkenlouis

The new commander – a cousin of Prince Eugene – was expected to make changes in the cautious strategy hitherto pursued. His personal resources were few, causing many to wonder why he had been selected by the emperor, who liked his commanders to supply a core of disciplined troops to the army. It was not just that Baden was a small princedom, but that he had to leave many of his troops at home to protect it against his neighbour, Louis XIV. The emperor understood this.

No one doubted Türkenlouis's capacity for leadership, but many were concerned that he was too daring – he was known to the Turks as the 'Red King' for his striking uniform that could be easily seen from any part of the battlefield, usually leading a devastating charge. To support him, Leopold raised a larger army than before – twenty thousand new men – and hired two thousand soldiers from Bavaria and six thousand from Prussia. Serbian volunteers joined as the army moved south, raising the total of Christian forces to eighty-five thousand men. The Ottomans matched that effort, then surpassed it. Mustafa Köprülü brought together ninety thousand soldiers, mostly cavalry, with five thousand camels and twenty-five thousand tents; the number of servants and slaves was almost beyond counting; there were more than 150 cannon, and many other firearms. But the grand vizier's strategy was defensive – to let the Christians exhaust themselves by long marches in the summer heat through depopulated regions that could provide neither food nor fodder, then find him waiting in a strong position. God would then deliver the Christians into his hands.

Türkenlouis advanced down the Danube in July, accompanied by a fleet of supply boats, until he reached the entrenched Ottoman forces at Semlin, between the Sava and Danube rivers. The imperial army was down now to about fifty thousand men, with at least five thousand disabled by disease, intense heat and poor food, and more falling ill every day. The Ottoman army was suffering, too, in spite of its legendary concern for hygiene. Nobody could avoid drinking polluted water. Indeed, nobody knew anything about germs. If the water looked clean, they drank it. This was one time when the Christian preference for alcoholic beverages proved an advantage.

In early August Türkenlouis put his troops into battle order – a somewhat risky formation based on long, thin lines – and moved towards the enemy fortifications. After closer study of the defences, which had been designed by French officers and protected by powerful cannon, he ordered his troops to pull back to Slankamen, to await the grand vizier's pleasure. No serious attack followed, though swarms of horsemen surrounded his bastions and harassed the men in the trenches.[10] News had just arrived that Suleiman II had died, making it difficult to know what his successor, Ahmed II (1642–95), would approve; and there was considerable doubt about what use the Tatar contingent would be – their recent record was not good. After two weeks the grand vizier shouted down those who advocated caution, then moved swiftly to seize the high ground on the Christians' right flank. That cut Türkenlouis off both from his supply base on the Danube and from the only good line of retreat; when the Ottoman fleet captured the Christian supply ships, Türkenlouis had to choose between surrender and fighting a pitched battle on Ottoman terms.

Sixty thousand Ottoman troops and thirty-four thousand Habsburg troops faced one another. Three times the Christian infantry stormed the Ottoman lines, only to be thrown back by the janissaries with heavy losses, the last time being followed back into their trenches, to be slaughtered almost without resistance until Türkenlouis's artillery broke up the attack. When the Christian forces on the left came forward only slowly and those on the right were almost wiped out, the Ottoman cavalry dashed forward to turn the retreat into a rout. However, the Brandenburg infantry stood firm, allowing Türkenlouis to rally his cavalry and charge into the flank of the attackers.

When the Turks fled back into their camp, the Christians attacked from all sides. As the Ottoman ranks fell into confusion and the grand vizier himself was endangered, the janissary band laid down their instruments and hurried to his rescue. The rest of the army, interpreting the sudden silence as a signal to retreat, fled the battlefield. Only the Ottoman cavalry made an escape; the infantry and most of the elite janissary corps was slaughtered. The next day twenty-five thousand Ottoman corpses were counted, against five thousand Habsburg fallen.

The Ottoman army would not recover from the disaster for years. The death of Mustafa Köprülü was almost as great a blow to Ottoman hopes as the losses in land and soldiers. Income from raids into Christian lands declined, and taxes and rents from Hungary ceased altogether. Still, as Rhoads Murphey explains, we know too little about war's impact on the Turkish economy – in Austria it stimulated production and created the growth of a class of middlemen who bought cattle, grain and other supplies and sold them to the army, and that was probably true for the Ottoman state, too, where the *Pax Ottomanica* provided the stability needed to encourage farmers and artisans to produce a surplus for the market. However, we cannot be certain, since contemporaries paid more attention to the drama of the battlefield than the counting house. There was certainly plenty of drama – the exotic nature of the 'other' was heightened by fascination with the famous leaders of the opposing armies.

By the time Türkenlouis had moved to Niš later in the month he had only sixteen thousand troops, a number insufficient for smashing what remained of the Ottoman army north of the Danube. More was not necessary, anyway. All Europe was celebrating the great battle at Slankamen: fireworks at the Vatican, the Order of the Golden Fleece for Türkenlouis, church bells ringing everywhere.

It was impossible, however, to follow up the victory the following year: Leopold needed all his resources to oppose Louis XIV's latest aggression. As the Austrians pulled back to defensible posts in Hungary, the Ottomans retaliated against Serbs who had risen in anticipation of a further Habsburg advance. To avoid annihilation, the archbishop of Peć led a mass migration of Serbs north into Croatia, where they were settled to shield the frontier against Ottoman attacks.[11]

When hostilities between the Austrian and Ottoman empires resumed in 1693, Leopold again entrusted Türkenlouis with command. Max Emanuel returned to Bavaria, where he made Munich into a centre of culture and the arts; the foremost of his achievements was enlarging the Nymphenburg Palace outside the city, a magnificent estate that had been started by his parents to celebrate his birth.

The man who became sultan in 1695, Mustafa II (1664–1704), was more fortunate than his predecessor – the Ottoman army had broken the two-year siege of Temesvar, a strategic city in Transylvania. The principal event of that year, however, as far as the Christians were concerned, was the presence of a new prince at the front – the twenty-five-year-old Augustus II (1670–1733) of Saxony, who brought twelve thousand finely appointed soldiers to Hungary. The elector's predecessors had made Saxony into a regional power. This permitted Augustus to hire more mercenaries than any of his rivals and equip them better.

He expected an easy victory. The Saxon army was the most modern in Europe: in 1686 it had introduced the first ring bayonets, and in 1687 the first flintlock muskets; it assigned a grenadier company to each regiment, and in 1692 created a new formation, the *grand mousequetaires* – mounted grenadiers. Augustus was also a larger-than-life figure – so powerful that he could bend horseshoes with his hands and women around his finger.

Unfortunately for Augustus's advanced corps on the Danube in 1695, he moved so slowly that it was savagely mauled by a more aggressive Ottoman army before he arrived. His tardiness can be somewhat excused, Rhoads Murphey explains, by the number of rivers and swamps that had to be crossed. Augustus was embarrassed, though his reputation as a lover was not harmed – a reputation more important to him than military glory. As a commander he had little to recommend him other than his birth and his well-drilled soldiers. Courage and determination meant little without energy and common sense.

Poland in Decline

As for Poland, after the death of Sobieski in 1696, the throne was clearly for sale again. It went to Augustus the Strong, whose Saxon lands bordered on Silesia, a historic province of Poland. There was the awkward fact that Silesia was an Austrian possession and lay between Saxony and the commonwealth, but Leipzig was still only a short journey from Cracow. A Saxon elector, now a convert to Catholicism, might just be the answer to Habsburg and Romanov aggression. At the very least, he was a very rich man.

Augustus the Strong's only serious competitor was Max Emanuel of Bavaria, but his marital and martial connections to the late king worked against him. Augustus, however, found that becoming king of Poland was easier than governing the country. Saxons were hard working and deferential, Poles were not – or, to put it less crassly, Saxons expected to keep the fruits of their labours, while recent Polish history suggested that whenever a Pole created something, some foreigner would show up to steal it from him. About all that could not be taken away was pride.

The first two decades of the next century were to be disastrous for the Polish–Lithuanian Commonwealth. Maurice de Saxe, the most prominent of Augustus's many illegitimate sons, linked the military weakness and the political paralysis. In *Reveries, or Memoirs on the Art of War* he looked back on his years of service there:

Poland is an open and extensive country, without fortified towns, well peopled, and abounds in grain, cattle, and all the necessaries of life; it has plenty of wood, a number of large rivers, all which are navigable, and great sums of money. The air is wholesome, it is entirely free from those disorders which are peculiar to other climates, foreigners enjoy as good health in it as the natives, and it is altogether adapted by nature for the seat and support of war.

This was perhaps too much of a good thing. Once a foreign ruler built a fortress inside the kingdom, the Poles could not get him out. The Poles had few cannon, little ammunition and – given the current government – no likelihood of acquiring more of either. They had the stores for campaigns, but could not provide them to their armies. Their cavalry was too swift to bother pursuing, but was also incapable of defeating well-organised troops. De Saxe remembered hearing of an incident in 1716, when a Polish uprising threatened his father's government. Twenty thousand Poles surrounded the queen's regiment of cavalry, persuading them by sheer numbers to surrender. A few hours later they murdered their prisoners, then marched against two regiments of Saxon dragoons. These Germans, knowing that surrender was no longer an option, managed to defeat the entire Polish army, capturing more than twenty pairs of kettle-drums and large numbers of standards and colours – clear proof of the extent of their victory.

At that very time de Saxe was in Lithuania, where a Saxon commander agreed to surrender his fort on honourable terms. He then drove out with a wagon loaded with money, a great temptation to the Poles, who debated for two days whether pursuing him was honourable or not, before setting off to steal the treasure. With only a guard of eighty horsemen the commander fought off ten times as many attackers.

Poles made poor infantry, de Saxe said, because though they offer themselves in droves, when the crisis comes, they run off, leaving their employer in the lurch. Worse, they would proceed to loot their own country, making it difficult for a commander to supply his men.

Could Poland defend itself? De Saxe said that a small tax on beer would suffice to sustain an army of 350,000 men, and sufficient men could be raised by requiring each parish to supply one man. However, it was impossible to persuade the Sejm to pass the laws or create the bureaucracy necessary to enforce them.

De Saxe was a German, of course, and his attitude reflected what became a long-standing German contempt of everything Polish. Reality was more complex. The professional infantry (*piechota łanowa*) was good, but – as de Saxe noted – there was never enough money to hire many of them. Efforts to replace them in emergencies by summoning all males to military service (*pospolite ruszenie*) were foredoomed to failure. Lastly, so many of the best Polish professionals were slain in the civil conflicts of this era that when the time came to face foreign armies, there were too few left, as well as too little money, for them to be effective.

Peter the Great of Russia

Although Peter was a gigantic figure (six feet eight inches tall, as well as throwing a great shadow over the events of his lifetime) he found it difficult to drag Russia into the West.[12] Finding tradition a major obstacle to his plans, he tried to abolish old forms wherever he found them – from his famous shaving of beards and requiring his courtiers to wear Western clothing to building a new capital at St Petersburg; from requiring wives to leave seclusion and attend court to naming foreigners to important offices. At first, he had little support outside his modest circle of military experts ('a tiny garrison in an alien land', as William McNeill called them in *The Rise of the West*). Peter enlarged this number by requiring nobles' sons to enter the military academy and the army, then rebuilding the military forces along the lines of Western armies, and selecting the most talented officers to staff his administration. The reformers' small numbers accounts for the relative moderation of their later internal disputes – if Westernisers took their quarrels too far, traditionalists would destroy them all. In *Europe's Steppe Frontier*, McNeill says that the Orthodox Church, shaken by the Old Believers' withdrawal from this world into ecstatic visions of the next, was shrinking back in fear of all change; but since those churchmen were fearful of peasant discontent, they did not oppose the tsar openly. As for the boyars,

Peter was able to bribe many of them, often offering their sons positions in his army and administration if they responded properly to training.

The task of reorganising both state and society, then taking the new army across the steppe to the Crimea was immense – too great, in fact. The army had to turn back when the Tatars burned the fields, depriving the horses of grass.[13] The next time he carried fodder with him.

Peter's timing was lucky – his aggressive moves against the Turkish and Tatar bases on the Black Sea coincided with Ottoman weakness and indecision, and with Poland–Lithuania's relapse into constitutional stalemate and economic recession. Peter's later invasion of Livonia was possible because Saxony, Poland and Denmark had agreed to attack Sweden in what they thought was a moment of weakness – a young and untried king, Charles XII, coming to the throne.[14]

As it happened, Charles XII was a military genius, a leader who routed superior forces again and again; his determination to prevail combined with a seeming invulnerability to allow him to overthrow his enemies' best mercenary armies. However, his political mistakes were also numerous – none worse than his assumption that the Turks would see how greatly they could profit by joining in his wars. Peter suffered repeated setbacks at the hands of the Swedes and failed to achieve easy victories against the Ottomans, but the seemingly endless resources of Russia, combined with his enemies' inability to concentrate their forces against him, allowed him to survive until his reforms took hold.

It was not easy to reform the Russian army, but, as was true in the past, Peter's mercenary officers did marvels with the peasant draftees. They could not make the common soldiers think, but in the warfare of the era that was not always essential – Russians could survive on little food and less clothing, they were courageous beyond reason, and good fighters when well led. They were, alas, also addicted to drink, prone to panic and at a loss what to do when their officers were slain.

It was no accident that Peter the Great favoured foreign officers for his army and navy. He could not trust the prominent boyars of his realm – individually, some saw themselves equally worthy of being tsar; collectively, they distrusted his policies. They were also traditionalists in military matters. Peter, who had travelled across Europe, understood the rapid changes that were occurring in military practices and believed that they could be implemented in Russia. Boyars were simply too proud to concern themselves with the petty details of command – inspection, supervision, supply, engineering and dealing with commoners. As for the soldiers, they were brave, uncomplaining and loyal; but promoting men from the ranks was impossible for every reason imaginable. Only foreigners seemed to have the knack for turning them into soldiers; moreover, foreigners were no danger to the boyars' traditional pretensions.

One of the first officers Peter recruited was Charles Eugène de Croy (1651–1703), the nephew of the governor of the Spanish Netherlands. However, since his uncle had been blessed with many sons, de Croy embarked on a military career. In December of 1676 he found himself serving the Danish king, fighting alongside Dutch mercenaries. At the battle of Lund, one of the most desperate engagements in Scandinavian history, he barely escaped the massacre (nine thousand bodies on the battlefield, other troops drowned), being saved, perhaps, by the merciful early sunset. In Austrian employ he fought at Vienna in 1683 and at the siege of Belgrade in 1690, after which he was named imperial field marshal. De Croy entered Russian service in 1697, but was defeated and captured at Narva by Charles XII in 1700. The Swedes held him prisoner in Reval until his death. His place was taken by his protégé, Peter von Lacy (1678–1751), an Irishman whose story of battles against Turks, Swedes and Poles is among the most fantastic of the era.[15]

Another adventurer was Patrick Gordon (1635–99), a Catholic Scot who had gone to Poland in 1651 to further his education and four years later sought to enlist in a Scottish regiment there. Unsuccessful, he was almost desperate when he heard that the Swedish army was looking for soldiers. The Swedes were willing to overlook his not being a Protestant, or, under the assumption that all Scots were Calvinists, had not asked. Wounded and discharged in Poland, he was on his way to join another regiment when he was captured. After weeks of captivity, he agreed to enlist in a Polish regiment. After serving long enough to learn Polish, he was captured by Germans in the Swedish army and persuaded to change sides again. After three years he was captured by Polish peasants and ended up once again in Polish employ. Not long afterwards he was captured by Austrian troops, but his wounds were sufficient excuse for not changing sides again until he was well enough to escape. After more complicated adventures, he went to Russia in 1660, married, and earned a great reputation as a battlefield commander. He was in charge of the troops in Moscow when the crisis arose over whether Peter or his sister Sophia would rule. He chose Peter, thus beginning a long friendship with the tsar, a friendship that allowed him to write a diary filled with intimate details of the tsar's habits. Gordon did not accompany Peter on his famous trip through Europe, but remained behind to see that the realm was protected from attack or domestic insurrection. Gordon populated the ranks of the Russian officer corps with sons and relatives.

Peter's practice was to time his wars with those of Austria against Turkey and of Saxony/Poland against Sweden. He was not chivalrous in the sense of desiring a personal duel with his foes – he was a fellow who put his feet up on fine furniture, patted the prettiest women and drank himself into a stupor. In short, not a gentleman – but Peter the Great held a rank higher than gentleman: he was the tsar of all the Russias.

Eugene Returns to the Balkans

The Treaty of Rijswijk brought an end to Austria's war with France in 1697. Almost immediately the emperor began transferring troops to the Balkan front. It was about time, contemporaries thought. The most recent campaigns, led first by Aeneas Silvius de Caprara (1631–1701), then Augustus the Strong, had been miserable failures; neither commander showed any spark of energy or genius – Augustus even carried a billiard table with him. After Augustus's departure, the emperor wanted to reappoint Caprara, but the president of the war council, Rüdiger von Starhemberg, persuaded him to give command for the 1697 campaign to Eugene of Savoy.

The imperial army was camped at Peterwardein, an almost impregnable fortress overlooking the Danube. Derek McKay in *Prince Eugene of Savoy* notes how the troops must have been struck by their young commander – a short, thin man wearing a modest brown tunic. The contrast to the flashy generals of the recent past could hardly be greater, but as they grew to admire his soldierly and human qualities, they called him affectionately the 'little Capuchin', or simply 'Prinz Eugen'. They knew that no one would mistake him for a Franciscan monk with a passion for pacifism; he was a cavalryman, with a cavalryman's enthusiasm for combat.

Prince Eugene's enthusiasm for his troops was more measured. Indeed, he had thirty thousand Austrian, Saxon and Prussian soldiers, but they had not been paid, fed or trained properly; discipline was miserable. All he dared do, he wrote, was to defend the fortresses along the Danube.

The Ottoman grand vizier had apparently come to the same conclusion as Eugene about the state of the Christian troops – and decided to deal with him as roughly as he had with de Caprara and Augustus. When the grand vizier crossed the Danube, he brought with him wagonloads of chains for the prisoners he intended to sell in the slave markets of the Islamic world.

Fortunately for Prince Eugene, his complaints and warnings had been taken seriously. The emperor authorised a determined recruiting effort, so that by the time the campaign began, Eugene had fifty thousand men at his disposal, most of them paid. However, it was not the larger numbers that made the difference, but rather Eugene's initiative in acting on intelligence. In September, learning that the Turks were having difficulty crossing the Tisza River, he hurried south to Zenta, driving his soldiers so hard that they arrived before the Turks even learned of their approach. Finding the enemy cavalry and artillery unprepared to meet him, and the infantry still on the opposite bank, he attacked immediately. The panicked Ottoman formations retreated to the river bank, where ten thousand drowned trying to swim across and twenty thousand were slaughtered trying to get to the bridges; the grand vizier, courageously attempting to rally his forces, was slain by his own panicked men. Prince Eugene lost only three hundred soldiers.

The emperor appreciated the fact that Eugene presented no challenge to his dynasty; therefore, he gave him increasing authority over all military affairs. As for Eugene, the income from his monasteries in Savoy allowed him to build a town house in Vienna, buy the gardens for his future palace at Belvedere, enjoy an impressive country estate and even acquire a respectable lady friend. As a churchman, he could not marry. Surprisingly, he did not even have children.

The Peace of Karlowitz (January 1699) gave the emperor all the lands north of the Danube and Sava rivers, while Poland received the lands north and west of the Black Sea, and Venice took part of the Dalmatian coast. The Ottoman Empire had survived, but the sultan retained only the southern half of the Balkans.

*   *   *

God's will, inscrutable and inescapable, had given victory to the infidels. What use was it to attempt reform? Man's fate was in God's hands, why should one struggle against it? As it happened, such fatalism was rewarded. In a sense, God did come to his people's aid, or at least religion did. With the Christian nations going to war with one another in 1700 (the Great Northern War) and 1701 (the War of the Spanish Succession), there would be a decade and a half of peace, during which the Ottoman army was able to revitalise itself in its traditional forms.

CHAPTER NINE

Summary
The Evolution of Warfare

Armies in 1700

By 1700 the rulers of states had their armies firmly in hand. Mercenaries were still common, but they were no longer in command or out of control; private armies had almost ceased to exist. Henceforth the kings and princes supervised military bureaucracies that allocated commands, provided arms and mounts, defined proper uniforms and dress, and even offered retirement benefits – in 1674 Louis XIV founded the Invalides in Paris for crippled, ill and aged veterans, and in 1682 Charles II (1630–85) founded the Royal Hospital in Chelsea. As garrisons were wintered at the same places year after year, the government either provided barracks or rented properties; this doubtless stimulated the local economies, and the sale of stimulants brought in even more money. As civilians were hired to haul supplies and to provide services such as butchering, cooking and baking, carpentry and blacksmithing, they brought their earnings home, offsetting considerably the taxes that supported the military, the court and other expenses.

Prostitutes did well, too, reducing the surplus of marriageable women that military service had created by taking away young males. What else was a young woman to do, once strangers had taken her virginity by rape or seduction? Prostitution, John Lynn II, reminds us, was always discouraged by rulers, churchmen and officers, who often imposed severe penalties on loose women as threats to the health and morals of the soldiers – and, perhaps more telling, because the men tended to fight over them. But, with young men being spirited (and often full of spirits), and marriage discouraged or even forbidden to soldiers, brothels abounded and the camp equivalents of street walkers were everywhere. Syphilis and other venereal diseases undoubtedly laid low more men than enemy gunfire, but men far from wives and girlfriends and without money for prostitutes were liable to desert.

This led to a most important development: the territorial rulers beginning to pay the owners of regiments a subsidy based on the number of men and animals on the pay rolls. Since the number of men actually in the ranks was never equal to the paper strength of a regiment, the noble owners could pocket the difference; this profit could then be enhanced by charging men for uniforms and equipment – a practice that probably began to discourage them from selling their possessions to support their drinking habits or to pay prostitutes. The owners often hired officers to perform the irksome duties of training and disciplining the men, and, when necessary, to face hostile fire and the hardships of campaigns.

Many nobles took their duties seriously, or would have – to the extent consistent with court responsibilities and safety – but rulers discouraged them from learning the arts of war by using subjects who were more valuable at home working and paying taxes. It was much better, as far as it was practical, to hire foreigners as commanders and recruit cannon-fodder from other nations as well. Of course, the nobles wanted opportunities to demonstrate their courage and competence, but once they had done the minimum, most were ready to hurry back to the extravagances of Versailles and its many imitations. Military service was dirty, dangerous (illness being the most serious threat) and boring.

The Future

The Christian armies of the wars just before 1700 had evolved significantly from earlier ones. First of all, they were much larger. Second, since it was now impossible (or highly undesirable) for soldiers to feed themselves from forage alone, commanders sent away most non-combatants. Women and boys attached to individual soldiers had once been essential, but now they were merely extra mouths to feed. Supplies could be transported easily by water, but once an army advanced overland, it became difficult to feed the large number of men and horses. Therefore, the importance of great fortresses that could serve as supply depots became critical.

Louis XIV had built an elaborate series of great fortifications along his western and northern frontiers, then pressed across the Rhine; he had been rebuffed until 1701 when he made a grandson king of Spain, then the next year made an alliance with Max Emanuel of Bavaria. With the anti-French alliance thoroughly shattered, the Sun King expected that he could finally overcome his hereditary Habsburg enemy, whose loyal German princes and Dutch and English allies were badly divided; his nobles, generals and priests urged him to exploit the moment to make himself master of the Holy Roman Empire. What he did not calculate correctly was that his aggression would cause his enemies to set aside their many mutual grievances in order to fight against him. The constant likelihood that the German–Dutch–English coalition would disintegrate encouraged him to persist, but thanks to gifted politicians and generals such as Prince Eugene and the duke of Marlborough,[1] Louis's golden opportunity eventually came to nothing, with France reduced to poverty and starvation, Holland bankrupted, Spain embarrassed, the German states frustrated and angered by their powerlessness, and poor Ireland left half-way between rebellion and occupation. Only the newly formed United Kingdom emerged victorious – with a vastly expanded maritime empire and, later, the acquisition of Hanover in Germany. The war debts were a heavy strain on the British budget, but commercial returns made them bearable. If Whigs were overjoyed, in time even the Tories came to accept the new circumstances as too good to risk upsetting.

Still, Britain's rise to supremacy was by no means assured. As Brauer and van Tuyll tell us in *Castles, Battles & Bombs*, Marlborough would choose to risk everything on pitched battles because he saw that he would lose a campaign of attrition. Had the French commanders been better, or had Marlborough suffered bad luck or become incapacitated, the superior wealth and numbers of France would have prevailed.

Such a statement might be remembered when someone doubts the importance of the individual in history, or when one hears that any given nation's success or failure was inevitable. Who in 1600 would have predicted the decline of Turkey or the rise of England?

Warfare After 1700

War implies – most of the time – a declared state of hostility between states, openly conducted by violent means, but limited by traditional practices, religious beliefs and the laws of war. The rules formulated by Hugo Grotius (1583–1645) to govern military conduct have been widely acknowledged to be universally applicable, but writing down the commonly accepted rules came less from theories than from acknowledging what was actually occurring, or following Roman precedents. Warfare had changed between 1500 and 1700 from a conflict between dynasties (rulers who viewed the state more or less as private property) to one between states (which involved important citizens and even many unimportant ones). This adjustment took place so slowly that even foreign mercenary officers found it relatively easy to accommodate themselves to it. Just as we needed to consider whether or not early contract armies resembled unions more than businesses, we need to be open to other new interpretations of old ideas. Our efforts to impose clarity upon practices of the past can lead to missing nuances; real life can be messy. Changes often occur over time, do not occur all at once, and sometimes occur in mysterious ways.

Bert Hall states in *Weapons and Warfare* that one of the advantages of the Swiss and German mercenaries was their social cohesion – both were recruited from lands with proud regional traditions. The same was true of Castilians in the Spanish armies. This phenomenon requires us to modify the widely held belief that mercenaries were usually foreigners. Yet even the Castilians were foreigners in a sense, because they so often served in Italy or the Low Countries. In general, when military units had to replace losses, they recruited wherever they were, thereby diluting the original ethnic core. The exception was the Swiss. When an employer hired Swiss, he expected to get Swiss. This made such units more expensive, but there were times when one got what one paid for.

A problem arose when it became clear that there were not enough Swiss for everyone to employ them as combat troops. More commonly rulers hired a small number as guardsmen. As foreigners they were not concerned with local politics and court intrigue, but more importantly, they were not easily corrupted and they excelled on parade and at ceremonial occasions.[2] Fortunately for rulers with limited incomes, their officers could find acceptable recruits almost anywhere. Good officers could fill the ranks, train the men and lead them into combat.

By the start of the sixteenth century mercenary armies were important for campaigns in foreign lands that lasted longer than knights were obliged to serve, and because professional soldiers were more competent than amateur ones. In the same sense, navies need trained, experienced seamen. When Charles V faced the combination of Ottoman and French fleets in 1541, and Venice was trying to curry favour with the sultan by remaining neutral, he hired Genoa's famed admiral, Andrea Doria and his slave-powered galleys. In time, though, the emperor learned that it was better to rely on military orders such as the Knights of St John, which had significant incomes of their own and, therefore, did not have as great a cash flow problem.[3] Without their ships the siege of Malta in 1565, the battle at Lepanto in 1571 and earlier Portuguese battles in the Indian Ocean would have been lost.

The early contract armies were less expensive than a standing army, and they could be raised relatively quickly, but often rulers did not have sufficient time before they had to confront enemies.[4] Moreover, the commander of a contract army – a Sforza, for example – might just take over the state. While this was rare after 1600, the potential of a Wallenstein or Cromwell coming forth was something that rulers dared not forget.

What was the alternative? It took time before something approximating modern armed forces was possible, but when standing armies were created, everything changed. The soldiers were always somewhat ready to fight, they rarely engaged in 'sit-down strikes', and an army could be larger because it was less dependent on pillage to feed itself. Such armies were also more easily co-ordinated because the officers were more dependent on the rulers' good will, and more deadly because of better weaponry and training.

As these armies began to represent national institutions, defending national interests, citizens began to see themselves not only as subjects of the lord to whom they owed taxes and services, but also as subjects of a more distant king whose armies were protecting them; or they began to think of themselves as Germans or Frenchmen or even Britons. National identity was still a nursling, but it had been born.

This shift in allegiance was especially noticeable among nobles, whose once-powerful class interests dissolved into competition for office. Feudalism, Brauer and van Tuyll note, was not abolished, but it was being superseded. Kings and princes remained wary of their immediate underlings, who were relinquishing their archaic rights as vassals only because the opportunities for self-advancement were greater if they became officials and officers.

Changes in social and intellectual life emphasised the lessened importance of monarchs, but this was obscured by the theatre of court life and pageantry. Field marshals, generals and colonels realised this, too – they paid little attention to intellectual trends, but they applied themselves to making their troops as splendidly garbed as possible, with flags, music and medals all contributing to impressing the public (and potential recruits) with the glory and utility of their profession.

As France came to replace Spain as the dominant nation in western Europe, the French language and French customs spread rapidly into the neighbouring states. To hold one's head up in polite society required that it be full of French ideas.

In this shift towards identifying oneself with a particular state, and often simultaneously copying French customs, western Europeans tended to identify with the Christendom that was expressed in the wars against the Ottoman Turks and against Muslims in Africa and the Indian Ocean.

Also, just as patriotism was becoming important, the professional warrior was becoming more prominent – demonstrated valour gaining on inherited status. This should have reminded people of why some individuals were noble and others not – that is, some had ancestors who had excelled on the battlefield and in court, while everyone else had to rely on talent, training and luck, which were not enough to break through the class barrier. It was not easy to persuade nobles that self-control and leadership were more important than impulsive deeds of derring-do, but well-aimed bullets tended to correct excesses in stupidity. Every battlefield casualty bled red blood; blue was only a figure of speech.

Officers and non-commissioned officers could make any kind of raw youth into fighting material quickly, then season him in victorious combats.[5] They could also manipulate larger and more complex armies, armies that could be raised only by drafting civilians into lifetime military service. These new armies embodied the nation-state in its early stages of development. Once rulers could dispense with foreign officers, they could become the heads of truly national armies, but since they wanted to have their citizens working, producing and paying taxes, they could not do away with mercenaries altogether. The usual compromise was to fill the ranks with a combination of local men drafted for service (usually ones who would be least missed by society) and hired foreigners.

This was followed by the almost total disappearance of camp followers, which included soldiers' wives and cohabiting women. This restriction on the sexual licence that drew some men into military service then led to an expansion of prostitutes.

Lastly, there were those rulers who rented out their armies at a profit. They were not mercenaries themselves – their role was more that of a pimp.

Who Was a Mercenary?

The answer to the question poised in the Preface – who was a mercenary? – might now be somewhat clearer. If we mean that a mercenary is someone who fights for money, for any employer willing to hire him, our answer will probably imply that he is the scum of the earth. That was an opinion as widely held between 1500 and 1700 as it is today, but, as often happens once we dig deeper into circumstances and motivations, we find that this definition leaves out a great many people, and includes others who, if they could come back to confront their accusers, would probably challenge them to appear on a field of honour. Duels were fought by some very reputable people in those days, as were wars. An accusation of being solely interested in money was not made lightly.

In Ancient Rome, in Machiavelli's Florence and in early modern times, the ideal soldier fought for his sovereign or for his native or adopted homeland, either voluntarily or when summoned to perform his civic duty, without regard for money and often at considerable personal sacrifice. Moreover, the expectation that soldiers should care nothing about money excludes almost everyone except figures in literature.[6]

Fritz Redlich demonstrates in *The German Military Enterpriser* that the men who organised war in this era were businessmen as well as warriors. They understood how to profit not only from cheating their troops and extorting 'contributions' from civilians, but also from the sale of weapons, clothing and horses. They had, however, financial limitations – when employers did not pay them, they could not pay their men; and when rulers had difficulties borrowing money, regimental commanders were even less likely to find bankers willing to advance cash. Iron laws, however, kept them in arms: war was not only the occupation they understood best, but it was the only way to prevent their savings – should there be any – from being stolen by other mercenaries.

Inflation was one reason for the instability of monetary values that bedevilled rulers, bankers and soldiers alike. For those who raised mercenary armies, it meant that interest rates were higher, making it difficult to borrow money; while this was a problem for rulers with limited incomes, at such times poor men were more willing to enlist, and for lower wages.[7] Thus, when times were bad, the recruiter's life was good. However, when the wages of a day labourer exceeded those of a soldier, and unpaid soldiers were going into debt to sutlers and merchants, recruiting was not easy. Still, military life always had its attractive aspects, one of which was job security; pay was relatively dependable, there were no taxes, and no skills were required – the army would teach recruits everything they needed to know.

It may be that soldiers are judged much as women used to be – that there were either honest women or whores, with no Hawthorne to point out how unfair it was to pin a scarlet A on any who fell short of purity. One might say that soldiers and women alike crossed the line when they became professionals, but it was not so long ago that the institution of marriage itself was being attacked as nothing more than a financial arrangement that should be abolished. Today one hears, it seems, from the same quarter, that armies are not necessary, either, nor even police. That pretty much closes out any rational discussion of mercenaries.

Criminal behaviour is the issue that lurks just out of sight here. The assumption seems to be that armed men will be criminals, and that unarmed men will be civilised. Cynics will say that the argument should be reversed; a middle position suggests that human beings are not always moral, but neither are they always evil, and rarely are they committed pacifists. In fact, the years between 1500 and 1700 were not easy for pacifists. Between feuding religious factions, taxes and recruiting sergeants, they were always looking for a refuge where armed rulers would defend them; they found this most dependably in England and its American colonies. In the next century Voltaire could praise the toleration of Ottoman Turkey, but without dwelling on the fact that Christians and Jews there were second-class citizens. Of course, Protestants were second-class citizens in France, as were Catholics in Ireland. Even Voltaire admitted that life at the top of Ottoman society was uncertain and usually short. Most people may have believed that any kind of civilian existence was better than army life, but soldiers knew better.

Army morals were a reflection of the three societies that made up the military. There were the youthful males, full of hormones, insecurities, bravado and vitality. Veterans were less exuberant: experience and hardship having made them grimly realistic about life and its apparent meaninglessness; they became the non-commissioned officers who were the heart of the new armies – professionals who could whip (sometimes literally) recruits into shape and who despised those civilians who (out of their hearing) deplored their occupation and their table manners. Then there were the officers, who were supposed to be gentlemen – but gentlemen in an era when 'drunk as a lord' was not necessary a condemnation. Good leaders set good examples for both men and officers, but combat had a way of blurring the distinctions between right and wrong. Religion was of some help, especially to those sitting around a campfire on cold nights in a strange land, pulling their cloaks tightly about them in a vain effort to keep off the rain and puffing on long curved pipes with metal tops covering the bowls, but less so to lusty men in a bar with pay in their pockets.

For various reasons today's armies have employed men who are often denounced as mercenaries. One reason is an effort to increase the 'teeth to tail' ratio (that is, fighting men versus support personnel); another is to avoid exposing men to danger. Therefore, modern military and political leaders 'outsource' supply service and hire contractors to provide experienced men willing to stand guard at heavily fortified compounds and buildings. Some commentators who dislike any required military service criticise 'volunteer armies' as encouraging enlistment for money alone. This is an intellectually consistent position only for pacifists, but it provides cover for those who believe that wars are only made for bad motives or who advocate wars that are not being fought over those currently in the news. Some Western nations have found a compromise in national service, with military duty as one of the choices. This is often accompanied by ignoring individuals who refuse to do anything.

Historians are especially challenged to explain how this came to be. An even greater challenge – and not just for historians – may lie in resisting pressure to see teaching as a revolutionary act – to prepare students for specific kinds of political and social engagement. Such political posturing tends to ignore military history. It is this author's opinion that judging men of earlier eras by today's standards is no more satisfactory than teaching a 'usable past' that speaks to current politics but not to possible futures. In the past men were moved by ideology or religious convictions, or even patriotism, to enlist in foreign armies.[8] If they were not able to pay their own expenses as volunteers, should we condemn them for that? By one definition they are mercenaries, by another they are not. For them money might be only a means to a noble end. Whether an end was noble or not depends on one's political beliefs. To close off discussion of this topic is to pretend that the future will not present us with new challenges.

This then is a partial answer to one question raised in the Preface – whether mercenaries of the early modern era have much to tell us about mercenaries today – yes, something. However, those were other lands, other customs, other times – today is today, and tomorrow will be tomorrow.

Why Were There Mercenaries?

Mercenaries were, by definition, serving for money, but they were far from alone in considering a dependable income important. As Marx tried to tell his followers who took his general principles as universal rules, money and class cannot explain all individual motivations. Our sources tell us quite a bit about military officers, but little about common soldiers. What we do know about officers indicates that many who served foreign lords picked employers whose political goals seemed to aid their homeland or their religion, or were at least not hostile to them.

Western mercenaries fought for the tsar, but would they have served the Tatar khan or the Turkish sultan in substantial numbers? Probably not – word about the silken cord had spread widely, and no officer could guarantee victory in every encounter. The tsar pressured his mercenaries to convert to Orthodoxy; the sultan did the same for Islam. Protestants and Catholics resisted as best they could – most importantly, probably, by taking employment elsewhere.

Revenge was a common motive – the Irish serving in French armies, for example, or Huguenots in British service. Poverty drove many to seek employment – Scots, whose lands were never rich but were being lost to enclosures; or inhabitants of war-ravaged lands who could feed their families from the enlistment bonus. Sometimes being in an army was the only safe refuge from enemies, much like inmates in prison joining a gang; sometimes perceived common interests, such as all Christians fighting 'the Turk', lasted only until the danger had passed. All these motives have to be taken into account, as well as adventurism, boredom and escaping personal and family problems. In all these cases the money was essential, but nevertheless of secondary importance. As James Miller says in *Swords for Hire*, loyalty could always be tested by a lack of pay, but other motives, usually mixed motives, were more significant.

In an age when only nobles were trained in the practice of arms, it was not always important that there be a war to keep them occupied; if they retired in middle age, their finances might be strained by efforts to keep up with their peers, but they rarely faced starvation. Should they decide to chuck it all in, there were plenty of male pheasants in the fields and female peasants in the barns. But when commoners were drafted or conscripted into armies as teenagers, after a few years of service they had no alternative profession to follow. For them the military life was all they knew; it was the only skill they had. When employers decided to dismiss their troops, those men had to seek out some new employer or, as often happened, ended up in the poorhouses and jails of their homelands. Communities were intolerant of idle or unemployed men, especially those in the habit of taking whatever they needed or wanted.

As Thorstein Veblen noted a century ago in *The Theory of the Leisure Class*, there was little difference between the upper classes of 1900 and the lowest ones, except money. Both saw leisure as the essence of the good life and both enhanced their status by acts of violence and wasteful spending; both happily wore uniforms and practised sexual promiscuity – but only the rich were lauded for these habits. The upper classes provided the officers, the commoners the cannon-fodder.

Casualties were high for both groups, from camp diseases and bad water as well as enemy action. Both groups were patriots, though many troops on actual service were (as best we can tell) often cynical patriots who became more prideful of their achievements in old age. This is not unknown even today.

Those great lords who rented out their armies sometimes resembled mafia gangsters; some were vain dilettantes, some were bored with any distraction from their personal pleasure. Noble though they might be, surely they were as much a part of the system as any criminals they might employ. They wore perfume, but they did not bathe often. And their morals stank.

What were their alternatives? One rose or one sank. Staying put was no option. Chekov's hopelessly useless family in *The Cherry Orchard* is a sad commentary on once-proud people who have lost their purpose in society, surviving only because a distant tsar protected the frontiers and maintained social peace.

A Military Revolution?

It is almost a truism that the states that survived the Darwinian political struggles of this era did so because those rulers were better able to utilise the human and natural resources of their lands than their rivals. This meant the development of bureaucracies that encouraged commerce, built roads and bridges, taxed their subjects and required them to perform military service. However, it is easy to exaggerate these developments. There was too much variety in Europe to extend generalisations from advanced countries to every corner of the continent. What was true in the Low Countries was not so elsewhere – the Balkans and the steppe presented such vastly different challenges that one should be surprised if western European practices were effective at all. Though we find mercenaries there aplenty.

Some scholars disagree with the connection of improved military technology with the rise of the nation-state. Jeremy Black, in *European Warfare, 1494–1660*, argues that there was minimal connection between war and absolute kings. This is an important statement because absolutism is the usual intermediate state between feudalism (aristocratic rule) and republics (democracies).[9] Instead, Black argues, rulers managed to co-opt the elites, a process that renders the term 'absolute' meaningless. Though Sweden and Holland made themselves into fiscal-military states, an alternative form of political organisation to absolute monarchy, they found few imitators. In short, the development of firearms led neither to a military revolution, nor one that affected the organisation of the state.

Geoffrey Parker, in *The Military Revolution: Military Innovation and the Rise of the West, 1500–1800*, notes that the capital ship, infantry firepower and the artillery fortress were all developed in the sixteenth century; the West built on these to dominate the world. He is reluctant, however, to apply the word 'revolution' to developments that took place over three long centuries.

Bert Hall, in *Weapons and Warfare*, observes that 'general political historians' find the term 'military revolution' useful. The comment was a nice touch – thereby suggesting that such historians do not know what they are talking about. Hall's own ideas emphasise a series of technological innovations and the increased professionalism of officers and men. War was not a part-time activity, but, like nineteenth-century industrialism, it changed everything.

Some find this debate fascinating, others tire of it quickly. What exactly does it have to tell us about today's world? Many of us see a connection between well-run militaries and well-run states, both in the centuries discussed here and today – just as in the chicken and egg problem, no matter which came first, one certainly led to the other. We do not see Cossacks and Tatars establishing national states, no matter how courageous and competent their individual warriors or their leaders were. Only those states that developed bureaucracies that could collect taxes and spend the money wisely remained powerful into the 1700s and even after the French Revolution.

John Lynn II, in *Women, Armies and Warfare*, notes the positions taken by Black and Parker, then dryly comments that if 'modernisation' has any meaning, it is that the new situation is more like that of today than it had been, and that was indeed the case in Europe between 1650 and 1700. Armies were more efficient and there was a state apparatus to support them; if the king was not an absolute ruler, he did have more authority than before, especially in organising the officers according to a hierarchy of ranks that limited the influence of noble ancestry and excluded private military entrepreneurs. The 'state commission army' not only was more efficient, but it reduced domestic turmoil and pillage abroad, thereby legitimising the state as the protector of the citizenry.

Fritz Redlich confirms this development in *The German Military Enterpriser* – officers were transformed from businessmen to state employees. Crude immorality and brutal behaviour gave way to the arts of the courtier; not surprisingly, the nobility saw its chance and took it – monopolising the officer corps and making it ultra-respectable.

Lynn notes that Louis XIV increased the size of the army four-fold, improved its weaponry and tactics, and brought every general under royal control, but failed fiscal policies eventually led the Capetian dynasty to decapitation.[10]

The French Revolution changed everything, or close to everything. It was not that the circumstances changed rapidly, because ideas and institutions can develop slowly but steadily. Nevertheless, the problems of French society eventually resembled water about to overflow out of a cup, hanging on the lip until at last, when one more drop was added, it spilled over on all sides. When nationalism and patriotism began to supplant money as a motivating principle, warfare evolved quickly. When Napoleon promoted soldiers and officers on the basis of competence rather than birth, the principle could never subsequently be fully revoked. Mercenary officers, who had been the standard for competence in warfare, were quickly devalued.

Rulers in Asia and North Africa did not hire mercenaries in the same way as Europeans did because circumstances differed. Tatars, for example, did not see infantry as useful, and though they eventually called upon the Ottoman sultan to send them janissaries, they were unwilling to fight on foot themselves. In this they were like most other hereditary warrior classes – it was acceptable to have slaves or auxiliaries do the dirty work, as long as the cavalry arm remained paramount. The Mamluks never had this problem because their Arab subjects were not allowed to challenge their military and political control.

The Mamluks fell before Napoleon's army, as did most of the eighteenth-century spit-and-polish European armies that relied on recruiting mercenaries. Then, when French armies were confronted by even larger ones motivated by patriotic and anti-French feelings, the French advantage vanished. The size and ferocity of the 1813 Battle of Nations in the heart of Germany could not have been imagined a generation before, and even Napoleon's genius could not prevail over the changed circumstances.

This was nothing new in European history. The miserably dressed hordes of the Thirty Years War gave way to the flashy uniforms and mitre caps of the 1700s, though even this change reflected more than an awareness of fashion. The mitre cap of the grenadier had its purposes: first, as a place to keep the fuses for grenades dry, and second, to make him appear even taller and stronger than he was. The uniform also attracted recruits and girls.

Why did mercenary armies disappear in Europe? This is the question that Charles Tilly asks in *Coercion, Capital and Europe*. The query almost comes as a surprise because the answer seems so obvious: if a ruler can raise soldiers cheaply and effectively by appealing to patriotism, the same emotion that allowed confiscatory taxation, national mobilisation of resources and the intimidation of dissenting opinion, why would he need mercenaries?

The problem was that the nation did not yet exist in 1700.[11] It may have been, as Richard Bonney suggests in *The European Dynastic States, 1494–1660*, that first the establishment of primogeniture, by preventing lands from being divided, stabilised each nation as a distinct entity; then the concept that the state was the dynasty's possession, to do with as the ruler wished, gave way to that of managing a state being a divinely imposed duty. Then propaganda (in the form of ceremonies), institutions, self-interest and rationality made subjects think of themselves as citizens. Certainly the nation was in the process of formation in this era, and royal armies would help mould a national consciousness, though in 1700 that was still in the future. Mercenary armies were still much better than citizen levies, and while militias were willing to defend their homes against raiders, they understood that untrained men with inadequate weapons stood little chance against professionals. Also, more men were seeing little point in sacrificing themselves for some titled dolt.[12] It would take several generations yet before industrialisation would provide the weapons, the uniforms and the ammunition, before population growth would provide the recruits, and before education and romantic nationalism would provide the motivation, but the process had been started.

For service overseas, especially in tropical climes, there had to be more than patriotism involved – since criminals sentenced to 'transportation' tended to die quickly or run away they did not make good soldiers. Professional troops were too valuable to be stationed abroad permanently. Consequently, colonial powers began to raise local bodies of armed men, such as the sepoys in India; even then, because it was desirable to have some

European soldiers present, colonial powers recruited men from marginal regions of the homeland. If mercenaries disappeared from the streets, they were not absent from the dusty roads of distant lands. Or even from Europe of the 1700s.

The result was that armies were somewhat more disciplined and methods of making war were somewhat more civilised. Men of irregular habits who had once signed onto mercenary armies were sufficiently 'street-smart' to avoid military service in national armies where there was little hope of loot; moreover, beatings and executions could make such men stand in line and fight for their lives, but not die like patriots. Wars might be less common in the 1700s, but they were still bloody and expensive.

There was no going back. Two centuries earlier, when vassals had objected to serving in foreign lands, where death or dismemberment was more likely than earning fame, rulers might be able to cajole, persuade, embarrass and threaten them, but there were limits on how long they would stay with the army. Now, when important nobles were all courtiers, no king wanted to return to the days when ordinary nobles and clerics had a strong voice in state affairs; it was hard enough to deal with representative assemblies and councils of advisers that usually dispersed quietly after making the customary complaints about bad government and high taxes. Sharing any significant authority with any parliamentary body risked sharing the fate of the kings of Poland–Lithuania. This attitude led to what historians long called the Age of Absolutism. If that name exaggerated the powers of princes, it still caught the essence of statecraft around 1700.[13]

Princes relied on mercenaries until the French Revolution overturned everything, but they kept the soldiers and taxpayers happy by avoiding war as much as possible. The Age of the Enlightenment overlapped considerably with the Age of Absolutism, and that made it possible for thinking people to believe that war was a passing aggravation and to conclude that the wars that came along were unavoidable. Those who relied on experience and conventional wisdom rather than intelligence and education knew better. All that everyone agreed on was that law and order were, on the whole, better than war and chaos.

Janice Thomson, in *Mercenaries, Pirates and Sovereigns*, emphasises the 'de-legitimating' of non-state violence. That is, just as individuals could not threaten, beat or murder other people over personal matters, they could not take up arms against the state or against other states.[14] Until then questions of sovereignty were sufficiently unclear that private enterprise in war continued – privateers being a prime example – and ended perhaps more as an unintended consequence of making state authority more effective than from state policy.

There had always been a contest between control and freedom. In the medieval village, most people worked under the direction of an overseer; in the cities, guilds set standards and regulated every aspect of life. As private property became more common and individuals could seek work elsewhere and put their resources at risk in new enterprises, they left the medieval world – and though they became less secure, they became much more prosperous. As liberty and economic opportunity became common, the restless desire for improvement and change embodied in these concepts had a profound impact on society, religion and politics. We often call this process modernisation. It was not always pretty, but, as Marx reminded us, neither was the poverty and ignorance of the village.

In recent years the concept that liberty and freedom are essential to progress has been criticised as being Eurocentric, reflecting Western values, and applying the concept of evolution to societies. Obviously, the debate over values that started in the late Renaissance and early Reformation assumed its modern form in the era of the Enlightenment after 1700 and is far from over.

Effective state authority also lies close to the heart of the concept of modernisation. One can disagree as to what the proper limits of government should be, how much a state should interfere in the lives of its subjects and about how these limits might change when subjects become citizens, but relatively few people today disagree that governments must perform tasks that individuals cannot do for themselves. First and foremost, this is the protection of life, liberty and property from foreign invaders and domestic criminals. After this come the practical matters of roads, waterways, trade and industry, care for the infirm and aged, and all those other matters that mark the differences between the developed and less-developed worlds today. This is far from total control over society and does not tell us whether central direction or local administration is better in every instance.

Between 1500 and 1700 the debate over these limits was still largely confined to basic matters, most important of which were religion and taxes. Because people still thought in local terms, rulers and churchmen tended to see all dissent as threats to national and religious unity. The new states were not yet secure – territories were still passed around by marriage contracts, treaties and conquest. As for the inhabitants of these states, the only effective means of resisting tyranny or rule by foreigners seemed to be rebellion, and that usually failed. There was no consensus that one duty of the state was to guarantee the citizenry protection against their governors – and their administrators who saw it as their duty to override customs and ancient rules that had protected groups from exploitation, but were now obstructing royal wishes. Governments did agree on the need to enforce laws and edicts, but accepted the fact that corruption was among the perquisites of office. Lacking an effective local police force and appropriate judicial traditions, rulers relied on the army to see that administrators and subjects alike obeyed the laws; and those states that would be important in the future all employed mercenary troops.

Brauer and van Tuyll say that state sovereignty was supreme as of the 1648 Peace of Westphalia. Afterwards, the Vatican could complain, but in vain – international law had trumped religious allegiance. In 1683 Protestants and Catholics could join to rescue Vienna from Turkish siege. By 1700 most armies were adopting bayonets, replacing matchlock muskets with flintlocks, employing more mobile field artillery, and severely limiting the number of camp followers. This 'military revolution' was not quite the same thing as 'modernisation', but the development of state institutions to support it led in that direction.

The full extent to which state authority would grow was not yet apparent in 1700 Europe, although strong governments had appeared in France, Prussia, England, Sweden, Austria and Russia. Spain still appeared strong, though its ministers were only barely managing to conceal its fundamental weaknesses; the self-deception would be revealed on the fields of battle, and even more so on the high seas. The Dutch were not to collapse so quickly, but the numbers and wealth needed to sustain a titanic struggle against Spain were exhausted in the fight against France. As lovers of mythology could have told them, the titans lost the war against the gods.

No sensible political observer of 1500, or of 1600, would have predicted that after 1700 England would be the greatest power in Europe. England did not have the manpower or the wealth of France. Nevertheless, it had developed its navy and its commerce, and after the 1707 union with

Scotland, it no longer had to worry continually about war in the north, or uprisings in Ireland. The United Kingdom was not yet a superpower, but that would be its status before the end of the next century.

England was able to achieve this because its monarchs had money, and because they invested this carefully in ships and regiments and in the men who commanded and filled the ranks. Colourful recruits from Gaelic regions continued to be seen in all branches of the royal service, men proud of their native lands. While the navy accepted sailors from every clime, many Englishmen signed on only at the insistence of the press gang and refrained from desertion only out of fear of the lash and the hangman. To find recruits for the more distant and dangerous scenes of combat, monarchs turned to the old recruiting grounds of mercenaries – Scotland, Ireland and county jails. Men were still ready to take the king's shilling, and did so for motives so mixed that it is difficult to determine to what extent they can be considered mercenaries.

Last Thoughts

Warfare had become a profession – an international business with interchangeable branches. An officer could move from army to army, as could an ordinary soldier – units from Protestant Germany could fight alongside Catholic Poles against Muslim Turks and Catholic Frenchmen – and everyone of importance could communicate in French. Troops wore uniforms, slept in tents and ate whatever the cooks provided.

While none of these characteristics was totally absent from the armies of 1500, they were dominant by 1700. An army from the early eighteenth century, were it somehow to encounter on the battlefield an army from two hundred years earlier, would literally blow it away. The army of 1700 was a killing machine, supported by another army of tax collectors, paymasters, supply officers and all the apparatus of support needed to get it to the place of battle with as many men combat-ready as possible.

The officers and men were professional, with all the virtues and vices of an elite fraternity, a fraternity divided rigidly by class – the officers being gentlemen (a rank not quite equal to noble, but which ennobled nobility in the sons of ancient families), the soldiers being at least proud of themselves and their units.

Some of these men could be called mercenaries, though they would not have used that word to describe themselves. That name smacked of money, and while money was both welcome and necessary, for officers it would have been gauche to mention it. After all, anyone who could afford to buy a commission should have enough private income to support himself and enough culture to behave as befits a gentleman.

This clouds the definition of mercenary somewhat. Janissaries and Mamluks were certainly not mercenaries, but neither were they volunteer citizen-soldiers. And what of the eunuchs in the service of Moors and other sultans? Or the Dahomey Amazons? Cossacks and Tatars were intermittent mercenaries, but often they were required to serve in the armies of the khans, the tsars and the kings of Poland–Lithuania under terms that did not seem to include regular pay. How do we classify warriors who fight on the promise of loot and plunder?

If the multinational empires of the Ottoman sultans and the Habsburg emperors found the strains of ethnicity too great to withstand, is this a warning to the modern world, where so many states are composed of jealous religious, racial and tribal entities? Habsburg efforts to force uniformity on their people proved counter-productive. When religious differences combine with linguistic and cultural ones, is the only practical policy to allow institutional diversity, regardless of how it cripples administrative initiatives? When groups are guaranteed a veto over taxes and policies, can the result be anything other than governmental paralysis similar to that which threatened the very survival of Poland–Lithuania? Must every Louis XIV crush his equivalent of the Huguenots? Was a mercenary army the only means that a government had to ensure loyalty and impartial treatment of all citizens?

There is also the matter of public works. By 1700 most recruits must have assumed that they would spend less of their time shooting people who looked like them than working on fortifications, raising crops for their own food, building roads and bridges, and labouring on similar useful tasks. While local entrepreneurs and skilled labourers would benefit from the demand for their goods and services, some of the hardest work was performed by soldiers. To what extent was military service becoming a part of the welfare system – a means of assuring full employment and building infrastructure cheaply? Were mercenaries actually cheaper than hiring skilled labourers, or merely available? Did that encourage desertion to such an extent that it hurt the army's principal function – war? Or was the labour fairly moderate compared to that typical of civilian life?

There is still much to think about.

Authors are not encouraged to end books with questions, but in the scholarly world the answers constantly change. The only continuity is in the questions.

Notes

Preface

1 See Braudel, *The Structures of Everyday Life*, an enchanting but difficult read, full of surprises, paradoxes and strong opinions.
2 My own *Medieval Mercenaries: The Business of War* (2006) posed similar questions about definition.
3 See the contrasting arguments of Geoffrey Parker and Jeremy Black in the Summary.
4 Some national groups hated traditional enemies, a habit that led to both fearful massacres and occasional willingness to die rather than surrender, but often this was tempered by respect for one another's courage and competence.
5 Daniel Goffman, in *The Ottoman Empire and Early Modern Europe*, decries this attitude, without suggesting that contemporaries could have avoided having it.
6 Edward Said's condemnation of Western bias will have an impact on some historians' judgements of the Oriental world for some decades to come, but the twenty-first century is less willing to see the West as aggressive and evil, and the East as passive and moral, than when he was writing. Already Roger Crowley (*Empires of the Sea*) and Barnaby Rogerson (*The Last Crusaders*) have demonstrated that there are at least two valid sides to the conflicts between the Christian and Ottoman worlds.

Chapter One

1 After Cem failed to persuade the Mamluks in Egypt to support him, he had fled to the Knights of St John (later called the Knights of Malta) on Rhodes, then from 1484 to 1492 was a hostage of the pope, who used him to assure peace with the sultan.
2 The immediate reason for the invasion was Emperor Maximilian I's 1493 marriage to Bianca Maria Sforza, giving him a claim on Milan – a claim shared by many other dynasties, including the Spanish monarchs. By his first wife, Mary of Burgundy, Maximilian had obtained the richest lands in northern Europe, lands he gave mostly to his son, Philip the Handsome (1478–1506), with some territories given to France to buy peace. A double marriage contract included Philip marrying the Spanish princess, Juana – their sons, Charles and Ferdinand, each becoming Holy Roman emperor. The French king wanted

to prevent the extension of Habsburg power, especially into the rich lands of Milan that would complete the surrounding of France.

3 Younger sons often became churchmen, but, given their obvious disinclination to a clerical life, such offices would not have been offered to them had their fathers not been important. Fighting for money was distasteful, but better than sitting idly at home and listening to how others were earning glory.

4 Jurgen Brauer and Hubert van Tuyll's *Castles, Battles & Bombs* is recommended reading for this argument.

5 He might have lived longer, had his young wife been less passionate or if he had recognised that he was not capable of meeting all her demands.

6 Geoffrey Barraclough reminds us in *The Origins of Modern Germany* that early on Charles had announced his intention to be the sole ruler of the Holy Roman Empire, but that Germans had seen no national benefit from the Habsburgs' dynastic plans. As a result, Germany limped into the modern era burdened by a lack of unity, an excess of incompetence and a failure to institute effective governance. This would be corrected only much later by the emergence of states within the larger framework of the empire, states that were national in almost every sense except that they were unable to unify Germany.

7 Turkish cavalrymen received revenues from lands assigned to them in return for military service. This meant that upon their deaths the revenues would be assigned to another warrior, and not necessarily to their heirs. It also meant that they often dwelt at a distance from the estates that provided their incomes. Both of these practices varied profoundly from those of the European knightly class, but, most importantly, hereditary warrior classes rarely saw anything but military service as honourable. See Daniel Goffman, *The Ottoman Empire and Early Modern Europe*.

8 Such is the contention of Rhoads Murphey in *Ottoman Warfare, 1500–1700*. Venice, of course, had a vulnerable island empire temptingly close to Ottoman shores.

9 Kenneth Chase, in *Firearms: A Global History to 1700*, estimates that in 1527 the sultan had a standing army of 11,000 infantry, 5,000 cavalry and 2,000 artillerymen; by 1609 this had increased to 47,000 infantry, 21,000 cavalry and 8,000 artillerymen. The production, transport and storing of supplies was carefully managed, and shipyards turned out many fine warships. Barnaby Rogerson, in *The Last Crusaders*, argues that Suleiman was fortunate both in inheriting a magnificent war machine and weak and/or incompetent enemies. He owed much to his boyhood companion and brother-in-law, Ibrahim Pasha, but in 1533 invited him to a private meal in the palace, then murdered him. Rogerson speculates that this was done at the behest of the sultan's wife, who wanted to protect her sons against their elder half-brother, whom she persuaded her husband to assassinate twenty years later. Nothing went as well afterwards as before. Rogerson commented that 'turning the pages of Ottoman dynasty history is like descending into the most violent dream cycle, wading

through a living paranoia, fed by real fears . . .' But behind these murders was a determination to forestall civil war.

10 David Chambers notes that Pope Julius tore down St Peter's to make way for a much larger church at the Vatican, he bullied the sculptor Michelangelo to paint the ceiling of the Sistine Chapel, and his rumoured sexual behaviour was not what one expected of a pope, however typical it was in fact.

11 *Austriae est imperare orbi universo* and *Alles Erdreich ist Oesterreich Untertan.*

12 The achievement is all the more impressive if Kenneth Chase's estimate is correct – that two hundred wagons were needed to carry the munitions and supplies for each cannon.

13 The recommended reading is Francis Hackett's lively and engaging *Francis the First.*

14 The issue had been regarding who was at fault for Trivulzio having taken Bologna without a fight. The cardinal, who had not been promoted to his high rank because of any suspicion of piety, had accused della Rovere of losing all the artillery and supplies, and then demanded that he be executed.

15 The number of electors had been seven since 1356, but in the Thirty Years War the vote belonging to the count Palatine would be given to the duke of Bavaria; since it was awkward to take this vote away later when the Peace of Westphalia promised to restore the Palatinate's vote, the electoral college would be expanded to eight; in 1692 it was expanded to include the duke of Hanover.

16 Maximilian's own journey to Rome in 1508 had been blocked by Venice. As for Charles, he knew Paris better than Germany, he spoke French and Dutch as a native (but his German and Italian were only halting), and he understood that any pope would hold out for concessions before agreeing to his coronation.

17 Charles borrowed the money. Richard Bonney, in *The European Dynastic States*, reports that the Fugger family in Augsburg earned an average profit of 54 per cent annually, but because the Habsburgs demanded ever greater loans, the profits existed solely on paper. It was no surprise, then, that when the emperor defaulted, the Fuggers went bankrupt.

18 Roger Crowley, in *Empires of the Sea*, called his appearance that of 'vacant idiocy'.

19 This was thought to be disloyal, perhaps, but not treason. In *The Emperor Charles V*, Karl Brandi reminds us that in the era before national states were considered indissoluble entities, a lord whose rights were abused could change allegiances freely. The queen took possession of his lands.

20 Karl Brandi called him a *condottiere* in the Italian fashion, suggesting a certain willingness to serve anyone who offered money, but also possessing a personality with flair.

21 Bert Hall argues that heavy cavalry based on a rider employing a spear and sword began to disappear only after 1550 when the wheel-lock pistol appeared. A cavalryman armed with two or three pistols was more effective than an armoured horseman who, in any case, was reluctant to charge his horse into

massed pikes. Moreover, a pistol was expensive, delicate and required the constant care of servants – the perfect weapon for nobles. This monopoly did not last long, Hall argues, and once the lower classes had access to pistols, warfare was changed forever.

22 Karl Brandi calls him a born dawdler, but he had little incentive to come to this pope's rescue.

23 Pompeo Colonna (1479–1532) had tried to seize Rome after the death of Julius II, but had relented upon being appointed vice-chancellor. In 1530 he would be named the imperial governor of Naples. Among his notable literary accomplishments was the composition of a long Latin poem in praise of women (*De laudibus mulierum*). Though normally a better politician than a general, he had miscalculated badly.

24 As Chase points out in *Firearms*, the accuracy of a ball depends partly on the length of the barrel, but also on the amount of spin, which eliminates the unpredictable resistance of the air on the ball's surface; a ball fired from a smoothbore moves erratically up and down, and from side to side, the farther it flies.

25 Fritz Redlich, *The German Military Enterpriser and his Workforce*, volume I, demonstrates that most mercenaries enlisted young, and died young. They had no barracks, no regular commissary, no hospital facilities and, of course, no guarantee of permanent employment.

26 She also made contact with the Ottomans, proposing a joint attack on the Habsburg domains. Complicating matters was the emperor's desire to consummate his marriage with his promised Portuguese bride, fear that Francis's illness would rob the emperor of every advantage in having him prisoner or that he might escape, French legal traditions requiring that every treaty be approved by the court of Parlement (which was unlikely to agree to any extreme concessions), demands that the last Sforza be returned to Milan, and papal hostility. Lastly, there was an Ottoman threat to Hungary, where his sister was queen.

27 Bert Hall notes a circular process: larger armies required more taxes; taxes caused wages to lag behind prices; popular discontent led to riots that could be suppressed only by larger armies, etc., etc.

28 Fritz Redlich sought in vain for a commander after 1600 who could raise an army in the fashion of Italian *condottieri*, then negotiate with potential employers. The closest he could find to that traditional model were men who changed sides after not being paid, or because they concluded that their employer's policies were thoroughly wrong-headed.

Chapter Two

1 Legal incorporation of Lorraine into France was achieved only by Louis XV, though Louis XIV advanced the frontiers to the Rhine.

2 Educated Italians living in 1500 would never have recognised this French word for 'rebirth'. As far as they were concerned, they were living in the 'modern' world, with the dark middle ages separating them from the glories of the classical era. By the nineteenth century there was insufficient room in historians' minds for two modern ages, so a French historian invented the 'Renaissance'.

3 Jurgen Brauer and Hubert van Tuyll tell us in *Castles, Battles & Bombs: How Economics Explains Military History* that a *condottiere* was by definition a 'contractor' (*condotta* meaning contract).

4 Fritz Redlich, *The German Military Enterpriser*, volume I, called professional officers 'innovators' for having broken the monopoly of nobles and city councils in raising troops.

5 Similar to, say, Mussolini, Hitler or Stalin, three modern leaders whose nations paid dearly for their pride and ignorance. It is rare that any amateur, in any field, however gifted, can perform as quickly and efficiently as a professional. But in the days when memories were still fresh of feudal armies being led to victories by amateurs, young rulers were apt to think of themselves as romantic heroes. One of the lessons of this era is that war is a profession, and that it had to be conducted by professionals.

6 A Swiss historian, Burckhardt (1818–97) emphasised the Renaissance-era discovery of the individual. For example, paintings of real people replaced saints and the Virgin. What Burckhardt had done was to set up a formulaic Middle Ages that scholars knew was never quite accurate. In return, scholars have set up a Burckhardt with little subtlety, a portrait that is not entirely accurate, either. His influence on art history and cultural studies has been profound – that is, that nothing can be studied in isolation, but only in context.

7 Bert Hall, in *Weapons and Warfare in Renaissance Europe*, explains this in sociological terms – that only men reared to value the community over individual interests could overcome the fear and greed that caused most infantry bodies to dissolve when faced by either defeat or the prospect of plunder.

8 See my *Medieval Mercenaries: The Business of War*.

9 Geoffrey Parker lists the needs of one two-thousand-man garrison in a north German fortress during the winter of 1627–8 as: 313,000 kg of bread, 33,500 kg of cheese and 1,674 barrels of cheap beer. It appears that they believed the best cure for diarrhoea was constipation.

Chapter Three

1 There were additional problems such as keeping bowstrings dry, preventing arrows from warping and obtaining good wood for longbows. Carrying large stocks of arrows was somewhat harder than hauling powder and balls. Powder had problems, too, such as settling during transport.

2 Roger Crowley, in *Empires of the Sea*, notes that Turkish janissaries employed a heavy firearm that was slow to load, but more accurate and more deadly.

3   As Kenneth Chase noted in *Firearms*, muskets gave us the saying, 'lock, stock and barrel'.

4   Bert Hall notes in *Weapons and Warfare* how difficult it was, and is, to predict what combinations of troops will work best. See also Kenneth Chase, *Firearms: A Global History to 1700*.

5   Some castles, like Colditz castle on the Elbe and Ehrenbreitstein overlooking the Rhine, were essentially impregnable to assault, and with well-stocked stores any siege would obviously be a long one.

6   Jurgen Brauer and Hubert van Tuyll estimated that it only took about two months before the employer of a besieging army was approaching bankruptcy.

7   His observation that a prince should lie when necessary was misunderstood as a general endorsement of deceit. Quite the opposite – a lie is only effective when everyone believes that the prince always tells the truth.

8   John Lynn II, *Women, Armies and Warfare in Early Modern Europe*, reminds us that quartering was one means that Louis XIV later used to punish Protestants.

9   John Lynn II illustrates how useful camp women were in collecting food, keeping possessions orderly and safe, washing, tending the ill and basically freeing the soldier to concentrate on fighting.

10 Peter Wilson in *The Thirty Years War* argues that the *tercio* was more flexible and practical than most historians recognise, and that Gustavus Adolphus's adoption of linear tactics was more to prevent being outflanked than to increase firepower. The greater problem was to feed, house and pay the large armies in a war that was marked as much by truces, extended negotiations and retirement into winter quarters as by sieges and battles.

11 In *Firearms*, Kenneth Chase analyses a miniature painting of the battle, noting that the sultan was protected by cannon and janissaries behind a line of wagons, and that one gunner was wearing European clothes – obviously a turncoat mercenary. László Vezprémy, in *European Warfare, 1350–1750*, reports that a recently discovered Italian document suggest that the Hungarian army was better equipped with cannon and other state-of-the-art armaments than believed, including 7,000 mercenaries. In the end, it was a general overconfidence in their own prowess that led the Hungarians to their doom.

12 Roggendorf (1481–1541) built a palace on Herrengasse in Vienna; he has a memorial at the military invalid hospital in Heldenberg. Salm (1459–1530) was mortally wounded in the fighting, his ankle crushed by a stone cannonball; Archduke Ferdinand built him a splendid marble tomb in the Dorotheerkirche that can be seen today in the baptistery of Vienna's Votivkirche.

13 Rhoads Murphey attempts in *Ottoman Warfare, 1500–1700* to correct impressions based on later Turkish military backwardness.

14 Roger Crowley, in *Empires of the Sea*, makes an excellent case for Charles giving this war priority over problems in Germany and the Balkans, and Barnaby Rogerson, in *The Last Crusaders*, demonstrates how close to success he came.

15 Swedish historians see this as the first standing national army in Europe, but Michael Roberts, in *Gustavus Adolphus*, notes that it did not meet the king's need for troops willing to fight outside the kingdom and who would not insist on debating constitutional rights. This could be done only by hiring foreign mercenaries to augment the royal army.

16 Livonia encompassed the modern states of Estonia and Latvia; when the Livonian Order divided over whether to become Protestant or remain Catholic, the Livonian Confederation ceased to operate effectively. The civil war was followed by pressure from Poland–Lithuania, then a Russian invasion. Danes and Swedes then entered the conflict.

17 James Miller reports in *Swords for Hire* that seventy survivors made their way to Russian lines, only to be mistaken for Swedes and sent on a death march towards Moscow. When the English ambassador explained to Ivan that they were not Swedes, the tsar enlisted them as mercenaries, stationing them near the Kremlin in Moscow.

18 John Lamphear, the editor of *African Military History*, noted that post-colonial scholarship revised, or tried to revise, almost everything we thought we knew about Africa. Some scholars in this volume even say that the European impact on African peoples was minimal or exaggerated.

19 The capture of Ceuta in 1415, a rich trading port opposite Gibraltar, was a chivalric exploit that Barnaby Rogerson used to open his book, *The Last Crusaders*. This inspired Henrique o Navegador (1394–1460), the grand master of the military order who had acquired the lands belonging to the Templars, to organise a school for sailors and map-makers at his residence on Point Sagres.

20 Alan Scholefield, *The Dark Kingdoms*, calls them mercenaries, though one might suspect that they were royal agents trying to demonstrate their importance to a potential ally and trading partner. Whatever interpretation one puts on it, the central fact was that Europeans using firearms were important in the king's victory. The king did not remain Christian long – polygamy was necessary to create close ties with important chiefs, and the Portuguese disapproved. John Thornton in Lamphear's *African Military History* describes the rise of a specialised military class in Angola, followed by the hiring of local mercenaries, and calling on Portuguese aid. In one battle in 1585 the Portuguese recruited nine thousand archers and soldiers to assist their three hundred men; each fought in their own style, with the Portuguese winning the victory.

21 Kenneth Chase in *Firearms* notes that matchlocks cannot be used effectively on horseback, while their heavy cavalry was very effective against the light cavalry they encountered in battle. As for musketeers, the Mamluks despised them not only because they used firearms, but because most of them were black; even when a special unit (the fifth class or the 'motley force') was created of sons of Mamluks and foreigners, they rarely paid them promptly.

22 John Glubb, *Soldiers of Fortune*, remarked on the breakdown of law and order as a result of insurrections. Believing that disasters are often preceded by

decadence, he was not surprised that spoiled and ill-mannered young Mamluks were rioting against military service; considering them disturbingly similar to students in the 1960s and strikers in labour disputes, he remarked, 'These problems are too complicated for my understanding, but they are worthy of more thought than they seem to receive.'

23 There were four brothers known as Barbarossa (red beard) who established the pirate tradition on the Algerian coast, the two most famous being Baba Aruj (1474–1518) and Hayreddin Pasha (1478–1546).

24 See Roger Crowley, *Empires of the Sea*, a page-turner about the climactic struggle between Christendom and Islam for control of 'the Center of the World'.

25 Perhaps best at explaining this is Admiral G. A. Ballard, whose 1927 *Rulers of the Indian Ocean* combines both an engaging style and a sailor's expertise in sailing vessels. He can be frustrating, using 'Mohammedan' and 'Hindoo' and extolling the superiority of the 'White Race' over the 'Brown', but he conveys that sense of excitement, daring and fear that the first Europeans felt in their encounters with the East.

26 Barnaby Rogerson's *The Last Crusaders* spares us no detail in the murders, robberies and rapes that were customary in the sack of any town, but were especially brutal when committed by sailors and soldiers at the end of a long and harrowing sea voyage.

27 See Geoffrey Parker, *The Military Revolution*, and Admiral Ballard, *Rulers of the Indian Ocean*.

28 Marshall Hodgson, *The Venture of Islam*, does not see the Portuguese impact as profound, but rather a European reading of world history as part of European history. Stay tuned – historians make their reputations by correcting their predecessors.

29 Admiral Ballard's reflections on this situation are worth considering – not for their accuracy, but because they reflect a widely held view that affected European policies. He wrote of these children of Portuguese men and native women: 'When led by European officers they were able to deal with such enemies as Malays and Arabs, or even Turks. But racial superiority is quite as much dependent on the female as on the male element and the rule of oceanic areas is too great a prize to remain in the hands of a mixed breed.' Such racist views saved Europeans the trouble of actually considering the talents and desires of people of diverse ancestry, whether part-Indian, part-African or fully American. As for those of 'pure native blood', they could be dismissed out of hand.

30 Admiral Ballard, *Rulers of the Indian Ocean*, contended that the Dutch lost their near-monopoly on trade after the ship-of-the-line became too large to be outfitted in their harbours; it was not just that France and Britain had larger navies, but they also had more powerful warships.

31 Muscovy was, as Lloyd Berry and Robert Crummey, the editors of *Rude & Barbarous Kingdom*, described it, 'in English eyes, a strange and barbaric realm'.

32 As Kenneth Chase notes, disease was as deadly to Native Americans as it was to Europeans in the Caribbean, Africa and Asia. Native Americans tried to preserve their rapidly declining numbers by avoiding close combat in which casualties would be high. Their diet of Indian corn (maize) lacked two essential amino acids, making them susceptible to disease unless they could hunt successfully – guns helped both in killing large game and in the competition for hunting grounds. The European settlers did not have an especially healthy diet either, but they had one great advantage – Native Americans had to buy guns and gunpowder from them.

33 Gold is not found in Virginia, and such as was possessed by any Native Americans on the Atlantic coast came from Spanish shipwrecks. It took decades for this to sink in; meanwhile, every explorer and colonists dreamt of finding 'El Dorado' – a name that underlines the fact that the Spanish owned the rich mines of Mexico and Peru.

34 Christina Snyder, *Slavery in Indian Country*, demonstrates that many early slaves were Native Americans, the institution having been central to Indian culture for centuries.

Chapter Four

1 See Russow's *Chronicle of Balthasar Russow* for entertaining, if disheartening, anecdotes representing the Protestant point of view.

2 The Sejm was composed of a senate (royal advisers, important nobles and leading clerics) and a chamber of deputies (elected by the nobles and gentry), and the king. The tradition of expecting unanimous consent encouraged losing parties to form legal 'confederations' that could forcibly resist the oppression of the majority.

3 Some bishops were already following German models, preparing to become secular nobles themselves.

4 David Kirby, in *Northern Europe in the Early Modern Period*, describes historians' puzzlement about Ivan's motives. For quite a while it was believed, probably incorrectly, that, like Peter the Great later, he wanted ports for trading with the West. However, this motivation is hard to square with Ivan holding back from serious efforts to occupy all of Livonia; instead, he sought truces and recruited Livonian nobles to promote a plan that would guarantee their traditional rights under Russian suzerainty. Some Russian historians regard the war as a mistake, using resources that should have been employed against the Tatars, who burned Moscow in 1571, a raid that was possible only because Ivan had diverted troops to other fronts.

5 The conquest of Kazan had been relatively easy because Ivan could transport supplies down the Volga River, but it was difficult to reach the Crimea, where the Tatars' fortifications provided them security. See Michael Khodarkovsky, *Russia's Steppe Frontier* and Kenneth Chase, *Firearms*.

6   It is fashionable to say that differences can always be reconciled, but some differences are so fundamental – such as the steppe peoples' predatory habits – that our ancestors would find it difficult to understand the modern faith in everyone being able to get along. It is easier to be tolerant and forgiving at a great distance in time and geography, without Cossacks pounding on the door.

7   See Brian Davies, *Warfare, State and Society on the Black Sea Steppe, 1500–1700*, and Kenneth Chase, *Firearms*, on how such artificial barriers made firearms practical against the swift attacks of steppe horsemen.

8   Barnaby Rogerson, *The Last Crusaders*, describes the fortress at Famagusta on Cyprus as having twenty-metre-high stone walls, sheltered by five metres of earth to absorb cannonballs, reinforced by thirteen bastions and with a moat twenty-five metres deep. The long siege, culminating with an assault from May to July of 1571, cost the Turks fifty thousand dead and wounded, and the Venetian defenders eight thousand. No wonder foreign engineers recommended building fortresses.

9   This organisation was created by the tsar in 1565 to eliminate all potential opposition, most importantly to crush the spirit of boyars. Like the contemporary Spanish Inquisition, it was secret and terrifying; the anonymous agents wore black cloaks like monks and rode black horses, spreading terror wherever they went – beating, killing, raping, stealing – until they were disbanded in 1572.

10 Shuisky (1552–1612) was a member of ancient aristocracy, but without royal bloodlines or a strong party. He remained in power only until the opposition could decide on which of them should replace him. Jacob de la Gardie (1583–1652) was the son of a French mercenary who had entered Swedish service after being captured, then subsequently married the illegitimate daughter of the king. He was born in Reval (Tallinn) in Estonia, and grew up in Finland. In 1606 he went to Holland to study the military arts under Maurice of Nassau, returning in 1608 to command the army invading Poland and in 1610 the army invading Russia from Finland.

11 Many Scots came, too. James Miller, in *Swords for Hire*, notes that Scots defending Dünamünde in 1609 were opposed to Scots in Polish employ; when the Scottish sappers directed by French engineers blew open the gates, the garrison soon surrendered, then changed sides.

12 Norman Davies, in *God's Playground*, called these friends loudmouths, and as destructive as the pompous courtiers surrounding the weak Stuart kings.

13 A recruiting captain in Scotland, after subtracting the initial hiring bonus, the cost of clothing, food and transportation overseas, would make about one pound per man – a substantial sum in those days. James Miller, in *Swords for Hire*, reports that between 1620 and 1630 the king offered eight riksdaler per man, but this fell to six in 1631, after he took the army to Germany, and to four within a few years.

14 See my *Bayonets for Hire* for the story of his father's incredible career.

15 Geoffrey Parker calls him a 'braggart and a brute', adding that he was 'utterly devoid of scruples or honour'. This judgement reflects the sentiments of those who later condemned him to death.

16 Grand hetman of Lithuania, Chodkiewicz (1560–1621) studied war first under the duke of Alba, then Maurice of Nassau. A brilliant general, he succeeded in driving back the Swedes in spite of receiving almost no money or supplies from the Sejm, until at last his mercenaries deserted him. He had a similar experience in a subsequent invasion of Moscow.

17 Redlich, in *The German Military Enterpriser*, volume I, was puzzled by Fahrensbach (the alternative spelling), whom he considered as bad as the worst mercenaries, if not worse, but whose powerful connections shielded him from punishment. His wife, born the Countess Eberhard (of Pomerania), was as politically astute as he was, and as ruthless; since so many mercenary officers were related by blood or marriage, they tended to protect one another. Cowardice could not be forgiven, nor (in Farensbach's case) treason.

18 Some of the gunpowder shipped to him was lost in 1619 when the English ambassador's residence in Yaroslavl caught fire during a drunken revel; everyone seems to have been trying the latest exotic import – tobacco.

19 'Mad Ibrahim' (1616–48) was strangled with a bowstring; his fatal mistake was not paying his janissaries.

20 William McNeill, in *The Rise of the West*, writes that once the janissaries were no longer recruited from the Christian subjects, a cultural gap opened between Ottoman administrators and Christian subjects; thus, capable boys who would once have risen high in Ottoman office now became bandits and leaders of the unhappy and oppressed peasants.

21 With promotion in all aspects of the government based largely on competence, it was a sophisticated system, but it was so difficult to understand that Thomas Barker, in *Double Eagle and Crescent*, admits to an inability to determine exactly where power lay.

22 One might wonder here whether the traditional Turkish enjoyment of alcoholic beverages was reinforced by the newcomers or by the habit of disdaining Arabs and their customs. Ferdinand Schevill, in *A History of the Balkan Peninsula*, mused over the difficulties of ruling the Balkan peoples, noting that the Ottoman Empire was merely the most recent effort to impose peace and order by force; for doing so, he said, it deserves 'a modicum of sincere, if cold respect'. Sultans ruled by dividing their subjects and relying on their despotic powers lasting forever. According to this time-honoured explanation, the empire had the appearance of a diseased tree, seemingly sound, but rotten at the core.

23 Orientalists were Western scholars of Middle Eastern cultures. Many were trained as Biblical scholars or archaeologists, but almost all expressed sadness over the peoples they loved failing to move into the modern world. Post-modern scholars argue that there was no way that such persons could truly understand the cultures and thought of this complex region.

24 Daniel Goffman identifies them as 1) Isaac Basire de Preaumont, probably originally from France, who earned a bachelor's degree at Cambridge in 1636 and left the country after the parliamentary victory in 1646; 2) Robert Frampton, a royalist veteran of the Civil War. Each had incredible adventures, and each reminds us that the Ottomans were not tolerant in the modern Western sense. Suraiya Faroqhi provides a more detailed study of source materials, but notes that some accounts of captivity are propaganda and some tell us nothing about the military. Clearly most travellers and traders avoided opportunities to be mistaken for spies. James Miller, in *Swords for Hire*, recounts the experience of James Keith, a Russian general who in 1739 was addressed in a broad Scots dialect by a Turkish vizier. It turned out that the vizier was the son of a Scottish bellringer.

25 Lord Kinross, in *The Ottoman Centuries*, credits Mehmed IV with reintroducing the tulip to Turkey. It had gone to Holland in 1593 under the Turkish word for 'turban'. Within thirty years individual bulbs were fetching high prices. As the Thirty Years War dragged on, speculators saw tulips as better investments than land or commerce. In 1637 the bubble burst, bankrupting many investors.

Chapter Five

1 Unless you were a young boy who could sing beautiful high notes. *Castrati* were in high demand for their ability to sing like a soprano, only sometimes higher, and with greater force.

2 When Charles's half-sister, Margaret of Parma (1522–83), became governor she learned that she was expected to support the activities of the Inquisition. When some two hundred Protestants asked for an audience to discuss their grievances and she was reluctant to meet with them, one of her courtiers asked why she should be afraid of such 'beggars'. When the petitioners left unhappy, they adopted that name as a reminder of Habsburg arrogance, bearing it proudly into battle.

3 This reassured Dutch republicans that he would not become a king, and it left room for a compromise settlement with the Spanish king. William the Silent's implicit recognition that only well-established dynasties were legitimate avoided his becoming a model for ambitious nobles everywhere.

4 Martin van Creveld notes in *Supplying War* that when Alba enlarged the army it became even harder to pay the troops, or provide them with food, clothing and lodging; by John Lynn II's count in *Women, Armies, and Warfare*, the army in Flanders mutinied forty-five times between 1572 and 1607 – in 1574 slaughtering eight thousand civilians in Antwerp. In 1594 the troops complained that they had not been paid in one hundred months!

5 The surprise was that a Dominican friar had been the assassin. Conspiracy theorists expected all assassins to be Jesuits.

6 Simms remarks that by confession Henry was a Catholic, but his political

strategy was Protestant. Apparently, Ravillac had it right, but it was a disaster for France.

7   A magnificent history of her reign can be seen in the Louvre – in 1621 Marie commissioned a series of paintings from Peter Paul Rubens to commemorate the most important events of her life.

8   He astounded his contemporaries by not taking a mistress; instead, rumours connected him to handsome adolescent males who took themselves far too seriously.

9   Philippe (1640–1701) became the most notorious homosexual of the century (more for his bad taste, grotesque fatness and insulting behaviour than for his sexual orientation, which was not all that unusual). In spite of this he married twice and founded the Orleans dynasty. His success as a general was so great that the jealous king ceased to entrust him with commands.

10 Giulio Mazarin (1602–61) was trained by the Jesuits, had some military experience, then demonstrated great skill as a papal diplomat. This brought him to the attention of Richelieu, who needed help during his long final illness. He was very successful at introducing his talented nieces, the Mancini sisters, to powerful men: Olympia was the mother of Prince Eugene of Savoy, Hortense became a mistress of King Charles II of England, Laura was the mother of Mary of Modena, the future wife of King James II of England, and Marie so infatuated Louis XIV that she had to be sent away from court.

11 Henri de la Tour d'Auvergne, vicomte de Turenne (1611–75), was a Huguenot who learned the military arts under William the Silent (his father-in-law) and Maurice of Nassau. In 1630 he entered French employ and became a favourite of Cardinal Richelieu. After leading an army composed of French, German, Dutch and Swedish mercenaries to numerous victories, he was named marshal in 1643. His present place of internment, in the Church of the Invalides, not far from Napoleon, confirms contemporary assessments that he was the greatest general of his era.

12 Actually, it had been murdered by literary purists, who objected to all new words and who made sport of anyone who spoke it badly.

13 Louis II of Bourbon-Condé (1621–86) was known as the duc d'Enghien until his father's death, after which he was called the Great Condé. He had married Richelieu's niece and filled his chateau at Chantilly with one of the greatest art collections of the era.

14 Molière mocked them in *Précieuses ridicules*, first performed at Condé's chateau at Chantilly.

15 Morris Bishop, in *The Life and Adventures of La Rochefoucauld*, tells how Mazarin, after obtaining Rochefoucauld's surrender at Bordeaux, offered him a ride north. With a laugh the cardinal remarked how strange it would have seemed, a week ago, that they would be in the same carriage. Rochefoucauld answered, '*Tout arrive en France*' (Everything happens in France), a phrase that became a byword.

16 Fritz Redlich reports in *The German Military Enterpriser*, volume I, that the private contractor vanished, replaced by princes; colonels still became rich, but they were now as much businessmen as warriors – corrupt businessmen, Redlich notes, but laying foundations for future industrial and commercial development.

17 One of the advantages of unifying the country was that each region could produce what grew best or was easiest to manufacture, then exchange these goods for those of other provinces. Twenty-first-century enthusiasts for eating only locally produced foods should study seventeenth-century France.

18 As Robert and Isabella Tombs note in *That Sweet Enemy*, Louis XIV may not have been brilliant, but he worked hard. Also, his domestic policies were cleverly designed to humble the nobles without destroying them, to curb the Catholic Church without angering it, and, less successfully, to expand his influence without war.

19 Michel Le Tellier, marquis de Barbezieux (1603–85); François Michel Le Tellier, marquis de Louvois (1641–91). In *European Warfare, 1350–1750*, David Parrott argues that their system of venality was at the heart of the compromise that brought crown, ministers and elites together.

20 David Bell notes that Fénelon thus opened the way for later writers who could find no justification for any war.

21 Michael Khodarkovsky, in *Russia's Steppe Frontier*, represents the Russian view well; Western historians share the views of John LeDonne, *The Grand Strategy of the Russian Empire*.

22 See the two-volume study by Fritz Redlich, *The German Military Enterpriser*.

Chapter Six

1 Knowledge of mathematics and geometry eventually became so obviously useful that in 1679 Louis XIV established an *École d'Artillerie*. The 'Great Elector' of Brandenburg, Frederick William (Friedrich Wilhelm, 1620–88) wanted young nobles and gentry to be educated for careers in the military and the bureaucracy. Other states copied and expanded these models in the early eighteenth century.

2 Michael Roberts, in *The Swedish Imperial Experience 1560–1718*, notes that Swedish historians have divided over this into two groups: the 'old school' emphasising political problems, most importantly Sweden's being caught between Denmark, Russia and now Poland; and the 'new school', strongly influenced by Marx, emphasising economic interests. There is no resolving this now, or perhaps even in the near future, but readers should be aware of the ways that historians see themselves as belonging not only to national camps, but to schools of interpretation. Readers might note how few historians are interested in military history.

3 Geoffrey Parker, in *The Thirty Years War*, notes how useful it would have been if Wilhelm Kettler had appeared now, to take Friedrich's place as duke,

thereby ending the issue of legitimacy, but Wilhelm preferred his quiet exile in Mecklenburg.

4 Brendan Simms, in *Three Victories and a Defeat*, called the Palatinate a Protestant boot on the throat of the Spanish Road, meaning that Frederick could choke off the supply of soldiers from Italy to the Low Countries.

5 Fritz Redlich heaped scorn on Frederick's 'ungrateful and cowardly' actions, while Peter Wilson condemned his reliance on Biblical prophecy, assistance from his distant father-in-law, King James I of England, and vague promises of support from Protestant princes. The fate of central Europe was decided by institutional checks and balances, the lack of imagination (or too much) and the vastly varying talents of leaders on all sides.

6 This is the traditional story in the English-speaking world, a narrative challenged by Peter Wilson in *The Thirty Years War*. Wilson emphasises the combination of ambition and fear, with Ferdinand being as much in danger of losing everything as any of his noble subjects.

7 Wallenstein had been educated in Protestant schools and Italian universities. Although he was converted to Catholicism by Jesuits during his service with the Habsburg army in Hungary, he was never really trusted by those who used their zealous partisanship to rise in Ferdinand's favour. Two marriages to very wealthy women provided him with the funds to raise troops at the start of the war. Afterwards his genius at warfare made for a swift rise in imperial favour.

8 Fritz Redlich called this 'quasi-ownership', a practice that would last for many decades. However, increasingly the rulers determined who was allowed to own such regiments. This could serve to moderate our tendency to think of businessmen as coming only out of the middle class – such people were considered unsuitable for military command.

9 The term 'prince bishop' became common in this period, referring to clerics whose lifestyle was virtually indistinguishable from their secular peers. Some were not even priests, and most held office thanks only to family influence.

10 Hans Jakob Christoffel von Grimmelshausen (1621–76) wrote *Simplicius Simplicissimus* in 1668. It was a somewhat autobiographical tale of a young boy's picaresque adventures during the war.

11 French prisoners were a problem, Redlich notes, because of the language barrier; the solution was to butcher them.

12 Peter Wilson argues in *The Thirty Years War* that political concerns, not religion, dictated the motives of the emperor, the Protestant and Catholic leagues, and the principal figures in Germany, Denmark, France, Spain and Holland. While he perhaps overstates his powerful case – one can hardly blame the Protestants for being unable to separate Ferdinand's programme to increase imperial authority and his desire to restore Catholicism – he makes it clear that the war was more complex than traditional narratives have made it.

13 Such is the analysis of Jurgen Brauer and Hubert van Tuyll in *Castles, Battles & Bombs* and Peter Wilson in *The Thirty Years War*.

14 George William (1595–1640) of Brandenburg was Gustavus Adolphus's brother-in-law. He had married the sister of Frederick of the Palatinate, and his sisters had married the rulers of Courland and Hesse. He attempted to remain neutral in the war, but failed miserably.

15 Michael Roberts notes in *Gustavus Adolphus* that the king loved every aspect of life – joking, talking, dancing and making war. The chancellor did his duty.

16 We assume that the challenge lay in the quantity of the wine, not its quality, and that poison was not suspected. Since 1650 the citizens have celebrated their delivery by an annual recreation of the event. Today it is a popular tourist attraction.

17 As Max Boot put it, he 'thought big'. Wallenstein was the most successful of the military enterprisers described by Fritz Redlich; he was a man who raised large armies, created industries to arm them and enforced discipline ruthlessly.

18 Van Creveld demonstrates in *Supplying War* that strategy revolved around protecting and taking the fortresses where stocks were kept, stocks that were regularly renewed by boat and barge.

19 Some historians believe that Germans did not recover from the trauma for centuries, but yearned for a strong leader to protect them. In the late nineteenth century, when Germans felt secure again under the Second Empire, many eagerly embraced the militarism of the Hohenzollern regime.

20 John Lynn II is good at asking questions such as these, which are seldom posed. What did soldiers think about torture? How else were they to discover where valuables were buried? How else to take revenge on troublesome peasants and burghers?

21 Ronald Asch, in *The Thirty Years War*, wrote that nobody could quite figure out what Richelieu wanted, other than to satisfy his own ambition, but most historians believe that it was a matter of state (*raison d'état*) – breaking the Habsburg circle around France was a cause more sacred than crushing heresy. Biographers' opinions diverge – some consider him an evil man, others a great one.

22 It might be noted that silverware was still so rare that nobles brought their own implements to table with them, carrying them in special wooden boxes; the lower classes and soldiers used their fingers. It was the same with underwear and all other fashions – the rich led the way. Uniforms were an exception, with the nobles resisting them as long as they could because they were too drab. Uniforms allowed commanders to distinguish one unit from another at a distance – and especially in close combat – but Fritz Redlich reports in *The German Military Enterpriser* that when peace undercut colonels' income from selling their men weapons and armour, they made up for the losses by entering the clothing business. Cavalry commanders similarly could do well from buying and selling horses.

23 Daniel Goffman, in *The Ottoman Empire and Early Modern Europe*, blames the hurried expansion of the army for these problems. He also notes the presence

of student anti-war protestors, who rioted when they were not sitting around smoking, drinking wine and discussing heretical ideas. Troops had to be stationed in every large town to maintain order, making the once proud army into an ineffective police force.

24 Jeremy Black noted in *European Warfare, 1494–1660* that the Habsburg policy of imposing Roman Catholicism caused Protestant Hungarians and Orthodox Serbs to seek protection from the sultan. German Protestants, of course, did not want the emperor strengthened, nor did French Catholics.

25 Chase in *Firearms* notes that the Safavid dynasty was originally Turkish, or Turcoman, and Turkish remained the language of the army and court into the 1670s. This, as well as practical considerations, explains their giving more attention to the lands north of them than to the Ottomans. This would pull them into Afghanistan, then India.

26 Modern Muslim scholars, according to Marshall Hodgson in *The Venture of Islam*, often criticise Akbar's tolerance and especially the idea that it was a successor's intolerance that led to the break-up of his empire; rather, they believe that Akbar betrayed his Muslim followers. Such ideas were especially important in the creation of modern Pakistan, and hence significant in tying the problems of the past to those of our own times.

27 Chase points out in *Firearms* that India's heat and disease were deadly to equines; this made small numbers of heavy cavalry more attractive than trying to raise swarms of light horse.

28 Max Boot, in *War Made New*, points out that at the end of the century the flintlock musket made possible closer formations with faster and more concentrated fire, and the ring bayonet allowed musketeers to defend themselves against cavalry and pikemen without ceasing to fire volleys. As artillery became lighter, it was more easily brought into the line of battle.

29 In this sense, according to Max Boot, in *War Made New*, and Kenneth Chase, in *Firearms*, the gunpowder revolution had less to do with explosives than with those who employed them.

30 This was an entirely rational position, according to Kenneth Chase, in *Firearms*, because firearms were too slow and inaccurate to be effective against nomadic warriors.

31 He was, as Thomas Barker says in *Double Eagle and Crescent*, 'yet another of countless examples of unhappy chance in human affairs'. See the chatty histories of Pawel Jasienica for more details.

32 The phrase, meaning 'I forbid it', had its force from the tradition of having every decision unanimous. It was not used often, and then only when a deputy to the Sejm believed that he could safely do so. However, when foreign ambassadors saw in it a method of paralysing the Polish government, it became more common.

33 When the tsar tried to pay his soldiers with copper coins, they refused them; he then had to abandon the war, bankrupt.

34 In *God's Playground* Norman Davies notes that public dismay at the multiple crises was all the deeper because they contrasted so strongly with the prosperity and pride of previous decades.

35 Norman Davies remarks that a fitting summary of Jan Casimir's reign was the fact that he allowed swindlers to flood the country with devalued coins, wrecking the economy. It would not be the last time that incompetent rulers assumed they could hoodwink the marketplace, nor the last time that inflation would ruin credit, bankrupt ancient firms and impoverish the peasantry. Coin collectors, should they wish to obtain a cheap reminder of financial folly, can buy Jan Casimir's shillings cheaply, then compare them to equally disgraceful Swedish ones, and marvel at the unfairness of life.

Chapter Seven

1 Matthew Smith Anderson, in James Cracraft (ed.), *Peter the Great Transforms Russia*, emphasises the desire of the peasantry for a better life, no matter what the hardships and risks. Such was the origin of the Cossack brotherhoods. However, since the nobles, government officials and towns were equally desirous of keeping their labour force from leaving, serfdom was the means of doing so. LeDonne, in *The Grand Strategy of the Russian Empire*, asserts that serfdom was the logical basis of the 'cult of awesomeness' upon which tsarist power and Russian hegemony rested. No individual, no state could resist the tsar's arbitrary power or that of his representatives.

2 Drummond was a common name among Scottish mercenary officers. They were Covenanters at this time, opposed to Charles I; hence, many of them were exiles.

3 Anderson quotes an Austrian ambassador who said in 1661 that there were over one hundred foreign officers in Russia; an official list of 1696 gives the names of 231 foreign cavalry officers and 723 officers of infantry. A detailed description of Russian and Polish forces through this era is given in Brian Davies, *Warfare, State and Society on the Black Sea Steppe, 1500–1700*, estimating that in Russia foreign formations included more than 54,000 men and officers in seventy-five regiments – just under 80 per cent of the total field army.

4 His father had followed Sigismund into Polish exile, leaving him in Sweden under the care of well-connected relatives; starting his career as one of Gustavus Adolphus's pages, he advanced through a mastery of artillery tactics and an obvious talent for command.

5 Michael Roberts, in *The Swedish Imperial Experience*, reports that she quoted Biblical commands to instigate war – the Old Testament presumably.

6 Roberts, in *Gustavus Adolphus*, estimates that only six of his thirty-nine regiments were composed of Swedes.

7 Although Frederick William's Prussian lands had been subject to Polish kings for a century and a quarter, the tie had grown weak. When it appeared

that Charles X was going to be master of all Poland Frederick William, along with many prominent Polish nobles, including Jan Sobieski, swore loyalty to him.

8 Contemporaries would never have believed that the Hohenzollern dynasty of Brandenburg–Prussia would make itself dominant in Germany, but in hindsight historians can see the origins of that development here.

9 Robert Citino, *The German Way of War*, calls this battle the decisive moment in Brandenburg history.

10 Thomas Barker, in *Double Eagle and Crescent*, calls him a 'rough and ready type of lowly Albanian origin', but ancestry and class meant less to Ottomans than ability and spirit.

11 Most of the soldiers actually came from the Rhineland. Jean de Coligny-Saligny (1617–86) was a highly respected soldier from a traditionally Huguenot family. Johann Philipp von Schönborn (1605–73) was one of the most powerful and respected churchmen in Germany, who had once urged the electors to select Louis XIV as Holy Roman emperor. Leopold-Wilhelm of Baden-Baden (1626–71) was a professional soldier, loyal to the Habsburgs.

12 Rhoads Murphey, in *Ottoman Warfare, 1500–1700*, uses both Turkish and European sources to get a better understanding of this era than the former reliance on Christian sources alone.

13 He had been born in Hungary and had Hungarians in his retinue, but the very name of his religious order (der Deutsche Orden, that is, the German Order) bespoke his alien orientation. Thomas Barker, in *Double Eagle and Crescent*, notes that the grandmaster actually set up an office in Pressburg (Bratislava), close to the frontier.

14 Kara Mustafa Pasha (1635–83) was Köprülü's adopted brother and brother-in-law.

15 The only way to control the Cossacks, William McNeill suggests in *Europe's Steppe Frontier*, was by cutting off their supplies of weapons and gunpowder – the Cossacks could not produce such war materiel themselves. This was practical in the short term, but with various rulers willing to provide the materials of war, it was not easy to sustain.

16 Brian Davies, in *Warfare, State and Society on the Black Sea Steppe*, notes that the tsar's introduction of a copper coinage had resulted in runaway inflation. The Swedish king had been able to persuade his soldiers to accept such coins, but, being tied into the European economy, they could exchange them for whatever they needed; Russian soldiers could not.

17 This was also the moment when Sweden became dependent on France for monetary subsidies. This diversion of Swedish attention from the conflicts in Russia to the war in the Netherlands and Germany benefited Poland greatly.

18 Brian Davies says that many of these cavalrymen were foreigners, that is, mercenaries. The *Wagenburg* was an old technique, but Czech Hussites had shown how effective it could be. Their fifteenth-century armies were almost

unbeatable, but only when in defensive positions, with the draught animals, the cavalry and the supplies inside the circle. Wagons on the move could be stopped by killing the horses.

19 Kazimierz Siemienowicz (c.1600–51), who made the rockets, came from a minor Lithuanian family, studied in Vilnius and was sent by the king to Holland to study the most recent developments in the art of war. His book on artillery and rocketry would be a standard reference work for many decades.

20 Marie Casimire Louise de la Grange d'Arquien (1641–1716) had been the widow of one of Lithuania's most prominent magnates, and knew the personalities and politics of the commonwealth well. When she returned home to give birth, she explained her husband's daring strategy to fight the Tatar–Cossack army to the Great Condé, who exclaimed that it was madness. Louis XIV was godfather to the child, James.

21 It was an effort, Norman Davies says, which succeeded brilliantly, but left his nation exhausted.

22 The Ukrainian quagmire – Brian Davies's phrase – swallowed up entire armies of Poles, Russians and Turks.

23 Thomas Barker, in *Double Eagle and Crescent*, calls him a good military officer, but has little else to say in favour of this arrogant, proud, self-confident autocrat. Those interested in psychological studies would find him a good subject. Having been adopted into the powerful Köprülü dynasty, he felt both the burden of tradition and a need to prove his abilities.

24 Brian Davies says that two-thirds of the 110,000 soldiers in the Russian army were mercenaries, many of them drawn from Swedish service.

25 One of the Russian generals was Patrick Gordon (1635–99), a Scot who was sent to Braunsberg in Ermland at age fifteen for a Catholic education, there being no such schools at home. In 1655 he started for home on foot, but made it no farther than Hamburg, where he enlisted in the Swedish army. In the war with Poland, he was captured, then joined the Polish army; captured once more, he returned to Swedish service. In 1661 he entered Russian service, fighting against the Turks and Tatars; in 1679–84 he was in command of the Kiev district. Pay for this campaign had been raised significantly, with bonuses for converting to Orthodoxy.

26 The prince of Orange was not considered the equal of kings, hence the difficulty of arranging a royal marriage, but he was highly respected by Protestants. The 1646 marriage ended a long dispute over Jülich-Berg in Brandenburg's favour.

27 His original intent had not been to enlist in an army, according to Robert Citino, in *The German Way of War*. While trying to cross a river, he lacked the fare necessary to pay a ferryman to carry him across, and was told that soldiers received free passage. That determined his career.

28 Citino considers this flexibility the essence of *The German Way of War*, citing Frederick William's views that wars should be 'kurtz und vives' (short and lively).

29 The playwright Heinrich von Kleist used this episode in *Der Prinz von Homburg*, the story of a hero accused of having violated orders in launching a victorious attack.

30 Fritz Redlich notes in *The German Military Enterpriser*, volume II, that Duke Johann Friedrich of Braunschweig-Lüneburg (1625–79) was the first German prince to engage in this practice, renting army units to Venice.

31 As Jurgen Brauer and Hubert van Tuyll analyse the situation in *Castles, Battles & Bombs*, no commander was willing to risk everything on the outcome of a single battle. Each was willing to fight when conditions were extraordinarily favourable, but it was a rare occasion when both commanders believed they had an advantage (or one was desperate enough to be foolish).

32 The minor states of the empire were divided into regions called 'circles', each group being responsible for contributing fixed resources to imperial defence.

33 It was a very curious diplomacy that Gabriel Joseph de Lavergne, count of Guilleragues (1628–85), pursued. Determined to avoid the humiliations heaped on his predecessor and refusing to pay a large bribe to see the vizier, he had to make contact indirectly. That he was able to influence Turkish policies somewhat gave him a great reputation as a diplomat.

34 When her father and husband were executed for treason, Leopold had seized their possessions; she was fourteen years old and an enthusiastic Catholic, who might in time have moderated Thököly's Protestantism, but Leopold was not interested.

35 Thomas Barker, in *Double Eagle and Crescent*, reports that the commander cursed Thököly to his face. His fate was not reported.

36 Charles V (1643–90), having been driven out of his ancestral lands by Louis XIV, had become a professional soldier for the Habsburg emperor, serving capably in wars against both the Turks and the French. He had married the widow of King Michael of Poland.

Chapter Eight

1 That is the opinion of Rhoads Murphey, in *Ottoman Warfare, 1500–1700*, who is as sceptical of Ottoman decline as most Christian observers were at the time.

2 As Thomas Barker noted, it was not until after Charles's death, when comparisons could be made with his successors, that observers came to appreciate his talents.

3 They hired a thousand Saxons and a Swedish field marshal. After a year of combat and disease on the Peloponnese, 761 men came home – this death rate did not discourage future armies from entering Venetian service.

4 Protestant princes were willing to take papal money once it passed through imperial hands, but they were wary of deep-laid Catholic plots. Tales of conspiracies were as common as beliefs in witches.

5 After a final and unsuccessful campaign into Moldavia in 1691, Sobieski retired to his private estate and let state affairs stagger on without him. Norman Davies compares the king's physical deterioration – grossly fat and flabby – with that of the republic. Sobieski's granddaughter later married James Edward Stuart (the Old Pretender), thus combining the fortunes of two dynasties that failed to pass their crowns on to their posterity.

6 Commanders wore distinctive uniforms so that troops could easily identify them. Max wore blue, possibly the 'Blau-Weiss' of the Bavarian coat-of-arms; Bavarian troops wore a more practical, darker shade of blue.

7 Maria Antonia did not inherit her father's pronounced Habsburg chin. Their surviving son was heir to the imbecilic last Habsburg king of Spain, a relationship that led to Max Emanuel being appointed governor of the Spanish Netherlands, but when the son died in 1699, the elector's hopes of further advancement vanished. Max Emanuel threw in his lot with Louis XIV in the ensuing War of the Spanish Succession. By then Leopold was too aged to have another legitimate child (in 1701 he would have been sixty-one), but too young to be expected to die soon. If French and Bavarian troops could have driven down the Danube to Vienna, the elector, standing at the right hand of the king, might well have become the emperor's successor.

8 In *The Venture of Islam* Marshall Hodgson argues that the decline of absolutism was not all bad, but it led to a perennial dispute between the adherents of two contrasting approaches to governing this vast and diverse empire – centralised authority and local responsibility. Since there was no easy way to compromise on this issue, grand strategy oscillated between the two extremes.

9 As Kenneth Chase noted in *Firearms*, all great empires of this time fared poorly when facing diverse hostile forces on widely separated frontiers. It is unfair, he argues, to single out the Ottomans as a failure – largely on religious grounds – because the empire's repeated revivals suggest that much of what the sultan's servants did was well considered.

10 According to John Kinross, in *The Ottoman Centuries*, there was an intense debate in the Ottoman camp whether or not to await the arrival of a large Tatar reinforcement. Tatars were good allies in the open field, and especially useful for sweeping plundering expeditions deep into Christian lands, but when it came to pitched battle, they were often prudently doing something else. At this moment, hard fighting was expected, so the Tatar presence would hardly be missed.

11 This would become important in 1991 and afterwards, when Serbians, Croatians, Bosnians and Kosovars fought over who had the better claims to their lands.

12 Peter Alexeyevich Romanov (1672–1725) was declared tsar in 1682, but actually ruled alone only after 1689. In 1696 he captured the port of Azov; in 1697 he made a long trip through western Europe to observe not only the courts, but the industry and commerce that made military success possible. When he returned

home he began to implement his plans to reform both society and state. It should be noted, however, that Brian Davies, in *Warfare, State and Society on the Black Sea Steppe*, believes that his successes owe much to his predecessors; even Peter's employment of mercenaries was no innovation.

13 Kenneth Chase in *Firearms* estimates that in 1687 Peter fielded an army of 110,000 men for his invasion of the Crimea; the march across the steppe took a month, the troops carting along twenty thousand tons of grain, which required twenty thousand wagons pulled by a hundred thousand horses.

14 Karl XII (1682–1718) became king at age fifteen, with all the unfortunate habits of a teenager except having an interest in alcohol or women. His enemies quickly regretted their decision that he could be easily dispossessed of his land – Charles XII could make cold-blooded calculations, inspire men to extraordinary acts of valour, and he never tired.

15 See my *Bayonets for Hire*, which also briefly describes other mercenary officers at Peter's court.

Chapter Nine

1 John Churchill (1650–1722) received the ducal title after winning the battle of Blenheim in 1704.

2 Awkwardly, today we think of a 'bodyguard' as someone resembling a recently retired wrestler, not someone who would look good in a Renaissance costume. However, 'guard regiments' were exactly that – they were there to accompany the ruler and keep him and his family safe.

3 The grandmaster of this religious order, which was also known as the Hospitallers or Knights of Malta, attracted Catholic volunteers to serve in his navy, and he coerced captured Ottoman subjects to row the vessels, but he could also talk the pope out of subsidies to hire mercenaries. Since semi-independent entrepreneurs representing city-states could not do this, they evolved into privateers and pirates. Muslims saw little difference between the military orders and secular pirates – both captured merchant vessels and sacked coastal communities.

4 This reflects the modern debate between private enterprise and government-owned industries and services. The advantage of private companies is that if they are badly managed, they go bankrupt, while government programmes just go on losing money forever; the advantage of government programmes is that they *can* go on forever – and are ready for use when the need arises. Since modern states need armies ready to use quickly, we may outsource many services, even hiring contractors as bodyguards, to perform dangerous guard duty and give convoys protection, but we keep the professional core a government monopoly. Armies are expensive and they are often unable to do everything politicians want them to, but the search for an alternative remains as elusive as it did between 1500 and 1700.

5   As Kenneth Chase explains in *Firearms*, the West had gained an advantage in military technology, but its decisive advantage was in discipline and drill.

6   Don Quixote was mocked by his author, not praised. My earlier publication, *Medieval Mercenaries*, showed that money was important for poor knights and rich nobles alike. Nobles may have thrown money away, but they understood that they could not scatter coins that they did not have.

7   Bert Hall notes that with real income declining by 30–50 per cent, young men saw only two ways out of their poverty – to tramp the roads in search of employment or to enlist in an army.

8   Think of Yanks in the RAF or the Flying Tigers in China. Other examples are Lafayette and von Steuben, heroes of the American Revolution, or the Wild Geese from Ireland.

9   The Athenian historian Thucydides noted that governments went through a cycle, changing whenever one form became corrupt. Kings gave way to aristocrats, aristocrats to a tyranny, a tyrant to democracy, and democracy to a king. Whenever people tried to skip a step, as from aristocracy to democracy, brutal civil conflict would result.

10 Louis XVI (1745–93) was not a Capetian, but every Frenchman knew that such was the name of the first dynasty. When the revolutionaries named him Citizen Capet, it was also a very appropriate joke for a hated king about to be beheaded.

11 Benedict Anderson in *Imagined Communities* associates the rise of nationalism with print-capitalism and the widespread use of vernacular languages. Peter Wilson, in *The Thirty Years War*, informs us that newspapers appeared in Germany during that conflict, but did not become common elsewhere until later.

12 Most subjects probably still respected their lords, but one may pay taxes out of respect and still not volunteer to be shot.

13 Absolutism often refers to the bulk of the seventeenth and eighteenth centuries, but with the Age of the Enlightenment becoming more important as time passed, absolutism is more appropriate to Louis XIV than Louis XVI. Obviously, there were limits to royal authority, especially in the ruler's right to raise taxes and demand loans. Charles I of England is a textbook example of the contest between 'divine right' and parliamentary rights.

14 This was actually achieved only in the nineteenth century, codified in a variety of treaties and legislation such as the United States Neutrality Act of 1794.

Readings

Anderson, Benedict. *Imagined Communities: Reflections on the Origins and Spread of Nationalism*. London: Verso, 1991.

Arnaldi, Girolamo. *Italy and its Invaders*. Translated Antony Shugaar. Cambridge, MA: Harvard University Press, 2005.

Asch, Ronald. *The Thirty Years War: The Holy Roman Empire and Europe, 1618–48*. New York: St Martin's Press, 1997.

Ashley, Maurice. *The Glorious Revolution of 1688*. New York: Charles Scribner's Sons, 1967.

Axworthy, Michael. *The Sword of Persia: Nader Shah, from Tribal Warrior to Conquering Tyrant*. London and New York: I.B.Tauris, 2006.

Ballard, George Alexander. *Rulers of the Indian Ocean*. London: Duckworth, 1927.

Barker, Thomas. *Double Eagle and Crescent: Vienna's Second Turkish Siege and its Historical Setting*. Albany, NY: State University of New York Press, 1967.

Barraclough, Geoffrey. *The Origins of Modern Germany*. Oxford: Blackwell, 1957.

Barzun, Jacques. *From Dawn to Decadence: 500 Years of Western Cultural Life, 1500 to the Present*. New York: HarperCollins, 2000.

Baxter, Stephen. *William III and the Defense of European Liberty, 1650–1702*. New York: Harcourt, Brace & World, 1966.

Bell, David. *The First Total War: Napoleon's Europe and the Birth of Europe*. New York: Houghton Mifflin, 2006.

Berry, Lloyd, and Crummey, Robert, eds. *Rude & Barbarous Kingdom: Russia in the Accounts of Sixteenth-Century English Voyagers*. Madison, WI: Wisconsin University Press, 1968.

Bishop, Morris. *The Life and Adventures of La Rochefoucauld*. Ithaca, NY: Cornell University Press, 1951.

Black, Jeremy. *European Warfare, 1494–1660*. New York, Routledge, 2002.

——, ed. *The Origins of War in Early Modern Europe*. Edinburgh: John Donald, 1987.

Bonney, Richard. *The European Dynastic States, 1494–1660*. Oxford: Oxford University Press, 1991.

Boot, Max. *War Made New: Technology, Warfare, and the Course of History, 1500 to Today*. New York: Gotham, 2006.

Brandi, Karl. *The Emperor Charles V: The Growth and Destiny of a Man and a World-Empire*. London: Jonathan Cape, 1963.

Braudel, Fernand. *The Structures of Everyday Life: Civilization and Capitalism, 15th–18th Century*. London: Fontana, 1992.

Brauer, Jurgen, and van Tuyll, Hubert. *Castles, Battles & Bombs: How Economics Explains Military History*. London and Chicago: University of Chicago Press, 2008.

Buchanan, Brenda, ed. *Gunpowder, Explosives and the State*. London: Ashgate, 2006.

Chambers, David Sanderson. *Popes, Cardinals and War: The Military Church in Renaissance and Early Modern Europe*. London and New York: I.B.Tauris, 2008.

Chase, Kenneth. *Firearms: A Global History to 1700*. Cambridge: Cambridge University Press, 2003.

Citino, Robert. *The German Way of War from the Thirty Years War to the Third Reich*. Lawrence, KA: University of Kansas Press, 2005.

Clark, Christopher. *Iron Kingdom: The Rise and Downfall of Prussia, 1600–1947*. Cambridge, MA: Belknap Press, 2005.

Collins, James. *The State in Early Modern France*. New York: Cambridge University Press, 1995.

Cracraft, James, ed. *Peter the Great Transforms Russia*. Lexington, MA: D. C. Heath, 1991.

Creveld, Martin van. *Supplying War: Logistics from Wallenstein to Patton*. Cambridge: Cambridge University Press, 1977.

Crowley, Roger. *Empires of the Sea: The Siege of Malta, the Battle of Lepanto, and the Contest for the Center of the World*. New York: Random House, 2008.

Davidson, Basil. *Black Mother. The Years of the African Slave Trade*. Boston, MA: Little, Brown, 1961.

Davies, Brian. *Warfare, State and Society on the Black Sea Steppe, 1500–1700*. London: Routledge, 2007.

Davies, Norman. *God's Playground: A History of Poland*. New York: Columbia University Press, 1982.

Duffy, Christopher. *The Fortress in the Age of Vauban and Frederick the Great, 1660–1789*. London: Routledge & Kegan Paul, 1985.

Faroqhi, Suraiya. *The Ottoman Empire and the World Around it*. London: I.B.Tauris, 2004.

Ferguson, Niall. *Empire: The Rise and Demise of the British World Order and the Lessons for Global Power*. New York: Basic Books, 2002.

Finkel, Caroline. *Osman's Dream: The Story of the Ottoman Empire 1300–1923*. New York: Basic Books, 2005.

Fisher, Godfrey. *Barbary Legend: War, Trade and Piracy in North Africa 1415–1830*. Oxford: Clarendon Press, 1957.

Fletcher, C. R. L. *Gustavus Adolphus and the Thirty Years War*. New York: Capricorn, 1963.

Flores, Jorge, and Vassallo e Silva, Nuno, eds. *Goa and the Great Mughal*. London: Scala, 2007.

Fortescue, John William. *A History of the British Army. Volume 1: To the Close of the Seven Years War.* London: Macmillan, 1910.

Foster, Robert Fitzroy. *Modern Ireland, 1600–1972.* London: Penguin, 1988.

Fowler, Kenneth. *Medieval Mercenaries. Volume 1: The Great Companies.* Oxford: Blackwell, 2001.

France, John, ed. *Mercenaries and Paid Men: The Mercenary Identity in the Middle Ages.* Leiden: Brill, 2008.

Gipson, Lawrence Henry. *The British Empire before the American Revolution.* Caldwell, IN: Caxton, 1936–70.

Glubb, John. *Soldiers of Fortune: The Story of the Mamlukes.* New York: Dorset, 1973.

Goffman, Daniel. *The Ottoman Empire and Early Modern Europe.* New York: Cambridge University Press, 2002.

Gray, Richard, ed. *The Cambridge History of Africa. Volume 4: From c.1600 to c.1790.* Cambridge University Press: Cambridge, 1977.

Guthrie, William. *The Later Thirty Years Wars: From the Battle of Wittstock to the Treaty of Westphalia.* Westport, CT: Greenwood, 2003.

Hackett, Francis. *Francis the First.* New York: Literary Guild, 1935.

Hall, Bert S. *Weapons and Warfare in Renaissance Europe.* Baltimore, MD: Johns Hopkins University Press, 1997.

Hellie, Richard. *Enserfment and Military Change in Muscovy.* Chicago: University of Chicago Press, 1971.

Hodgson, Marshall. *The Venture of Islam: Conscience and History in a World Civilization. Volume 3: The Gunpowder Empires and Modern Times.* Chicago: University of Chicago Press, 1974.

Hughes, Lindsey. *Peter the Great: A Biography.* New Haven, CT: Yale University Press, 2002.

Ingrao, Charles. *The Habsburg Monarchy, 1618–1815.* Second edn. New York: Cambridge University Press, 2000.

Jasienica, Pawel. *The Commonwealth of Both Nations.* 3 vols. Miami, FL: American Institute of Polish Culture, 1987–92.

Jardine, Lisa. *Going Dutch: How England Plundered Holland's Glory.* New York: Harper, 2008.

Kagan, Frederick, and Higham, Robin, eds. *The Military History of Tsarist Russia.* Basingstoke: Macmillan Palgrave, 2002.

Keegan, John. *Fields of Battle: The Wars for North America.* New York: Knopf, 1996.

Kennedy, Paul. *The Rise and Fall of the Great Powers.* New York: Vintage Books, 1989.

Kenny, Kevin, ed. *Ireland and the British Empire.* Oxford: Oxford University Press, 2004.

Khodarkovsky, Michael. *Russia's Steppe Frontier: The Making of a Colonial Empire, 1500–1800.* Bloomington, IN: Indiana University Press, 2002.

Kinross, Lord Patrick Balfour. *The Ottoman Centuries: The Rise and Fall of the Turkish Empire.* New York: Morrow Quill, 1977.

Kirby, David. *Northern Europe in the Early Modern Period: The Baltic World 1492–1772*. London: Longman, 1990.

Lamphear, John, ed. *African Military History*. London: Ashgate, 2007.

Laroui, Abdallah. *The History of the Maghrib: An Interpretive Essay*. Princeton, NJ: Princeton University Press, 1977.

Leach, Douglas. *Arms for Empire: A Military History of the British Colonies in North America, 1607–1763*. New York: Macmillan, 1973.

LeDonne, John. *The Grand Strategy of the Russian Empire, 1650–1831*. Oxford: Oxford University Press, 2004.

Lewis, Bernard. *What Went Wrong? The Clash Between Islam and Modernity in the Middle East*. New York: Oxford University Press, 2002.

Lynn II, John. *Battle: A History of Combat and Culture from Ancient Greece to Modern America*. Cambridge, MA: Westview, 2003.

—— *The French Wars 1667–1714: The Sun King at War*. Oxford: Osprey, 2002.

—— *The Wars of Louis XIV*. New York: Longman, 1999.

—— *Women, Armies and Warfare in Early Modern Europe*. Cambridge: Cambridge University Press, 2008.

Maland, David. *Europe at War, 1600–1650*. Totowa, NJ: Rowman and Littlefield, 1980.

Massa, Isaac. *A Short History of the Beginnings and Origins of these Present Wars in Moscow under the Reign of Various Sovereigns down to the Year 1610*. Toronto: University of Toronto Press, 1982.

Massie, Robert. *Peter the Great, his Life and his World*. New York: Knopf, 1980.

McKay, Derek. *Prince Eugene of Savoy*. London: Thames and Hudson, 1978.

McNeill, William. *Europe's Steppe Frontier*. Chicago: University of Chicago Press, 1964.

—— *The Pursuit of Power: Technology, Armed Force, and the Society Since A.D. 1000*. Chicago: University of Chicago Press, 1984.

—— *The Rise of the West: A History of the Human Community*. Chicago: University of Chicago Press, 1963.

Meserve, Margaret. *Empires of Islam in Renaissance Historical Thought*. Cambridge, MA: Harvard University Press, 2008.

Mill, James. *The History of British India*. New York: Chelsea House, 1968.

Miller, James. *Swords for Hire: The Scottish Mercenary*. Edinburgh: Birlinn, 2007.

Mitford, Nancy. *The Sun King*. New York: Harper & Row, 1966.

Mortimer, Geoff. *Eyewitness Accounts of the Thirty Years War*. New York: Macmillan, 2004.

Murphey, Rhoads, *Ottoman Warfare, 1500–1700*. New Brunswick, NJ: Rutgers University Press, 1999.

Oliver, Roland, ed. *The Cambridge History of Africa. Volume 3: From c.1050 to c.1600*. Cambridge: Cambridge University Press, 1977.

Parker, Geoffrey. *The Army of Flanders and the Spanish Road, 1567–1659*. Second edn. Cambridge: Cambridge University Press, 2004.

—— *The Military Revolution: Military Innovation and the Rise of the West, 1500–1800.* Cambridge: Cambridge University Press, 1996.

—— *The Thirty Years War.* New York: Barnes & Noble, 1993.

Parvev, Ivan. *Habsburgs and Ottomans Between Vienna and Belgrade (1683–1739).* New York: Columbia University Press, 1995.

Pincus, Steve. *1688: The First Modern Revolution.* New Haven, CT: Yale University Press, 2009.

Redlich, Fritz. *De Praeda Militari: Looting and Booty, 1500–1815.* Wiesbaden: Franz Steiner, 1956.

—— *The German Military Enterpriser and his Workforce: A Study in European Economic and Social History.* 2 vols. Wiesbaden: Franz Steiner, 1964–5.

Renner, Johannes. *Johannes Renner's Livonian History, 1556–1561.* Translated Jerry C. Smith and William Urban. Lewiston, NY: Mellen Press, 1997.

Reston, James, Jr. *Defenders of the Faith: Charles V, Suleyman the Magnificent, and the Battle for Europe, 1520–1536.* New York: Penguin, 2009.

Roberts, Michael. *Gustavus Adolphus: A History of Sweden 1611–1632.* London: Longmans, 1953.

—— *The Swedish Imperial Experience 1560–1718.* Cambridge: Cambridge University Press, 1978.

Rogerson, Barnaby. *The Last Crusaders: The Hundred-Year Battle for the Center of the World.* New York: Overlook Press, 2009.

Russow, Balthasar. *The Chronicle of Balthasar Russow.* Translated Jerry C. Smith and William Urban. Madison, WI: Baltic Studies, 1988.

Schevill, Ferdinand. *A History of the Balkan Peninsula.* New York: Harcourt, 1922.

Scholefield, Alan. *The Dark Kingdoms: The Impact of White Civilization on Three Great African Monarchies.* London: Heinemann, 1975.

Setton, Kenneth Meyer. *Venice, Austria, and the Turks in the Seventeenth Century.* Philadelphia: American Philosophical Society, 1991.

Showalter, Dennis. *The Wars of Frederick the Great.* London: Longman, 1996.

Simms, Brendan. *Three Victories and a Defeat: The Rise and Fall of the First British Empire.* New York: Basic Books, 2007.

Skrynnikov, Ruslan. *The Time of Troubles: Russia in Crisis, 1604–1618.* Gulf Breeze, FL: Academic International Press, 1988.

Snyder, Christina. *Slavery in Indian Country: The Changing Face of Captivity in Early America.* Cambridge, MA: Harvard University Press, 2010.

Staden, Heinrich von. *The Land and Government of Muscovy: A Sixteenth-Century Account.* Stanford, CA: Stanford University Press, 1967.

Stone, Daniel. *The Polish–Lithuanian State, 1386–1795. A History of East Central Europe, Volume IV.* London and Seattle, WA: University of London Press, 2001.

Stoye, John. *The Siege of Vienna.* New York: Holt, Rinehart and Winston, 1965.

Stradling, R. A. *The Spanish Monarchy and Irish Mercenaries: The Wild Geese in Spain 1618–68.* Dublin: Blackrock, 1994.

Tallett, Frank, and D. J. B. Trim, eds. *European Warfare, 1350–1750*. Cambridge: Cambridge University Press, 2010.

Tanner, Marcus. *Ireland's Holy Wars: The Struggle for a Nation's Soul, 1500–2000*. New Haven, CT: Yale University Press, 2001.

Thomson, Janice. *Mercenaries, Pirates and Sovereigns: State-Building and Extra-Territorial Violence in Early Modern Europe*. Princeton, NJ: Princeton University Press, 1994.

Tilly, Charles. *Coercion, Capital, and European States, A.D. 990–1990*. Cambridge, MA: Blackwell, 1994.

Tombs, Robert, and Tombs, Isabella. *That Sweet Enemy: The French and the British from the Sun King to the Present*. New York: Knopf, 2007.

Urban, William. *Bayonets for Hire: Mercenaries at War, 1550–1789*. London: Greenhill, 2007.

—— *The Livonian Crusade*. Chicago: Lithuanian Research and Studies Center, 2004.

—— *Medieval Mercenaries: The Business of War*. London: Greenhill, 2006.

Waterson, James. *The Knights of Islam: The Wars of the Mamluks*. London: Greenhill, 2007.

Wedgwood, C. V. *The Thirty Years War*. Garden City, NJ: Doubleday, 1961.

Wilson, Peter H. *The Thirty Years War: Europe's Tragedy*. Cambridge, MA: Belknap Press, 2009.

Wolf, John. *Louis XIV*. New York: Norton, 1968.

Index